The Heroic Path to Self-Forgiveness

The Heroic Path to Self-Forgiveness

Change Your Story, Change Your Life

Marion Moss Hubbard, Ph.D.

Orion Publishing Company
San Diego, California

Unless otherwise referenced, pseudonyms have been used for the people whose stories are included in this book to protect their privacy.

This book was printed in the United States of America.

Published in the United States by Orion Publishing Company and distributed through Heroic Journey Consulting, www.heroicjourney.com.

Library of Congress Control Number: 2012931133

Hubbard, Marion Moss.
The heroic path to self-forgiveness: change your story, change your life/
Marion Moss Hubbard
Includes bibliographical references and index.
ISBN 0-9631341-9-1 Trade Paperback

To **Susan Ellis**
for guiding me in taking my first
soulful steps of self-forgiveness,

To **Robert E. Lang**
for heroically facing your past and
creatively moving into your future, and

To **Elisa Christensen**,
my soul sister. I lovingly pass this baton of wisdom
to you to support you on your unfolding journey.

CONTENTS

Apendices (Continued…)

Figures, Tables and Lists

Exercises and Tools

Exercises and Tools (Continued)

Stories and Articles

Stories and Articles (Continued)

ACKNOWLEDGMENTS

"Every collaboration helps you grow."
—**Brian Eno**
English musician, composer, and
innovator of ambient music

This book has been a collaboration of so many people. I am eternally grateful to each of them for their individual insight and heart-felt connection that made this book possible:

- **Edie Eger**, my dear friend, whose amazing life and in depth conversations acted as catalysts for the writing of this book.
- **Catherine Cleary**, my cherished colleague and friend, for her thoughtful and detailed multiple edits of the manuscript that pushed me to dive deeper within than I thought possible to clarify what I wanted to convey.
- **Holly Bell**, my dear lifelong friend, whose amazing knowledge of me and our mutual journeys in personal growth, gave her the insight to clearly articulate in her manuscript edits what I was trying to say.
- **Elaine Rozelle**, my soul friend, whose parallel journey in personal growth and self-forgiveness work, brought insights to her manuscript edits that helped me more clearly communicate the inner terrain of shadow work.
- **Rose Cuschieri**, my heart-centered friend, whose expertise in education, training and personal growth work, helped me clarify through her edits how to better structure chapters, exercises, and appendices to make them more relevant and useful for readers.
- **Lynne Wilkins aka "Locksmith Lynne,"** my new friend and wise woman, whose keen mind and incisive comments in her manuscript edits helped me lock into place some key elements of this book.
- **All those who contributed self-forgiveness stories**, for taking the time to write your stories and submit them for inclusion in this book, I applaud your courage and celebrate your journeys!

- **Susan Ellis**, extraordinary *Bioenergetics* therapist, whose expert guidance at a critical time in my life helped me step onto the path self-forgiveness and claim my inner wisdom.
- **Robert E. Lang,** whose introspection and candor about his personal journey in his correspondence with me, have demonstrated what heroic courage is all about and the power that can come from diving deeply into the areas of our life that are most challenging to face.
- **Elisa Christensen**, my soul sister, whose personal journey inspired me to write many of the chapters in this book.
- **The Urban Grind,** particularly under the new ownership of Sam Khorish and his partner Pascal Courtin, and staff members Vanjya, Johanna, Sandra, Andrea, Jordan, Loren, Ernesto, Johnny, and all the others, for providing me with the space to write this book, a community of amazing people, and enough tea to help me float away.
- **Richard Hubbard**, my husband, chief editor, and partner in love and growth, who has endured my late nights and weekends of writing, and supported me at all levels in writing this book.
- **Other Family Members and Close Friends** including my sister Lisa Aldrich, niece Carolyn Sinclair, and friends DJ King, Lisa Longworth, Ruth Kornhauser, Judith Larkin Reno, Morgan Hunt, Nina Fishman, Linda Erwin-Gallagher, Robin Hotchkiss, Patricia Sierra, Lynn and Rick Bradshaw, and all the others too numerous to mention, who have supported me on my journey and brought greater meaning and joy to my life!
- **My Inner Wisdom** for being my strength and forgiving presence when I fall short of living up to my own expectations.

"Not until we tell ourselves a story
can we make sense of our experience."
—Jerome Bruner
American psychologist

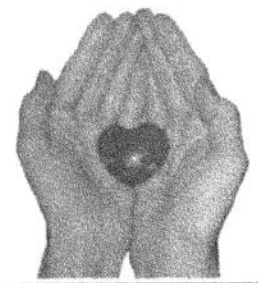

INTRODUCTION

Author Photo

"Life is an adventure in forgiveness."
—Norman Cousins
American political journalist,
professor and author of *Healing Heart*

The seeds of this book began to germinate long before I thought of writing it. But, the title first came to my conscious awareness several years ago when I was working on a project with a friend. We discussed how easy forgiving others had been in comparison to forgiving ourselves. I realized that it has sometimes been much easier for me to walk in the shoes of others rather than my own.

At this point, several incidents flashed into my mind. The first one was when I was a sixteen year old high school student and a dear friend was abducted from her home and violently murdered. She was missing for three agonizing days before police found the person who they believed was responsible for taking her. When the police confronted him at his home he immediately confessed to killing her and took them to where he had left her body.

The murderer was a seventeen year old heroin addict, who was in the midst of a robbery where he thought no one was home. My friend was asleep when she was awakened by sounds in another part of the house. She got up to investigate and when he realized she was home he forcibly took her away in his car. When she wouldn't stop screaming, he drowned her in a bayou in a remote area on the other side of town.

I was numb and distraught when I heard the gruesome details of how my friend had suffered before she was killed. I put myself in her shoes and imagined how horrible it must have been for her to endure those last hours of her life. I also put myself in the shoes of her killer. I felt compassion for him when I found out that he had been a good kid until he had fallen in with a group doing drugs. Even though I wanted justice for what he had done, I felt sad about how tragically his senseless act of violence had, in effect, killed his own life as well as that of my dear friend.

I flashed to another incident when I was nineteen. I was away in college and my parents called to tell me that my sixteen year old sister had been shot twice in a hold up at a fast food restaurant where she worked. She was in critical condition and in the intensive care unit at our local hospital. My sister was fortunate. Even though her injuries were serious, her long term prognosis was good. I was so grateful and relieved that she was alive and thankful that she would eventually recover. I put myself in her shoes and I wasn't sure I would have acted with such bravery as she did at the time of the shooting and during her long recovery. The gunman who shot my sister was also seventeen and had gotten in with a bad crowd. I put myself in his shoes and felt so sad that yet another family, in addition to my own and the family of my murdered friend, had been irrevocably changed as a result of adolescent stupidity and lack of judgment.

I flashed several years forward to another incident when I was twenty two. A young man about my age, with rape on his mind, attacked me in the parking lot of my college apartment complex as I was exiting the car I was driving. With a screwdriver (which I thought at first was a knife) digging into my ribs, he attempted to get me back into the car. I was determined not to let him take me anywhere, especially after how my friend was murdered. I made a vow to myself that if he was going to harm me, he would have to do it right there. Because of some quick actions I took, he wasn't able to get me into the car and because someone else came along at just the right time and called for help, he wasn't able to rape or physically harm me other than some bruises and a small cut from the screwdriver. He got away and was never caught. For many years I had what I now know was PTSD (post traumatic stress disorder). I remember that right after the incident, while I was still shaken and reeling from the attack, I put myself in my attacker's shoes and I had empathy for how disturbed he must have been to attack me.

In thinking back about all of these incidents, I realized that I was so busy standing in other people's shoes, that I often was not standing in my own. I have easily forgiven each of these people who committed horrible acts of violence that severely affected me and my family and friends. However, I have often not had that same level of compassion for myself and my own humanness. I have sometimes not allowed myself to fully feel my feelings, particularly anger, which still at times seems taboo to express. I am my own harshest critic. I have sometimes been merciless at punishing myself for relatively minor offenses. Many times I have felt that I "should" be more evolved, more aware, better able to communicate, or able to instantly change my behavior. I have been frustrated with myself for not learning my personal lessons more quickly. Sometimes I have felt shame for hurting others because of my inability to be a more enlightened human being.

At the point that I made this connection, I asked myself the hard question: "*Why am I unwilling to feel the same level of compassion and forgiveness for myself that I have had for attackers and murderers?*" Once I asked this question, another question popped into my conscious awareness, *"If I forgive myself completely, how will it change my life?"*

My desire to answer these questions and share with other people what I have learned from my personal self-discovery so far is what gave me the impetus to write this book. I did not embark on this writing journey lightly. I knew from years of personal growth work and other self-help books I have written that writing about this topic would take a heroic level of commitment. I also knew from using the *Heroic Journey* as a context for my change process, that diving deeply into my self-forgiveness work would probably change me in ways I could not imagine. I had no idea, however, how profound this change would be!

One of my first areas of exploration was to discover what I even meant by self-forgiveness. I see self-forgiveness as *ceasing to harbor resentment against ourselves*. Without denying responsibility for what we may or may not have done, it is about *no longer believing we can change our past*. Self-forgiveness is instead about changing our perception of the past, so it reflects a meaningful present and more librated and joyful future.

Self-forgiveness allows us to cease blaming ourselves for our humanness, flaws or errors in judgment. We release the need to do penance for past grievances we committed against others. We quit working so hard to make up for past personal mistakes. Self-forgiveness is a profound act of self-love and self-compassion that lightens our burden of guilt, calms our feelings of self-rejection, and ends our need for self-destructive behavior. It also *frees our heart from self-inflicted pain and suffering.*

One aspect of myself that needed forgiveness had been within me for as long as I can remember. It literally changed overnight as a result of the specific self-forgiveness technique I developed during the writing of this book. I was able to get to the root cause of my pain, feel compassion for this part of me and help transform forever my relationship to it. Since then I have felt freer, lighter, and more joyful than I have ever felt! (See *Marion's Story*, pages 157-158 for more detail.)

Although the specific details of my story are unique to me, I know that I am not alone in the need for self-forgiveness. The evidence of the immense need for it is all around us. In the coaching and organizational work that I do with individuals and groups, I see the pervasiveness of self-sabotaging behaviors, depression, emptiness, hopelessness and lack of resilience and self–confidence, much of which is rooted in a lack of self-forgiveness. I see in the people I know and society at large how this is played out externally through dysfunctional relationships, lack of personal values, leadership scandals in business on ethics and integrity, and war between nations.

We each have had our share of traumas and dramas that call us to heroically meet our personal forgiveness challenges. *Forgiving others is one piece of the forgiveness puzzle. Forgiving ourselves is the other piece. We need both to be truly at peace, flourish, and fulfill more of what we are on this planet to do.*

This book is designed to help you create your own heroic story of self-forgiveness. It will provide guidance for how to quit punishing yourself so harshly for minor offenses or lapses in judgment. If you are a perfectionist, it will give you techniques for becoming kinder toward yourself when you fall short of your expectations. If you are using drugs, alcohol, sex or other methods of self-medication to cover your pain, it will provide alternate tools to help you lovingly and gently get to the root of your true feelings, so you can become more authentically yourself. Even if your signature pattern of self-sabotaging behaviors has been longstanding, this book will provide examples of how to replace them with life-affirming patterns that can give you a sense of wholeness, joy and self-fulfillment. In some of the chapters I share poignant stories of individuals who have struggled with self-forgiveness. While the details of their stories are personal, I hope that you will be able to relate to the *subjective experience* of the storytellers that is common to all of us.

Throughout this book I will capitalize and italicize *Heroic Journey*, as a guiding principle for the transformational process we undergo to experience self-forgiveness. In *Part 1,* we will discuss the significance of the *Heroic Journey* for all of us as human beings and I will provide more details about my use of the *Heroic Journey* as a context for change in my personal development and my body of work.

I know from personal experience that self-forgiveness work can be challenging, as well as life changing. It is my hope that this book will help you plumb the depths of your own self-forgiveness challenges, so you can release the tight grip of the self-judgment shackles. Self-forgiveness is not only a gift you give to yourself. It is ultimately a gift to humanity. Each personal change you make shifts a small piece of human consciousness, which makes self-forgiveness easier for others now and in the future.

Marion Moss Hubbard, Ph.D.
February 2012

PART 1
CREATE YOUR HEROIC STORY OF SELF-FORGIVENESS

Movie Reel/Photos.com

"What depths of the human spirit are revealed in these places of darkness! And that seems to suggest that the beauty is what lasts. And somehow, even in the grossest of places, beauty reveals itself to humanity, and if we can attune ourselves to that beauty, we may find our way through."

—James O'Dea

Past president of Institute of Noetic Sciences
and co-director of the Social Healing Project

The ability to create and tell stories has likely been with humans as long as we have gathered together around fires. This uniquely human form of communication connects us to one another, helps shape our understanding of ourselves and the world around us, and allows us to make meaning of our day-to-day existence. Stories do this by providing a framework, or *context*, that helps structure our thoughts and actions and gives form to our dreams and aspirations.

Unlike the reporting of facts that engages our logical mind, storytelling engages us at all levels of our being, including body, mind, emotions and spirit. While facts may convey statements of "truth" based on empirical data, facts are bound by physical reality. By contrast, stories are boundless in their ability to connect us to the mythical and mysterious aspects of human experience. They allow us to tap into statements of *"Truth,"* which reside at a deeper, more timeless and immutable level of our shared humanity. (Throughout the book, I will distinguish between the two types of truth by capitalizing and italicizing timeless and immutable *Truth*.)

In any good story, there is a beginning, middle and end. In the beginning, we learn about the setting of the story and the characters involved. We are introduced to some challenge, conflict or problem that the main character must face. As the action or suspense builds, so does our interest in the story. In the middle part of the story, the main character comes face-to-face with the primary situation to be addressed, decides how to deal with it, and faces the consequences of actions taken or not taken. As the story comes to an end, the challenging situation is resolved. The crescendo of the action winds down and the loose ends are tied up. If the story is told well, it helps us identify with the main character. Like a tuning fork, a great story resonates with us, connects us to a deeper *Truth*[1] and allows us to draw something valuable from the character's experience.

Throughout history and in cultural traditions around the world there have been many stories of heroes and heroines. In his book, *Hero with a Thousand Faces*,[2] the great mythologist, Joseph Campbell, discussed the universal motif of the *Heroic Journey*. He believed that as human beings we need stories of heroism to bring meaning and purpose to our struggles. We each have opportunities to develop our heroic character and, while not everyone will choose to do it, we each have the capability to transform our lives in remarkable ways.

In her books, *The Hero Within*[3] and *Awakening the Hero Within*,[4] author and educator Carol S. Pearson makes a case that the heroic archetype is a master archetype for other archetypal character traits that we play out in our lives. She also describes what is required of us on our *Heroic Journey*, "Heroism for this age requires us to take our journeys, to find the treasure of our true selves, and to share that treasure with the community as a whole—through doing and being fully who we are."[5]

From a heroic perspective, every person and situation we encounter gives us an opportunity to gain something valuable from the experience, if we choose to experience our lives in this way. In our society, however, we have often confused true heroism for the "warrior"[6] or macho, charismatic figures portrayed in film and on television, who gain power through dominance and control or who come out ahead by hurting or demoralizing others. Many people strive to be like these characters and idealize and romanticize the actors who portray these roles.

True heroism, however, is not about gaining power over anyone or anything externally. It is not manipulative. It is instead about gaining the wisdom to live our lives in an authentic way from our values and heart-felt connection to the world around us. Heroism is an *inside job* that requires us to stand naked before the *Truth* of who we are and examine our inner motivations and our outer behavior. In that moment of *Truth*, we can choose to make whatever personal changes are necessary to live a heroic life. What is required is leaping blindly into the unknown to follow our *Heroic Journey*, wherever it may lead us.

When we think of our lives as a *Heroic Journey*, our personal story has all of the elements of any good story. Unlike other stories that can become irrelevant as we change, the *Heroic Journey* never becomes outdated. This is because *the Heroic Journey is a story about transformational change.* The very nature of the *Heroic Journey* as a transformational story is that it evolves with us as we grow in wisdom and develop a more mature perspective.

Although our lives are continually changing, this does not mean that we are in a constant state of transformation. *Change just means situations become different over time. Transformation in this context means that we are changed in a positive and profoundly different way.* Our view of the world and ourselves is forever altered. Our frame of reference may change in ways not previously imagined. Our thoughts, feelings and actions begin to align to our new reality, sometimes with a minimum amount of effort or time involved. With this new, more integrated, level of awareness, we may experience a resolution of the internal stress caused from a previous feeling of conflict, agitation or discontent. Now that we are more integrated, our energy can be refocused on creating more meaning and purpose in our lives.

The power of the *Heroic Journey* is that it provides a *context for transformational change*, which helps us better align our outer reality with the core of our being. Using the *Heroic Journey* as a context for our lives helps us weave together the individual threads of our experiences into a unified whole. No longer are our thoughts, feelings, perceptions and actions detached "experience fragments" floating randomly within us. They are instead rearranged into new slots in our brains,[7] so they can become meaningful elements in our personal heroic plot and unfolding story.

Seeing our lives as a *Heroic Journey* helps us realize we have choices in life. We *choose* whether we courageously do whatever it takes to triumph over adversity. We *choose* whether our persistence prevails to continually clear outmoded beliefs and patterns of action. We also *choose* whether we feel like victims of circumstance or take personal responsibility for the consequences of our actions and how these choices shape our lives.

Examining our choices from a heroic perspective helps us see the conscious and unconscious stories we have been telling ourselves. We begin to ask whether those stories need to be altered to better reflect the heroism we want to experience. Are our beliefs and thoughts leading us in a direction that will help us fulfill our heroic potential? Are the actions we are taking reflecting the way we want to relate to the world?

The *Heroic Journey* offers a self-correcting course of action that helps us make the right choices in life. Forgiveness of others and ourselves is a key component of this decision-making process. *Chapter 1* will explore the benefits of forgiveness of others and self-forgiveness. You can decide for yourself whether it is worth it to embark on this heroic quest and make it your own.

CHAPTER 1
TO FORGIVE OR NOT TO FORGIVE... THAT IS THE QUESTION

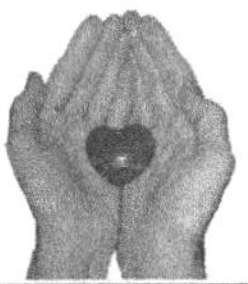

"To forgive is the highest, most beautiful form of love. In return, you will receive untold peace and happiness."
—Robert Muller
Professor of clinical psychology and
author of *Trauma and the Avoidant Client*

Forgiveness is a charged and often misunderstood word, especially in our culture. In October 2006, ten Amish school girls in the Nickel Mine School in Lancaster, Pennsylvania, were murdered by a gunman. The tragedy galvanized the attention of the world. Immediately after the incident the Amish in the community forgave the gunman and his family, which became even more of a focus of the story than the tragedy itself. People marveled at, and in many cases questioned, the authenticity and wisdom of the Amish for forgiving so quickly. What ensued was an international discussion about forgiveness and its ramifications.[1] Incidents like this point out how deeply emotional forgiveness can be and what an integral role forgiveness, or the lack of it, plays in the human drama.

We live in a culture fixated on vengeance, revenge and violent force against those who have committed real or perceived transgressions. This perspective is woven into our psyches through the popularity of the movies and news we watch, the books we read, and sometimes in the neighborhoods in which we live. In many ways, forgiveness of others and ourselves goes against the grain of how most of us were raised to relate to our exterior and interior world. Even though many spiritual traditions and moral codes have forgiveness as a central tenant, the actions and reactions of family members, peers, world leaders, and even spiritual leaders demonstrate for us an underlying belief system that is contrary to what is espoused.

One reason forgiveness is such a charged word, is that many people confuse it with forgetting. *Forgiveness is not about forgetting.* It is actually about choosing to remember clearly, but from a new vantage point. It is about placing experiences in a different context.

As authors Donald Kraybill, Steven Nolt, and David Weaver-Zercher describe it, "When we remember we take the broken pieces of our lives—lives that have been dismembered by tragedy and injustice—and *re-member* them into something whole."[2] Viewing our lives as a *Heroic Journey*, helps us rearrange the broken pieces of our lives that were split off when we experienced the anguish or pain from a particular incident and reassemble those pieces into an integrated and life-affirming perception of reality.

Another misperception about forgiveness is that it excuses behavior. *Forgiveness is not about condoning offenses, but it is also not about seeking revenge for what happened.* Lashing out in revenge, which is a common reaction that arises when we feel we have been wronged, is a desire to get back at another person or group of people to make them suffer as we have suffered. It may give us temporary satisfaction to "get even." Ultimately, though, the satisfaction wanes and we are left with the same anger, pain or sense of betrayal we had when we first felt wronged. In fact, the desire to "get even" keeps the incident in the front of our consciousness and often prevents us from freeing ourselves of a situation. It can sometimes spark retaliation that escalates into violence, as each side tries to become a winner and make the other person a loser. As Mohandas Gandhi said, "An eye for an eye makes the whole world blind."[3]

Emmett E. "Bud" Welch learned this *Truth* about forgiveness first hand after his daughter Julie-Marie was killed in the bombing of the Murrah Federal Building in Oklahoma City on April 19, 1995. After Timothy McVeigh and Terry Nichols were charged with the bombing, Bud recalls how angry he was:

> The first five weeks after the bombing are a blur to me. I wanted McVeigh and Nichols hanged, no trials necessary. I suffered from a temporary insanity. I would have killed them with my bare hands if I could have reached them…In January 1996, I asked myself, 'What is it going to do for me if McVeigh and Nichols are executed?' I repeated the question for about three weeks and kept getting the same answer: Their deaths wouldn't help me one bit.[4]

Bud Welch found the road to forgiveness and compassion difficult, but possible to traverse. The still-grieving father says that "revenge is nothing but hate and anger. We have to stop the carnage, stop ratcheting up the violence, stop all the killing..."[5]

Feeling rage about an injustice or great tragedy is a natural reaction. Recognition that we have rage may be an important first step toward forgiveness. Acknowledging the unfairness of offenses and our right to resentment may be another. Even though we have a right to be resentful, forgiveness is about choosing to move through resentment and ultimately give up irritation, outrage, or righteous indignation toward the offending person. We do this, not for the other person, but because holding onto the resentment hurts us. It festers inside of us. As Irish-American actor, writer and politician Malachy McCourt pointed out, "Resentment is like taking poison and waiting for the other person to die."[6] When we hold onto resentment for a long period of time, we may become bitter and obsess about the negative, rather than appreciate what we have now and feel hopeful about the future. Resentment can never bring back what was lost or fill the missing hole inside. It can, in fact, interfere with our ability to have a positive, enjoyable outlook on life. *Forgiveness can help us release offenses and return them to their rightful source*. It can also help us choose to *respond rather than simply react* to situations without thinking through the consequences.

In Western culture many of us have been taught that in a contentious situation the only options are either to fight or flee. The Japanese martial art of *Aikido* teaches alignment with life force and redirecting the attacker's force rather than meeting it head-on. Forgiveness acts as "psychic Aikido" helping us re-channel the energy, so we are not consumed with resentment.

Forgiveness is also not about letting others off the hook or condoning what they did. People still need to be accountable for their actions and deal with the consequences of their behavior. The appropriate level of consequences will vary depending on how egregious the behavior. For minor offenses, consequences may involve simply calling people on their hurtful behavior and asking for their commitment to stop in the future. For more serious offenses, such repeated offenses or causing long-term physical or psychological suffering, appropriate consequences may involve disciplinary or legal action or paying reparations for damage caused. For extreme offenses, such as inflicting intentional cruelty or causing death, the consequences may involve removing the offender from society to keep them from perpetuating harm on others in the future. Whatever the consequences for offenders, forgiveness allows us to feel compassion for their humanity that exists under their actions, even while we steadfastly hold them responsible for what occurred.

Sometimes people say they don't want to forgive because the offense feels too great, no consequences have been faced, or offenses are ongoing. Not only do some people think it is not desirable to forgive, but they also feel it would be disempowering for them to do so. One example cited is women who are in abusive relationships. Abused women sometimes stay and "forgive" their abuser over and over, while ignoring the continuing pattern of abuse. In these cases, forgiveness may be confused with letting abusers off the hook for their actions. Intertwined with this misguided perception of forgiveness, also may be low self-esteem, a profound sense of shame for getting into the situation, a lack of self-confidence, a belief that they are unable to be self-reliant, or a myriad of other reasons.

Women who find themselves in these circumstances also may fear, often with justification, that they will suffer repercussions if they hold their abusers accountable. At times like these, rather than focus on forgiveness, other actions may need to take precedence, such as leaving an emotionally damaging or potentially physically dangerous environment. Assessing the individual situation can help us determine whether forgiveness is the action called for in the moment.

Like grief, forgiveness cannot be forced. It often takes time to move through the associated anger, fear, and pain before we are ready to forgive. If we try to jump ahead of where we authentically are in the process, we actually may do more harm than good to ourselves and others. What we may create is an overlay of false piety that drives the anger, fear or pain underground. Like a pressure cooker, however, the energy and passion of these emotions cannot be totally contained. They may leak out in unconscious or passive aggressive ways that actually prevent us from experiencing authentic forgiveness.

Another reason sometimes given for choosing not to forgive is a desire to just move on and no longer focus on the past. It can be a good strategy to decide not to dwell on the past, especially for people who have spent a lot of time obsessessing about what happened without resolution. However, if feelings about a negative incident still have an emotional charge and these feelings are denied or just shoved aside without clearing them, the anger, fear and pain may go underground with unintended consequences. These negative feelings may instead leak out externally, such as when we treat others badly. They may also pool inside of us and manifest as self-loathing or self-destructive behaviors. *Focusing on forgiveness can bring the negativity to the surface to be cleared, so the emotional charge of the incident no longer has a hold on us.*

Although much of this chapter has been focused on forgiving others, forgiveness of others and forgiveness of ourselves are inextricably intertwined. In the *Introduction* I mentioned that forgiving others is one piece of the forgiveness puzzle and forgiving ourselves is the other piece. As we delve more deeply into challenges with self-forgiveness, we are bound to encounter the need to forgive others.

The reverse is also true. At some point as we find it in our heart to forgive those we believe have wronged us, it will likely touch a nerve that urges us to forgive ourselves. Maybe we will be called to forgive ourselves for making poor choices, having a lack of personal understanding, repeating a hurtful pattern as an adult that we experienced in childhood, or seeing the world through a judgmental lens. (See related article, *Jennifer's Story: Mistaken Identity* on the next page.)

The payoff of forgiving others and ourselves can be enormous. Researchers have found that the physical effects of forgiveness include "reducing anger, depression, anxiety, and fear and affording cardiovascular and immune system benefits."[7] Forgiveness of interpersonal transgressions has been linked with better sleep quality.[8] In individuals suffering from chronic low back pain, those who were more forgiving were found to have lower anger and pain.[9]

Forgiveness interventions also seem to be effective in reducing anger-induced myocardial ischemia in patients with coronary artery disease.[10]

Forgiveness also has positive psychological effects. Additional research found that "… HIV-infected patients took better care of themselves if they successfully forgave themselves and others. So did recovering alcoholics. People suffering spinal-cord injuries tended to cope better with their health situation and their treatments if they had forgiven."[11] Women who forgave others, themselves, and felt forgiven by God had decreased odds of depression.[12]

Forgiveness, whether it is focused toward others or ourselves, can be a transformative experience. It often bypasses our intellect and permeates through our emotions to reconnect us to the core of who we are. It redirects our attention away from the negativity and stress associated with repeatedly reliving past painful incidents and channels our energy instead toward enjoying the present moment and creating the life we envision.

Forgiveness can restore our ability to feel a wide range of emotions without needing to tiptoe around previously emotionally triggering incidents. With forgiveness comes freedom! We just need to know how to take the action steps to get from here to where this *Heroic Journey* can naturally lead us.

Jennifer's Story: Mistaken Identity*

In 1982, Jennifer Thompson was a college student living alone in an off campus apartment in Burlington, North Carolina. One night she was violently raped at knife point by an intruder while she was sleeping. During the incident, she studied the face, voice and other identifying features of her assailant, so she could help identify him if she survived. Ultimately, she was able to escape. She vowed to do all she could to make sure that the person who did this to her was put away for a very long time.

When she was asked to identify her assailant in a police lineup, Jennifer identified Ronald (Ron) Cotton, who had been arrested as a "person of interest." She again identified Ron at his trial and, despite his protest that he was innocent, he was found guilty and received a sentence of life in prison plus 50 years.

▶

While Ron was in prison, a new inmate arrived named Bobby Poole. Bobby, who looked startlingly like Ron, was serving consecutive life sentences for multiple brutal rapes. Ron asked Bobby where he was from and Bobby said he was from Burlington. Ron asked Bobby if he had raped Jennifer and Bobby denied it. But later, another inmate told Ron that Bobby had confessed to raping Jennifer. On that basis, Ronald was able to appeal and receive a new trial. At the second trial, with both Ron and Bobby in the courtroom, Jennifer again identified Ron as her assailant. Ron was once again convicted and this time he was sentenced to prison for two life sentences.

While Ron was in prison the second time, he was watching the O.J. Simpson trial when he heard about DNA testing for the first time. At Ron's request, his lawyer asked that the evidence in Jennifer's case be retested and compared to the DNA samples of both Ron and Bobby Poole. The tests revealed that it was Bobby's DNA that was the match and Ron was released from prison after serving 11 years.

The realization that she had made a horrible mistake about the identity of her assailant turned Jennifer's life upside down. She experienced a suffocating, debilitating shame. After some time passed, Jennifer asked to meet Ron Cotton. He agreed and they met at a local church. When she first saw him, she couldn't move and began immediately to cry uncontrollably. She said to him, "Ron, if I spent every second of every hour for the rest of my life telling you how sorry I am, it would never come close to how my heart feels. I am so sorry." Ron leaned down and gently took her hands. He said, "I forgive you. I do not want you to look over your shoulder. I just want us to be happy and move on in life."

Jennifer said that the minute he forgave her, physically her heart started to heal. She thought, "This is what grace and mercy is all about. This is what they teach you in church, that none of us ever get. Here was this man that I used to hate. I prayed for 11 years that he would die, that he would be raped in prison and someone would kill him." Now she was the one who was asking for forgiveness and receiving it from this amazing man who didn't seem to harbor resentment against her.

As a result of her meeting with Ron, Jennifer was finally able to begin to forgive herself for the effect that her mistaken identity had on Ron's life. She let go of the shame, remorse, and self-judgment she had carried since Ron was exonerated. She felt lighter and free to move on with her life.

▶

Now their lives are entwined in an unexpected way. Ron and Jennifer have become close friends and their families spend time together. They have co-authored a book, *Picking Cotton, a Memoir About Injustice and Redemption*. They also speak to law enforcement agencies about the role that false memory plays in convictions and they lobby to change state laws about how eye witnesses are interviewed by the justice system. Both of them have expressed how their lives have forever changed as a result of their poignant experience.

*Based on news stories and interviews.[13] [14] [15] [16]

CHAPTER 2
FOLLOW YOUR HEROIC PATH OF TRANSFORMATION

"As we become heroic ...we learn to view our challenges differently, and they subsequently lose their hold over us."
—Lorna Catford and Michael Ray
Authors of *The Path of the Everyday Hero*

When the idea of using the *Heroic Journey* as a structuring mechanism for the process of self-forgiveness first came to me, I was very excited. I had already been using the *Heroic Journey* as a metaphor for my life for some time. In fact, the dissertation I wrote for my Ph.D. in Transpersonal Psychology was titled, *The Workplace Labyrinth: A Heroic Journey to the Center of Yourself.*[1] What I found in my research and personal experience was that the *Heroic Journey* can provide a powerful context for personal and organizational change. I later wrote a book based on my dissertation, *Work as a Heroic Journey: Use the Workplace to Evolve Your Character and Consciousness.*[2] My goal in writing that book was to help individuals and organizations view their workplace, with its "labyrinth of experiences," as a heroic training ground to help them become all they are meant to be. One of the main premises I discussed was how everyday experiences present us with a variety of moral, ethical, psychological, and interpersonal tests to see how well we can put our principles into real life practice.

Placing self-forgiveness into a heroic context, shifted something profound inside of me. It was as if I had snapped a plumb line in my consciousness that aligned my awareness with my inner *Truth.* No longer were the personal "unforgiving threads" inside of me disparate "experience strands" that were unrelated. I knew that they all related to the core of my being and my personal evolution in some way, even though I didn't yet understand that relationship. I committed to exploring the dark corners of my life where the unforgiving parts of me lurked in the shadows. I also committed to discovering how these parts could be transformed into allies in my larger unfolding heroic story.

One tool that helped me enormously in this self-discovery process has been the *labyrinth.* (See **Figure 2.1**.) As a symbol, the labyrinth can act as a powerful graphical representation of the *Heroic Journey*. As a self-discovery tool, it can provide a visual map to help anchor in our minds the path to follow to be heroic.

Figure 2.1. The labyrinth is a universal symbol that can be used as a visual map for the route to follow to be heroic.

In cultures throughout the world, the *Heroic Journey* has been depicted by various forms of the labyrinth. In the ancient Pima culture in the American southwest, the labyrinth was referred to as *Tcuhuki*. It was considered the house of mythological hero *Tcuhu,* who is often shown on baskets guarding its entrance.[3] In one of the two major Sanskrit epics of ancient India, the *Mahabharata*, the labyrinth played a prominent role in the battle of Kurukshetra. To assure victory, warriors were lined up for battle in the formation of a labyrinth, which they believed "the gods themselves could not enter."[4] It is the retelling of this epic, with its description of the labyrinthine design, which may have helped spread the popularity of the labyrinth throughout the Indian sub-continent.[5]

One of the most well known Western civilization stories of heroism and its relation to the labyrinth is the Greek myth of *Theseus and the Minotaur.* In this myth, the Athenian prince, Theseus, heroically faces and kills the fierce Minotaur, who is a half man, half bull monster at the center of a Cretan labyrinth. Although the details of this myth vary depending on which version is read, the metaphorical essence of the story has remained basically the same since the ancients Greeks first colonized Crete circa 800-600 B.C.

This Greek version of the labyrinth myth was based on a more ancient Minoan civilization labyrinth myth in Crete (circa 3000 – 1100 B.C.). The Minoan myth is thought to vary dramatically from the Greek version.[6] According to Riane Eisler, cultural historian and author of *The Chalice and the Blade,* in the Minoan myth, the Minotaur was not a monster. Instead it was a cherished symbol of wholeness resulting from the sacred marriage of the female principle (represented by the Goddess) and the male principle (represented by the ancient Bull God.)[7] Eisler points out that, "In Minoan art are scenes of youths and maidens dancing with bulls in what appears to have been an important ritual of both athletic skill and religious devotion…a balancing act where these people's legendary love for life was symbolically poised against the ever-present possibility of death."[8] From this perspective, the labyrinth that housed the Minotaur would have likely been considered a sacred home for the Minotaur and the center would have symbolized the place of wholeness.

Around the world and throughout the ages, there are many variations of the labyrinth design from a single spiral coil, to more complicated labyrinths with eleven circuits or more. However, the classic seven circuit labyrinth depicted in **Figure 2.1** is one of the most popular. (See a related article on page 18, *The Universality of the Seven Circuit Labyrinth.* See also my previous book, *Work as a Heroic Journey,*[9] for more information about the many forms of the labyrinth and its metaphorical significance to our lives.)

The appeal of this particular seven circuit design in so many different cultures throughout history is likely linked to its archetypal nature. Archetypes are primordial imprints embedded within our human psyche. Like DNA, which acts as a blueprint for a particular aspect of our genetic makeup, an archetype can act as a blueprint for a particular aspect of human consciousness. It is my contention that this classic seven circuit labyrinth is "a symbolic representation of our heroic search for the currently hidden center of ourselves. An innate drive compels us to search, even though we are not sure what we will discover at the center or that we will have the strength and wisdom to appropriately use what we find."[10]

Melissa Gayle West, who wrote *Exploring the Labyrinth: A Guide for Healing and Spiritual Growth*, describes the value of using the labyrinth for our heroic search:

> There's something very elemental about the labyrinth that speaks to who we really are at our deepest level, a much deeper level than the shallow one of modern society.[11]...When [we] walk the labyrinth, [our] story is part of a much larger picture, one filled with mystery; the labyrinth opens [us] to the mystery of [our] life and the greater mystery in which all life is held...Seeing our life challenges as a journey into new life helps us walk into painful feelings as fires of transformation. These fires burn away the old and make room for new power and love and creativity, if we can allow the burning...This opening into the greater story frees us to actively choose to surrender to, rather than resist, our experience in the present moment, trusting that there is always learning, and redemption, to be gained [in] any situation."[12] The labyrinth... provides a strong and safe container for the ups and downs of our emotional lives. When we walk through the sacred space of the labyrinth, we are reminded that all the twists and turns, the highs and lows, of our lives are sacred as well.[13]

Unlike a maze that can be tricky to navigate with its dead ends, cul-de-sacs, and intersecting pathways, the labyrinth has a single path. There is no trick to figure out the route. It consists of a threefold process of winding inward, arriving at center, and winding back out again.

When we view our experiences as happening within the sacred space of a labyrinth, we see that there are no choices that are "wrong." There are no people "too difficult" to deal with. And there are no decisions that trap us. All of our experiences play a valuable part in creating who we are and shaping who we will become.

Symbolically, the labyrinth can help us transcend our conditioning that has fostered a belief that life is confusing, complex, and uncertain. Winding inward helps us shed what no longer serves us. Arriving at the center of ourselves shines the light of awareness on some previously unrecognized aspect of our knowing. Winding outward reunites our inner understanding with our outer reality. (See **Figure 2.2 - 2.4**.)

Figure 2.2. Winding inward, sheds what no longer serves you.

Figure 2.3. Arriving at the center, shines the light of awareness on some aspect of yourself.

Figure 2.4. Winding outward, reunites your inner understanding with your outer reality.

Synthesizing each of these three phases can help us experience a transformation in personal awareness. *It is this transformation that allows us to feel a sense of wholeness and helps us prove to ourselves that we are truly heroic.* From the heroic perspective, we are constantly reminded that what we think, feel, or do can either make us feel more or less aligned to the core of who we are.

The process of synthesis is not something to be done only once and never done again. The ongoing quest continues for the rest of our lives. We will repeatedly weave through all the heroic phases over the course of our lives. New situations will arise that challenge us to synthesize from a higher level of awareness.

When we use the labyrinth as a tool to focus on forgiveness and self-forgiveness, as we will learn how to do in the rest of the book, there is an introspective and often contemplative quality to our heroic story. We discover how to reach deeply within to clear away all that stands in the way of compassion for others and ourselves. Breaking through this invisible barrier can be life changing. It often affects the very way we see and interact with the world around us. We may find that our perceptions, feelings, or behaviors have drastically shifted. We may feel less conflicted or anxious within and less judgmental or resentful toward others. Even though we are walking in the same environment as others around us, our subjective experience of it may be so drastically different that it may seem as if we are living in a parallel universe. The rest of this book is structured to help you courageously walk the heroic path of self-forgiveness and take the personal steps needed to create a heroic story that makes you proud to claim it as your own.

The Universality of the Seven Circuit Labyrinth

The seven circuit labyrinth has been found throughout the world from ancient to modern times. European archeologists discovered the seven circuit labyrinth in Knossos Crete, on coins that were from the first or second century B.C. The same symbol has been used in temple carvings in India; on cliff dwellings and pueblos in the Native American indigenous cultures of the Southwest; on petroglyphs in Ireland; turf hedges in England; and stone layouts in Sweden, Finland, Italy, Iceland, Peru, Russia and Spain.

In recent times, there has been a resurgence of interest in labyrinths. Seven circuit labyrinths are being dug out of sand on beaches, inlaid in church courtyard mosaics, painted onto portable labyrinths for use at workshops, stitched into tapestry wall hangings, laid out in stones for backyard gardens, and carved into small wooden labyrinths that can be traced with fingers. As labyrinths grow in popularity, so does the part they play in opening us to the great mysteries of life and showing us how we fit into this ongoing human saga.

Cretan coin (circa 2nd century B.C.)

North American Hopi symbol for "Earth Mother"

Labyrinth petroglyphs in Ireland

Stone labyrinth layout in Sweden

CHAPTER 3
LET THE LOGIC OF YOUR HEART GUIDE YOU ON YOUR JOURNEY

"A path without a heart is never enjoyable. You have to work hard even to take it. On the other hand, a path with heart is easy. It does not make you work at liking it."
—Carlos Casteneda
From *The Teachings of Don Juan*

For a story to really connect to its intended audience and be memorable, it must be told with heart. The same is true for our heroic story of self-forgiveness. The path of transformation, which helps us connect to our internal self, is not a process that emanates from the head, but rather from the heart.

The heart has its own form of logic that many times differs significantly from what our head would like it to be. As storyteller and author Annette Simmons points out, *"People irrationally believe they are rational."*[1] [Emphasis added.] This is not to say we don't need rationality. Rationality is generally associated with the head through brain functioning and the ability to cognitively process information using our five senses.[2] The ability to rationally process information helps us successfully operate in the material world. Without this ability we wouldn't be able to learn and understand language, solve math problems, determine our spatial orientation when crossing the street, or make basic decisions that help us prioritize our day.

The idea that our cognition is limited to what we can rationally process through the material world does a disservice to us as complete human beings. It has skewed our perception of human intelligence and tends to reduce us to mere computers that use our brains to process information through our five senses.[3] Over-reliance on rationality, particularly in Western culture, has lead to a mistrust in our non-rational ways of knowing. This narrows our perception and interferes with our ability to tap into our broader intelligence. It has also profoundly affected the stories we tell ourselves when we receive knowledge outside of what we can rationally explain.

While our head, through rationality, tells us that we have to squeeze our knowing into our five senses, our heart is not constrained in this way. Kabir Helminski, author, translator, and Sufi sheikh, describes the heart as the "threshold between two worlds:"[4]

> The heart is an intelligence beyond intellect, a knowing that operates at a subconscious level, the only human faculty expansive enough to embrace the infinite qualities of the universe. Intellect can take us only so far; it can *think* about faith, hope, and love, for instance, but it cannot entirely *experience* these qualities. This is the function of the heart. The heart is the faculty of knowing that can apprehend a qualitative universe.[5]

Tapping into the logic of our heart gives us a portal into this universal qualitative realm. It allows us to experience our lives in the larger context of humanity and our connection to all that is. It acts as our entry point into the wisdom of the ages that is greater than we can rationally access. It is the place we experience *agape*, or unconditional love, which is more expansive than we can consciously comprehend.

While our heart is a portal into the universal realm, it is *not an external place* outside of us. We access it through the vast inner reaches of our existence. It is the source of our true power that is our natural internal reference point. It is this true power that acts as a beacon calling us back to the center of ourselves in all that we do.

In the vastness of this inner space, it is our heart that we can turn to for solace and refuge from the hustle and bustle of our daily lives. It is a peaceful place that is not available to us when we live solely in the frenetic and fragmented energy of the material realm. In the fullness of our heart space we are able to block out the external and listen deeply to our inner callings. This is where we can process incoming information in a more intuitive way than logic alone allows us to do. It is where we are able to sit in awareness without judgment.

It is also the place within us where there is no suffering, even when our body, emotions, or psyche cry out in pain or anguish.

It is in the spaciousness of our heart that the transformational process has room to take place. Psychologist, teacher and author Frances Vaughn, describes transformation as "a change in the sense of self…Transformation is multidimensional. It involves the heart, mind and spirit, and affects behavior and relationships in the world."[6] As experts in the field of transformation point out, though, "… who you are 'authentically' doesn't change—rather, as false selves are shed and buried elements of yourself are retrieved and integrated, your expression of yourself aligns with who you truly are. Thought patterns, attitudes, behaviors, and ways of being in the world that are incongruent with your core self may drop away."[7]

Transformation can't be consciously willed. It requires instead an act of letting go into the mystery of the unknown. The very act of releasing invites transformation into our lives and makes us more receptive to its gifts. In the transformational moment a *metamorphosis of spirit* occurs. Metaphorically a fermentation process takes place that shifts our energy from an old form of being to a new one that is less ego-bound and more aligned to our true nature.

In the process, we may feel as if a door into the wisdom of humanity has been flung open. Our perception may drastically shift. Our experiences may take on new meaning. We may feel a different sense of peace than was possible before this profound experience.

Although it may take us time to integrate transformational change into our daily lives and alter old habits, we always retain the knowledge of this experience in our heart. In the moments when we have the presence of mind to return to our heart, the original feelings may come flooding back into our awareness and bathe us in its radiant and ever present knowing.

There is a profound level of trust that is required to enter into a heart space and open to transformation. This is especially true if it is unfamiliar terrain or we haven't had any prior transformational experiences. For those who are more comfortable living in their heads, it can be a particularly scary proposition. It may seem cognitively illogical to lean into the unknown and purposefully risk vulnerability and potential pain for the mere hope that life will be better from having gone through this process. But, this is exactly what the heroic path of self-forgiveness often challenges us to do.

Although it may be uncomfortable in the beginning, following the logic of our heart also can be extremely rewarding. We may experience a surrender of our head to a deeper *Truth* within that cannot be logically explained, such as an experiential knowing that we are to fulfill a particular calling in life. We may feel a life force surge through previous walled off parts of ourselves that can now be reintegrated into our lives, such as an extreme trauma that we had previously blocked from our memory. There may be a sense of dissolving an invisible barrier between our outer persona and the core of who we are, such as feeling more comfortable with speaking our mind. However the logic of the heart presents itself in our life, following it can help us feel more alive, happy, and authentically at home in our own skin.

Research is beginning to show that "as people learn to sustain heart-focused positive feeling states, the brain can be brought into entrainment [synchronization] with the heart."[8] "[T]his increased synchronization may alter information processing by the brain during the experience of positive emotions."[9] *As our head witnesses the positive emotions of being in sync with our heart, the more it makes logical sense to actively partner with our heart.* This is especially helpful as it relates to processing experiences on our heroic path of self-forgiveness. We can use our logical mind to grasp and retain the individual strands of experience and we can use our heart to weave those pieces together into *meaningful* and *significant* elements in our unfolding self-forgiveness story.

Following the logic of the heart can help us experience more compassion for ourselves. As we soften to our own humanity, it becomes easier to forgive our shortcomings and acknowledge the fact that we are not superhuman. The moment this recognition moves from our head to our heart, we may find that it unlocks a compartment of self-love, which releases us from self-condemnation we may have harbored toward ourselves for years.

Giving up the unrealistic demand for perfection often makes us less judgmental toward ourselves. With less self-judgment, we are less defensive. We are more likely to bring to the surface previously unrecognized internal beliefs. We are also better able to clear behaviors and patterns that negatively influenced our relationship with ourselves and others. The less judgmental we are, the safer it feels to reveal to ourselves the root causes of our self-inflicted punishment, recrimination, and negative self-talk. This level of self-honesty often gives other needy parts of ourselves permission to come forth to be acknowledged and forgiven for being needy. As we attend to the needy parts of us, we help transform them into valuable allies on our *Heroic Journey*.

Our heart is naturally forgiving and free of internal conflict. Following the logic of our heart is a gift we give to ourselves, which helps us get out of our own way so we can access this inner knowing. *Part 2* is designed to help you get out of your own way, so you, too, can personally experience this gift from inside out.

PART 2
THE JOURNEY INWARD: SHED WHAT NO LONGER SERVES YOU

Just Hatched/Photos.com

"Sometimes in life we have to become less to be more. We become whole people, not on the basis of what we accumulate, but by getting rid of everything that is not really us, everything false and inauthentic."
—Harold S. Kushner
Author of *When Bad Things Happen to Good People*

Our heroic story of self-forgiveness begins when we are called to do something different in our lives. It may be precipitated by something external, such as a layoff from work that makes us doubt our self-worth, a life altering accident that makes us repeatedly punish ourselves for an error in judgment, or a health challenge that makes us feel shame for our lack of independence. It may be precipitated by something internal, such as getting fed up with feeling perpetually like a victim, feeling angry toward ourselves for putting up with being unhappy for so long, or being tired of living with self-loathing because we are afraid to change career paths.

Whether externally or internally driven, when we step inside our *Heroic Journey's labyrinth of experiences*, we are inexplicably drawn inward toward the center of ourselves. Winding inward on our self-forgiveness journey represents the *shedding* process. We are like hatching chicks, shedding shells we have outgrown. This is the phase when we make a conscious choice to release whatever hinders our personal growth or the evolution of our character. It may cleanse our lens of understanding or quiet our inner conversation. It may allow us to feel more comfortable with our natural pace. It may assist us in accessing our innate wisdom with greater clarity and ease. Or it may open us mentally, emotionally, physically, and spiritually to new possibilities.

The tightening spiral of the labyrinth's inward journey focuses our energy and helps us concentrate so we can become more introspective. This is a time to look deeply within to examine everything we emotionally hold close to see if it fits who we really are. As biophysicist and author Jill Purce explains, "The recurrent moments of crisis and decision, when understood, are growth junctures, points of initiation that mark a release or death from one state of being and a growth or birth into the next."[1]

Ultimately, this phase of our self-forgiveness journey helps us *deconstruct our current story so we can make room for a new story that better serves who we are becoming.* It can be disconcerting to shed elements of our old story. But, once we decide to step inside our personal labyrinth, there is no turning back. An inner force propels us toward the center of ourselves to find an integrated reality. If we fail to shed what needs to be discarded, the inner force is relentless in gaining our attention. The intensity of the pain we experience is, as psychologist Anne Wilson Schaef, says, "...directly proportional to the strength of our stubbornness, our control, and our denial."[2]

The resistance we encounter in the shedding process of self-forgiveness may be an indication of the intensity of our fear that if we discard our ego defenses we will be left vulnerable. The act of casting off, however, can actually free us from our *need* for defenses. There is no need to defend what comes from who we truly are. As a result we may feel less embarrassed about showing our imperfections, more comfortable with our bare face hanging out, or more open-hearted in our dealings with others.

As with a spiral's vortex, the closer to the center we get, the greater the momentum of the shedding. When we first begin to release what stands between us and self-forgiveness, it may seem painfully slow, tedious, and threatening. But the more we shed, the easier the process becomes. If we have the courage to stay with the process to completion, the sense of freedom and lightness we experience from the release eventually outweighs the perceived threat of being defenseless and vulnerable. We may experience this freedom as a great weight lifted off our shoulders, less tightness in our chest, or a feeling of being more grounded and present in our body.

Willingness is a prerequisite to shedding what no longer serves us. When we are willing to see the *Truth* and *willing to act differently*, our old ways lose their appeal. Like outdated garments that we no longer have interest in wearing, our old ways can be put away without any regret or remorse.

When we are called to embark on the heroic path of self-forgiveness, we may have doubts about whether this journey is worth it or if it will actually get us to our destination. We may also wonder where that destination is actually leading us or how we will know it when we arrive. Courageously taking the first step is generally the only action required. Like Indiana Jones in the movie, *The Last Crusade*, the action called for may be to take the initial step off of the cliff in blind faith, trusting that the bridge will appear under us as we go.

Through the uncertainty, relying on our heroic character can help us immensely to take each new step. Such traits as trust, fortitude, persistence, and openness become invaluable tools in this phase of our journey. They give us the strength to deal with the challenges we encounter and in the process help us become more mature and wise human beings. Even though we may not consciously realize what to do next or how to do it, if we call on our heroism and pay attention to the clues, we develop an internal sense of the action called for that will propel us toward the next chapter of our heroic story.

CHAPTER 4
DO YOUR EMOTIONAL HOUSECLEANING

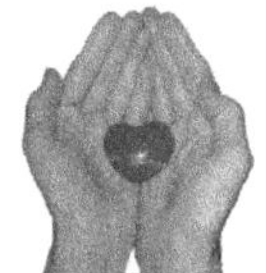

"Take control of your consistent emotions and begin to consciously and deliberately reshape your daily experience of life."
—Anthony Robbins
American self-help coach and
author of *Awaken the Giant Within*

As we step onto our heroic path of self-forgiveness, it may be helpful to understand the powerful role that emotions play in this process. We can forgive in our heads all we want, but it is not until we emotionally *feel* forgiveness, that it moves from being a mental construct to our heart space where it can become a reality that changes our lives.

Throughout the history of human evolution, emotions have acted as a sophisticated inner guidance system helping us deal with life. Emotions alert us to potential danger, assist us with decision making, help us gauge personal happiness, and allow us to communicate with and connect deeply to one another as human beings. While differences in beliefs and perspectives may divide us, emotions have the power to transcend these differences and unite us through our common bonds.

Emotions rise and fall within us depending on what is going on in our lives. As we begin to focus on self-forgiveness issues, we may find that the alarm in our emotional guidance system is triggered more than usual. If we commit to doing our emotional housecleaning as we feel triggered, we can accelerate the process of clearing what no longer serves us and move one step closer to the self-forgiveness we seek. Here are several tips concerning our emotions that can facilitate this housecleaning process:

- **Honor your emotions as they arise**. Emotions by definition are not rational. No matter how much we "wish" we didn't feel something (whether it is pain, anger, resentment, bitterness, guilt, shame, jealousy, etc.), pretending it isn't there does not make it go away. Ignoring the emotion only makes it go underground. Acknowledging our feelings brings them to the surface to be dealt with, shifted or even cleared.

- **Listen to the logic of your emotions.** Just like there is a "logic of the heart," emotions also have a logic of their own. Being open to what our emotions are trying to communicate can actually reduce their intensity. Like children who want to get a parent's attention, if we ignore what our emotions have to say, they will get louder and more persistent in an attempt to break through our conscious awareness. If we chronically ignore our emotions, they may affect us physically, or make us shut down to ourselves and others. Listening to our emotions honors this valuable aspect of our humanity and gives us a doorway into the needs and desires of the deepest and most vulnerable parts of ourselves.
- **Do not diminish what your emotions are telling you**. Our emotions by nature are dramatic. When our emotions first come to the surface, we may give ourselves a hard time about being "overly dramatic." We may discount the damage done to our psyche by a negative incident from our past. Or, we may tell ourselves that we *shouldn't* feel the way we do, since what happened to us was not nearly as bad as what someone else experienced. Our emotions, though, are *our* emotions. We have a right to feel just exactly as we do, whether or not we approve of them, agree with the reasons given, or consciously want to discount their effect on us. Owning the fact that we have a right to feel the way we do is sometimes all our emotions need to feel validated and to release what they have been holding onto, so they can move on.
- **You are not your emotions**. Years ago in a workshop I was presenting, I made this statement and a young woman sitting near the front of the room jumped up and yelled, "*I am, too, my emotions!!!*" She dramatically stomped out of the room. I could not have asked for a better example for the point I was making about how people often confuse the two. Our emotions are clues to our needs and who we are, but they are *not* who we are. Until we are able to fully understand this, we

may be caught up in the drama of our emotional whirlwinds and not be able to really hear the underlying messages that our emotional guidance system is there to help us acknowledge. If you feel like you are ruled by your emotions or have a hard time separating yourself from your emotions, you may find *Appendix A: Skills to Tame Unruly Emotions* helpful.

- **Look for the patterns in your emotions**. If we pay attention, we see that there are some common patterns of emotions that play out in people's lives. Some people are more prone to feel anger first while others are more prone to feel hurt or fear. Some people wear their emotions on their sleeves, while other people hold their emotions close to the vest. It can be helpful to recognize our own emotional patterns, so we can know how to best approach our emotional housecleaning. If you are more prone to anger, it may mean that you will be well served to look at your fear or pain that lurks in the shadows under the anger. If you are more prone to fear, it may be helpful to bring the anger "up and out" that has been seething under the surface. In both cases, once the underlying emotions are brought to conscious awareness, you may begin to feel clean from inside out.
- **Take responsibility for your emotions.** A significant step in your personal growth may be to acknowledge that no one can *make* you feel a particular way without your explicit or implicit consent. Examining the filters you use to take in information can help you own how you *choose* to experience a situation. Sometimes taking responsibility may involve owning your reaction when someone "triggers" a particular emotion within you. Are you someone who tends to emotionally lash out at others? Do you do a "dump and run," which leaves your emotions with someone else to deal with while you walk away? If so, the action called for may be to take responsibility for the negative consequences that your emotions have on others. Are you someone who often feels hurt by what others say? Do you cringe in fear when dealing with particular kinds of people? If so, you may need to examine how you are translating incoming information that

evokes such painful or fearful reactions within you. The simple act of taking responsibility for your emotions can help you take a major step forward in making the changes that will free you from longstanding emotional triggers.

- **Understand the relation between control and emotions**. Sometimes the emotions we consider negative emotions stem from the frustration that we cannot control our environment or the people in our lives. A story from someone who attended Alcoholic Anonymous (AA) meetings on a regular basis, illustrates this connection. Although the story was told anonymously, for simplicity of retelling the story, I'll call the people Bob, Sam, and Pete. One night at an AA meeting Bob was regaling his friend Sam with a story of how mad he was with someone in his life. Sam said, "Oh, you mean you didn't get your way." In describing the incident later, Bob said, "Then I was really mad. [Sam] had struck a nerve. I knew it, but I had no idea how to respond. A few weeks later, I mentioned the episode to another friend [Pete] who said, 'Oh, sure. *Anger* is "I didn't get my own way today." *Resentment* is "I didn't get my own way yesterday."...And by the way, *fear* is "I may not get my own way tomorrow."'"[1] If you experience one of these emotions, you may want to ask yourself if it is hitting one of your raw control nerves. If so, this very acknowledgement may help you take a giant step forward in owning your emotion and no longer being controlled by it.
- **Face your emotions rather than run away**. Sometimes as an ugly or painful *Truth* we have been hiding from ourselves comes to the surface, our tendency may be to turn and run away from it as fast as we can. It is natural to want to avoid pain, embarrassment, or shame. When we commit to our emotional housecleaning, we courageously face our personal *Truth*, look it squarely in the eye and thank our emotions for bringing what we needed to see to the surface. This acknowledgement often frees us to see a deeper *Truth* about ourselves and others under the ugliness or pain.

- **Feel compassion for your emotional self.** When dear friends come to you in pain, chances are you listen to what they have to say and you are there for them as they work through the issues associated with their feelings. Having compassion for your emotional self is the equivalent of being a best friend to your emotions. The more your emotions can trust you, the more honest they will be about what is going on inside. Self-honesty and self-trust make it easier to clear what no longer serves you and also builds your self-forgiveness muscles. (For an example, see *Edward's Story: Learning to be Patient with Myself* on the next page.)
- **Clear the emotions of others you have held onto.** Sometimes, especially if you tend to be empathetic, you may have taken on the emotions of others around you without even knowing it. For example, if you grew up with a father who routinely reacted to new situations with suspicion, you may find yourself as an adult also reacting in the same way. Even though your rational mind tells you that you don't need to be suspicious, you might be experiencing the situation through your father's reaction rather than your own. When you feel an emotion rise within you, it may be helpful to take an emotional inventory and ask yourself, "Is this my emotion or someone else's?" If it is your emotion, the intensity will likely remain. If, however, it belongs to someone else, the emotion may dissipate or lose its hold over you. If you determine the emotion belongs to someone else, you may benefit by lovingly, but firmly, imagining the emotion returning to its original source. Whether or not other people choose to deal with the emotions you send back to them, this small act can free you from the heaviness of carrying emotions that were never truly yours to deal with anyway.
- **Reframe your emotions as you progress on your heroic path.** In the *Part 1 Introduction*, we discussed how stories provide a context for our lives. They do this by structuring our thoughts and actions and providing a form for our dreams and aspirations. When we are stuck in negative emotions, the stories we tell ourselves may keep us from focusing on our

dreams and aspirations and in some cases may be completely debilitating. Experiencing your life as a *Heroic Journey* helps reframe your emotions in terms of how they contribute to your evolving heroic story. Within a heroic context, as emotions arise and you open to what those emotions have to tell you, you see their evolutionary nature. You honor the part they play in your personal growth. You also see how, rather than resisting your emotions, partnering with them can help you get to a deeper personal *Truth* and accelerate your emotional housecleaning process.

Emotions hold many keys to our forgiveness and self-forgiveness journey. Not only do they give us messages of what to forgive, but once we have forgiven, they anchor the change within our emotional guidance system. Once changed, we carry this "forgiveness feeling" with us through the rest of our journey, which makes future forgiveness and self-forgiveness challenges easier along the way.

Edward's[2] Story: Learning to be Patient with Myself

I was a child who grew up on a farm in the Midwest in the 1960s. Like many people, I came from a dysfunctional family. Even though my family had issues, I know that they did the best they could at the time. I was a child with a lot of health issues and that caused financial strain on my parents. My father was an impatient man and a bully. My mother was also impatient, but she was more passive. She used guilt to get what she wanted.

At fifty-nine years of age and after more than ten years of therapy, I still get impatient with myself when I fall into old patterns. One of my patterns is isolating myself from others. It is an issue I work on, but then I fall back into the old isolation rut. I get angry at myself for not following through with what I know I need to do.

▶

Feeling isolated also leads to a lot of problems with fear. In fact, that may be an underlying issue for me. Growing up around a father who was much larger than me, I was always intimidated by him. He knew if he made me angry enough, he could get me to work harder on the farm, and get his way. I always gave in to him and everyone else.

Learning how to forgive myself for being self-critical has been a lifelong process that I continue to work on. I find that even when I think I have escaped my father's tyranny, I still hear his critical voice inside of my head. My two kittens have helped me deal with self-criticism. I am learning to talk to them the way I would like to have been talked to as a child by my father. I am learning to be patient with my cats the way that my father and mother were not patient and loving with me. I still feel isolated quite a bit of the time. The book, *Removing Your Mask,*[3] has been helpful in teaching me how to allow my real self to come forward. I have read and reread this book many times. I have notes and underlines all through it. I think that this book was a fundamental step in helping me begin the process of self-forgiveness.

CHAPTER 5
LOOK FOR CLUES OF WHAT TO FORGIVE

"The keynote here is receiving: messages, signals, gifts. Even a timely warning may be seen as a gift."
—Ralph Blum
From the *Book of Runes*

As we wind inward on our self-forgiveness journey, the clues for what we need to shed to make peace with ourselves may come in many forms. They may be overt or subtle. Overt clues may include constant negative internal self-talk, debilitating depression, heavy drug or alcohol use, relentless migraine headaches, or immobilizing fear that makes it difficult to breathe or leave home. Subtle clues may include faint inklings that something inside of us is "off kilter," seeing more negative than positive about current circumstances, being bored, or having a nagging feeling that we are missing a meaningful component in life. Paying attention to both the overt and subtle signs can help us realize that something is ripe to be shed.

Self-forgiveness clues may also be inwardly or outwardly directed. Where we focus the blame for what is not going well in our lives can be a clue in determining whether we are more prone to pull the negativity inward and blame ourselves, or push negativity away from ourselves and blame others. (See **Table 5.1.**) No matter which direction we channel negativity, it may be a sign that self-forgiveness is the action called for to release blame.

Guilt and shame also often play prominently in this first phase of our journey. If they are present, it is a pretty clear sign that there is something to be shed. Guilt, as it relates to self-forgiveness, is a feeling of responsibility or self-reproach for having done something wrong. There is a punitive quality to guilt that involves having gone against a moral code, either perceived or actual. Often at the root of feeling guilt is a conflict between what we believe we should have done and what we actually did (or didn't do). The feeling of wanting to do penance or undo the harmful effects of past actions may play prominently with guilt.

Common Motives	Examples of Inward Directed Behaviors	Examples of Outward Directed Behaviors
Punishment	Self-destructive behaviors, such as inflicting physical or psychological pain on yourself	Chronically seeking revenge and paybacks, fighting or being argumentative
Sabotage	Keeping yourself from enjoying life or having what you want	Being manipulative or purposely hurting others
Denial	Discounting your perception and needs	Ignoring other people and their feelings or needs
Control	Keeping your environment so tightly ordered that, if anything changes, you become anxious	Instilling fear in others through violence and/or threat of violence, "my way or the highway" mentality
Distance from pain	Feeling numb, with little or no access to your emotions	Pushing others away who try to show you love
Judgment	Feeling that you are fatally flawed or evil at your core	Being judgmental or hyper-critical of others' behavior

Table 5.1. Examples of common motives and examples of associated behaviors that indicate self-forgiveness may be in order.

Shame is closely associated with guilt, but there are some major differences. Shame is pain arising from the feeling that we have done something improper, disgraceful, ridiculous, or regrettable. But, while *guilt is focused on our behavior or actions, shame is focused on who we are as a person*. With guilt, we have an intact sense of self. When we feel shame we have a splintered sense of self. Shame may include a sense of humiliation, self-loathing, or a feeling of defilement. It may come from childhood family patterns, traumatic incidents, or long term abuse. In extreme cases such as survivors of the Holocaust or African Americans' experience as a result of slavery, there may be a feeling of a "social death [or a loss of personhood]."[1] (See related example, *Eva's Story: Forgiving the Nazis* in *Chapter 7* on pages 50-52.)

Shame makes us feel less than in relation to others, flawed, and "not good enough," no matter how much we do. If someone loves us, we may ask ourselves, "How could they love *me*? I don't deserve it." When we are driven by shame, we may attract people and situations that reinforce our shame-based beliefs. Shame becomes our identity. Often what we think we deserve will be reflected in the way we present ourselves and how we allow ourselves to be treated.

Both guilt and shame play an important role in our socialization as human beings. They help us know what is socially accepted. When they are carried to an extreme, however, they can be harmful to our self-perception and ability to interact effectively with others. (See related example below, *Sheila's Story: My Silent Shame*.) We can use feelings of guilt and shame that arise within us as clues to a deeper understanding of ourselves and others. Once we follow where those clues lead, we go a long way toward shedding what no longer serves us on our journey to self-forgiveness.

Sheila's[2] Story: My Silent Shame

When I was sixteen years old, I was forcibly raped by a young adult male who had recently been released from prison. He was the older brother of the guy that I was dating. The rape took place at a party, in a back bedroom that I had to pass through to get to the bathroom. As I came out of the bathroom, he was waiting for me. Even though he was all over me pretty quickly, I felt that I could handle the situation discretely. Everything escalated so quickly, however, that by the time I tried to scream, my head was smashed so deeply into a pillow that I could barely breathe. It was an anal rape. The pain was beyond anything I could imagine and the experience was really outside my psychic vocabulary at the time. At that point, though, I was just trying to keep from suffocating and the pain became secondary. I am now fifty one years old and I can still hear his words, which alternated between calling me a "prick tease" to telling me it would be over soon.

▶

I did not tell a soul about this incident until I was about thirty years old. The disclosure arose from an epiphany that the whole thing was not my fault. For years I had been ashamed because I was a "prick tease," I should have been able to control the situation, I should not have even been at that party, etc. Once I vocalized what happened to my two best friends, though, I realized that it was not my fault. I do, however, sometimes still feel guilty for being in that situation.

I am not completely sure how this incident has affected my relationships, but I did not marry until I was in my forties. Perhaps I did have some trust issues. I do try not to blame anything in my life on that trauma. That day was one day out of many, many wonderful days and he was one person out of the many beautiful people I have in my life now.

Prior to meeting my husband, however, I did always seem to go for the guy that "I couldn't have." I suspect I may have been sabotaging myself. I did often feel unworthy in my youth and I lacked a sense of security. I believe I have slowly overcome all those feelings, although I am still very hard on myself.

CHAPTER 6
STOP BAD HABITS OF THOUGHT

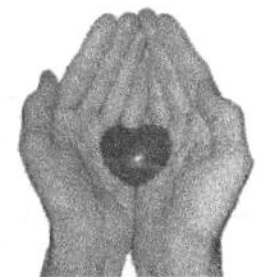

"By changing our thinking patterns,
we can change our experiences."
—Louise Hay
American new thought leader and
author of *You Can Heal Your Life*

As we begin to examine the effects that guilt and shame have on us, we may also realize that there is an associated undercurrent of negative self-talk. These negative sound tracks may be conscious or unconscious, but they can have a powerful influence in our lives. Like sound tracks that we play over and over, they can groove deeper and deeper into our psyches if left to run on their own. The thoughts we think, for better or worse, are the building blocks we use to create our life and the stories we tell ourselves about what we experience. Our thoughts also play a pivotal role in how easy or hard it is to forgive ourselves for our shortcomings.

Research has found that our bodies generally do not distinguish between thoughts that are real and those that are imagined.[1] As Oakley Ray, author and former professor of psychology at Vanderbilt University pointed out:

> …the body responds to the brain regardless of whether the beliefs and ideas are imaginary or based in reality, or whether they are positive or negative. What a person thinks does make a difference—sometimes it is good for him or her, sometimes it is bad… It is important to note that it is not the coping skills that individuals have or do not have that are important. What counts are the coping skills that individuals *believe* [emphasis added] they have or do not have.[2]

Canadian endocrinologist Hans Selye, who pioneered research on the effects of stress on human beings, validated the importance of beliefs, "It's not what happens [to you] that counts; it is how you take it."[3] This has been documented in numerous studies including in breast cancer patients who had higher rates of relapse or death within five years when they felt helpless,[4] the earlier death rate (by 1.3 to 4.9 years) among ill Chinese Americans who believed they were "fated" to die based on Chinese astrology,[5] and the extended longevity (by 7.6 years) among older adults who had positive self-perceptions about aging.[6]

The connection between beliefs and stress plays out in our bodies every day. Even though we all undergo stress, negative stress, which may result in anxious or fearful feelings, can cause an overload of adrenaline in our system. While being pumped full of adrenaline can help us survive in times of danger, if we are in chronic overload, our physical and mental system becomes distressed and can eventually begin to breakdown. Positive stress, by contrast, produces a number of chemicals including endorphins, serotonin and dopamine that help us feel more relaxed and enjoy what we are doing.[7]

One of the keys to shedding what no longer serves us is to make a conscious choice to change negative thought patterns that have helped create the negative stories we tell ourselves. Having negative thought patterns increases stressors in our bodies. Like any habit we want to change, whether it is smoking, overeating or lack of exercise, altering our thought patterns takes conscious *intention* and *attention*. This is especially true when the thought has been thoroughly ingrained in us for many years. No matter what the original source or how long it has been there, it is possible to change the negativity.

There is a powerful formula for transforming negativity into a positive force in our lives. The first part of the formula involves repeating *affirmations* to help reprogram our minds to think differently about ourselves. The second part of the formula uses *visualizations* to see ourselves as the person who has already internalized the affirmations into a new way of being.

Affirmations are positive forms of self-talk. They are statements that we declare to ourselves to be true, which are stated in the present tense. They are action-oriented and are defined as specifically as possible. An example is, "I now forgive myself for errors in thoughts, judgment, or deeds that I made in the past. I absolve myself of them to move forward in life."

Affirmations need to be repeated with commitment and fervor to produce a long-lasting change in our perspective. Anyone who has plays a musical instrument knows the importance of repetition to the learning process. Repetition of affirmations can quicken the release of old habits of thought by overriding the negativity that has been repeatedly coursing through our minds. By helping focus more of our energy on the positive, affirmations bring out our optimism. They boost our self-esteem. They also bring to conscious awareness our previously hidden potential. Muhammad Ali, one of the greatest boxers of all times, described how affirmations help with this process, "It's the repetition of affirmations that leads to belief. And once that belief becomes a deep conviction, things begin to happen."[8]

Affirmations can be especially effective at reintegrating our shattered sense of self that may have been splintered by shame. The positive energy of affirmations acts as a magnet, coaxing the scattered pieces back together. This reintegration not only shifts our thought process, but can also permanently shift the thought patterns that are associated with our emotions as well as ailments in our bodies. As Dr. Phil Shapiro, clinical psychiatrist, teacher, and administrator in mental health describes, "Positive thoughts act like medicine released from the brain's own pharmacy."[9]

When first beginning affirmations, we may not believe what we are saying because of our previous conditioning. With repetition over time, however, we reprogram our minds and begin to realize that our perception has shifted. We now see our situation in a more positive light. Self-development author and teacher, Wayne Dyer, talks about the power of belief in his book, *You'll See It When You Believe It*,[10] which turns inside out our notion of "you'll believe it when you see it." Repeating affirmations, even before we believe them, has the power to change not only our thinking, but also alter how our life unfolds.

Affirmations that have a particular resonance to you will often be the most effective for reprogramming your particular thought patterns. Below are examples and adaptations from Louise Hay's "little blue book," *Heal Your Body A-Z,*[11] that you may find helpful in shedding what no longer serves you. (See also *Appendix B* for *Affirmation Resources.*)

- *I recognize my innate self-worth.*
- *I love and approve of myself.*
- *It is safe for me to express myself.*
- *I accomplish anything I put my mind to.*
- *I am supported to live life fully.*
- *My life is peaceful and in perfect balance.*
- *I easily flow with change, knowing that I am always going in the right direction.*
- *I am passionate about life.*
- *I am excited about fulfilling my life's purpose.*
- *I let go of the past. I lovingly forgive myself and I am now free to move forward in life.*

While affirmations help change our perspective, visualizations take the abstract concepts in our minds and transform them into real and tangible changes in our lives. It has been said that before we can create anything, we must first imagine it. Visualizations engage our creativity and imagination to do just that.

Whether or not we are aware of it, we continually use visualizations to create our reality. Sometimes these visualizations are conscious. Many times, however, they are unconscious and based on pre-programmed scripts that focus on lack, limitations, stress, and difficulties.

Consciously created visualizations help us override outdated programming. They convert our affirmations into "mini stories" about how we have already achieved the positive results we want to create. These positive stories naturally engage our body, mind, emotions and psyche. They enlist our whole-hearted support in playing out the story with the positive ending we want to achieve.

Like anything we want to do well, conscious creation through visualizations may take practice at first. We may need to set aside time in our day to give our creativity and imagination permission to come forth and take the lead. As we become more adept, visualizations are incorporated into our continual state of awareness and become our way of being in the world. Shakti Gawain, a pioneer in the field of personal development and author of *Creative Visualization* says, "the ultimate point of creative visualization [is] to make every moment of our lives a moment of wondrous creation, in which we are just naturally choosing the best, the most beautiful, the most fulfilling lives we can imagine…"[12]

There are different ways of engaging our creative and imaginative process for visualizations. If you are a *visual learner*, you may actually see images and sometimes complete scenes in your mind's eye. An example of this is to imagine that you want to go to college. See yourself filling out the application for a particular college; joyously receiving the acceptance letter; listening intently in class to a professor while taking notes; studying in the university library; taking a test in which the answers come easily; and walking across the stage at the graduation ceremony to receive your diploma.

If you are an *auditory learner*, your visualization may take the form of hearing an inner voice like a radio broadcaster that describes a scene in vivid detail. For the example above of going to college, as an auditory learner, you might do best by speaking your visualization into a tape recorder and playing it back to yourself with your eyes closed or before you go to sleep. You may also find value in telling your friends the story of your visualization. Each time you hear yourself saying what you want it becomes more real in your life.

If you are a *kinesthetic learner,* you learn best by personal experience. The form your visualizations take may be more hands on. You may want to take a field trip to the local university. Go to the admission office, get an application, and fill it out. Hang out on campus in various locations so you can feel what it would be like to be a student. Go to graduation ceremonies and experience the emotion of what it will be like to cross the stage and shake hands with the dean as you are handed your diploma.

No matter which learning technique you use, visualizations activate your internal storyteller and help you create a new, more positive story about yourself. By enlisting your creativity and imagination, it becomes a fun and entertaining process that invites all aspects of your being to play. This playfulness makes it easier to release the old and evolve your story into something new and exciting. (See also *Appendix B* for *Visualization Resources.*)

Both affirmations and visualizations can play a significant role in shedding many of the negative patterns described in the following chapters. As affirmations become more woven into your thinking process and visualizations anchored into your way of being in the world, you may find over time that you have refocused more on the positive and you feel lighter since you are carrying less negative baggage. You may also realize that with less negativity there is more space in your psyche for self-forgiveness to take hold and flourish.

CHAPTER 7

RID YOURSELF OF THE VICTIM MENTALITY

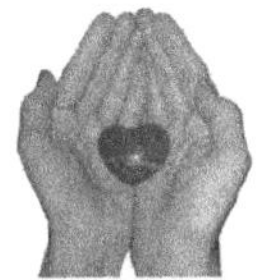

"I never told a victim story about my imprisonment. Instead, I told a transformation story - about how prison changed my outlook, about how I saw that communication, truth, and trust are at the heart of power."

Fernando Flores

Finance minister under Chilean president Salvador Allende and political prisoner after the military coup of General Augusto Pinochet

Everyone encounters challenging situations from time to time. There are situations you may find yourself in where you feel victimized, such as having a wallet or purse forcibly taken or having a co-worker betray you to get a promotion. There may be more extreme situations of victimization such as being abused as a child, violently raped, tortured, or falsely imprisoned. *There is, however, a difference between being victimized, and perpetually thinking of yourself as a victim.* When challenges are the norm, or there is a parade of new faces playing out all too familiar persecutor roles, it may be a sign that you are operating from a victim mentality. When you think of yourself as a victim, forgiveness of yourself and others is virtually impossible.

Some people are addicted to being a victim. Their lives are in constant crisis and full of high drama. There is no shortage of other people in their lives to blame or situations to point to as evidence for why situations are not going right for them. The victim stance is a childlike stance that keeps you feeling like you lack control over your destiny.

Taking full responsibility for your perception and behaviors can rid you of the victim mentality. It may be difficult at first to accept that *you are fully responsible for the way you perceive and respond to outside circumstances*. You may still have a tendency to think that what is happening is someone else's fault, your fate, karma, bad luck, oppression, etc.

Some people who operate from a victim mentality get angry at the suggestion that they bear any personal responsibility for creating their reality. They translate this through their internal filter as "blaming the victim." Since they see external situations as just happening to them, they may ask incredulously, "Do you really think I *want* to have these bad situations repeatedly happen to me?" To consider that they may have control over situations that they are just not exercising may cause them even more anxiety and shame. The mere thought of this may make it even harder to forgive themselves for their shortcomings.

I remember one time years ago being stuck in an elevator between floors of an office building. One of my women colleagues was in the elevator with me. As soon as it was clear that we were stuck, she began to panic. I tried to calm her saying I had pushed the call button for the maintenance personnel and I was sure they were on their way to help.

As the minutes passed, the woman began to have an anxiety attack. She started pacing the small space like a caged animal. I tried unsuccessfully to distract her with conversation. After a while I sat on the floor of the elevator just to get off of my feet. She huddled in the corner of the elevator crying and rocking herself.

After about twenty minutes, we could hear the maintenance personnel working to pry open the doors. When the doors finally parted, we realized we were a half floor up. We had to duck down and jump out of the elevator to make sure we cleared the darkened elevator shaft below. We went to our respective offices. I told my office cube mate that I had an exciting experience, which was a good break from the workday. I then went back to work.

A few minutes later I heard my fellow elevator colleague crying inconsolably to someone a few cubes away. I could hear her say that the experience had been one of the worst of her life. She described the jump out of the elevator as "almost dying." I have no doubt that this is how she experienced what happened. It just made it very clear to me what a difference our internal filters made to the stories we told ourselves about the same situation.

Accepting responsibility for your perception creates an opening for experiencing your life story from a new vantage point. You begin to see how the patterns of your thoughts and behaviors may in fact create experiences that reflect your victim stance. *Ridding yourself of the victim mentality helps you move from feeling passively powerless over your circumstances to being an active creator of a thriving life story.* (See **Table 7.1** to check where you fall on the continuum between victim and thriver. For more information about how you can rid yourself of the victim mentality, see my previous book, *Removing Your Mask: No More Hiding from Your Truth.*[1])

Victim ◄									► Thriver
Blaming									Accountable
1	2	3	4	5	6	7	8	9	10
Feeling weak and incapable						Feeling strong and capable			
1	2	3	4	5	6	7	8	9	10
Problem-oriented									Solution-focused
1	2	3	4	5	6	7	8	9	10
Rigid									Flexible
1	2	3	4	5	6	7	8	9	10
Stuck in pain and anger						Work through pain and anger			
1	2	3	4	5	6	7	8	9	10
Pessimistic									Optimistic
1	2	3	4	5	6	7	8	9	10
Focused on excuses						Focused on fulfilling goals			
1	2	3	4	5	6	7	8	9	10

Table 7.1. Where are you on the Victim/Thriver Continuum?

This chapter opened with a quote by Fernando Flores about how his imprisonment transformed his outlook about life into a positive and growth-producing experience. Being an active creator of your life story helps you choose how to filter a past negative experience. You decide whether to carry it as a life-deadening trauma or grist for the mill that is helping define who you are now and influencing your choice to create a more life-affirming and meaningful future. (*Eva's Story: Forgiving the Nazis* below provides an example of how one person used forgiveness and self-forgiveness to dramatically change her life story.)

Eva's[2] Story: Forgiving the Nazis

We are naturally attracted to stories of people who had harrowing or traumatizing experiences and used those experiences to their advantage. These stories speak to the resilience of the human spirit. They also remind us of the heroic capacity we all have to transform negative and seemingly unbearable experiences into a positive force of good for ourselves and the world.

Eva Mozes Kor's story is one of these inspiring stories. It is especially poignant as it relates to forgiveness and self-forgiveness. During World War II, ten year old Eva and her twin Miriam, along with their parents and two older sisters were forcibly taken to Auschwitz Concentration Camp. The rest of their family was sent to their deaths in the gas chamber. Eva and Miriam were kept alive for the sole purpose of being human guinea pigs in the sadistic twin medical experiments conducted by the notorious Dr. Josef Mengele, known as the "Angel of Death."

Eva almost died in one experiment. It took every ounce of her strength to stay alive. She knew that if she died, her sister would be killed, too, so a double autopsy could be performed. In another experiment Miriam was injected with a substance that made her kidneys stop growing. Despite the odds the sisters survived their horrific experience and were liberated from Auschwitz in 1945, just before their eleventh birthday. In 1993 Miriam died from bladder cancer that resulted from the childhood experiments inflicted on her.

After her sister died, Eva had an opportunity to visit with Dr. Hans Munch, one of the doctors at Auschwitz during her time there. Dr. Munch told Eva that he had nightmares every day of his life because of what he witnessed in Auschwitz. It was a very healing experience for Eva. She hadn't realized until that moment that it had been a bad experience for some of the Nazis, too! She asked Dr. Munch to join her at the 50th anniversary of Auschwitz. As a gift to him, Eva decided to write a letter of forgiveness and read it to him at the ceremony.

▶

She said, "I knew it would a meaningful gift, but it became a gift to myself as well, because I realized I was NOT a hopeless, powerless victim. When I asked a friend to check my spelling, she challenged me to forgive Dr. Mengele too. At first I was adamant that I could never forgive Dr Mengele but then I realised [sic] I had the power now…the power to forgive. It was my right to use it. No one could take it away…As I did that I felt a burden of pain was lifted from me. I was no longer in the grip of pain and hate; I was finally free. The day I forgave the Nazis, privately I forgave my parents whom I hated all my life for not having saved me from Auschwitz. Children expect their parents to protect them, mine couldn't. And then I forgave myself for hating my parents. Forgiveness is really nothing more than an act of self-healing and self-empowerment. I call it a miracle medicine. It is free, it works and has no side effects."[3]

As a result of her profound experience, Eva Kor has become very outspoken about Auschwitz and the atrocities of the Holocaust. She has also founded the C.A.N.D.L.E.S. (Children of Auschwitz Nazi Deadly Lab Experiments Survivors) Holocaust Museum and Education Center in Indiana, which focuses on shedding light on the effects of hatred and prejudice.

There is an interesting side note to Eva's story. After her public announcement that she had forgiven Dr. Munch and the Nazis, she received an immense amount of criticism from Holocaust survivors and others, who were appalled and angry with her declaration of forgiveness. They said she had no right to forgive the Nazis for what they did.

It should be reiterated, that forgiveness does *not* excuse or condone offenses. (See *Chapter 1* for more detail.) Perpetrators of political acts of violence, and indeed *any* act of violence, need to be held accountable for their actions. They should be appropriately sanctioned to prevent further violence against innocent people. Eva's decision to forgive the Nazis was an act of empowerment she did for herself *in addition to* holding them accountable for the atrocities they committed. Eva's act of forgiveness freed her from continuing to carry the pain they inflicted on her and her family. Without that heavy burden she felt lighter and more buoyant. She was able to refocus her attention on creating the future rather than continually reliving the past.

▶

Forgiveness and self-forgiveness cannot be forced, whether from external or internal pressure. They are choices we each make at our own pace when the time is ripe. Just knowing forgiveness and self-forgiveness are options, though, can profoundly shift our victim mentality and open the door to a more empowered mindset.

CHAPTER 8

FIND THE CORRECTIVE VALUE IN CRITICISM

"Don't mind criticism. If it is untrue, disregard it; if unfair, keep from irritation; if it is ignorant, smile; if it is justified it is not criticism, learn from it."
—Author unknown

As human beings we undoubtedly have found ourselves in situations where we received a mixture of positive and negative feedback, whether the critique has come from parents, teachers, friends, employers, or people we didn't even know. When we are unforgiving of our shortcomings, it may be very difficult to hear what people are saying, much less learn and grow from their feedback.

There are a variety of reactions we can have to criticism, some of which impede our learning and growth. Luckily there are also tools we can use to help us get out of our own way, so we can let in the feedback that will promote our personal evolution.

- **Fixating on negative feedback**. No matter how much positive feedback some people receive, they totally discount the positive. Instead they focus on the negative, even when it was only a minor part of the overall critique. Sometimes the negative becomes so amplified in their minds that they are consumed by it. They may continually mull over in their minds what they "could have" or "should have" done better. If you are someone who lets negative feedback ruin your entire day, you may benefit by stepping back and consciously shifting your focus to the positive. Take in the positive and celebrate your triumphs large and small. To put negative feedback in its proper perspective, you may want to ask yourself, "How important is this negative feedback in the whole grand scheme of things?" By seeing the feedback from a more balanced perspective you are more likely to find the value of both the positive and negative critique that you receive. From a more balanced perspective you also may find yourself more forgiving of yourself for having human flaws.

- **Feeling wounded to the core**. Some people who consider themselves highly sensitive may feel deeply hurt by comments they perceive as negative. Even when something was said off-the-cuff with very little thought going into the feedback, people who come from this perspective may take to heart what is said. In some cases, they experience negative feedback as a reflection of their innate worth as human beings. If you feel wounded to the core, you may be slipping into a belief that you are a victim at the mercy of what others say or do "to" you. (If this is the case, you may want to review *Chapter 7: Rid Yourself of the Victim Mentality* for strategies to transform your mindset.) Feeling wounded may also indicate you are focused on the pain, rather than spending your energy separating out the feedback others give you from your core sense of self. The following exercise may help you refocus your energy.

  Exercise: Wounding Arrow. The next time you feel wounded by someone's negative feedback, see the feedback as an arrow that pierced your heart. Visualize pulling the arrow out of your heart, while your heart heals the physical wound. Examine the arrow in your hand. Ask yourself whether it reminds you of any past heart-wounding experiences. If so, you may find *Chapter 12: Quit Holding Yourself Hostage to Your Past* particularly helpful. Does the arrow represent a piercing of your sense of perfection? If so, you may find *Chapter 9: Release Perfectionism* particularly helpful. This simple exercise can help you reduce the emotional charge from feeling wounded. With less emotional charge it is easier to honestly examine the feedback and take to heart any opportunities for growth it presents. As you become more skilled at not feeling wounded by criticism, it also becomes easier to forgive yourself for having taken in the heart-piercing arrows in the first place.

- **Fixating on positive feedback.** Rather than take in corrective feedback that could be helpful, some people totally gloss over it and hear only the positive. In doing so they may miss a valuable opportunity to learn and grow from the the appraisal from others. Sometimes people who are unwilling to take in criticism have such a high opinion of themselves that they develop an unrealistic view of how they come across to the people around them. In failing to see their own behavior patterns, they may inadvertently hold themselves back from succeeding in life. Instead they remain oblivious about why they are continually overlooked for promotions, have personal relationship challenges, or feel a sense of internal emptiness. If you are someone who has this tendency, you may benefit from asking yourself what critique you have previously been ignoring that would be helpful for you to hear now. Think back about feedback you received from people in different parts of your life. Was there something that was consistently told to you as a child by your parents, coach, teacher, etc. that you are still being told today? You may want to ask a few trusted friends or family members to share what they see as your biggest blind sight that hampers your personal growth. By honestly looking at yourself, you may finally hear helpful feedback that, if taken to heart, could change the direction of your life.
- **Failing to develop good "feedback filters."** As the examples above illustrate, some people see criticism as all or nothing. They either take all of it in or they reject all of it. To effectively deal with criticism, we can all benefit by filtering the feedback we receive. Feedback from others can be a mixed bag. Some of it may have validity for us and some of it may actually say more about our critics than it does about us. Others may project onto us their own shortcomings or negative baggage. They may deliver feedback with the same cruel edge they experienced as children. They may have ulterior motives unrelated to us, such as wanting to cut other people down to size to elevate themselves. It is up to us to choose how we process criticism that comes our direction.

When we have good feedback filters, we consider the source of the feedback. Does the person have our best interest at heart? Are they trying to get through to us to let us know something important we need to hear? Or, do they have their own agenda that has nothing to do with us? As we sort through the feedback to determine what is worth processing, the following exercise may be helpful.

Exercise: Sort the Laundry. Visualize two empty laundry baskets in front of you. One is labeled "mine." The other is labeled "theirs." Before you take in criticism from others, ask yourself if it belongs to you or if it belongs to them. If the criticism is theirs you may feel an internal sense of relief. If so, throw the criticism into the basket labeled "theirs" and don't even bother to think about it anymore. If you honestly get a sense it is yours or there is even a grain of *Truth* that is yours, throw it in your basket. Only then do you need to process the feedback to determine what relevance it has for you.

- **Internalizing criticism**. Having good feedback filters not only helps us better filter external criticism, it also helps us become more skilled at filtering internal criticism. There are some similarities between being wounded to the core by external criticism and internalizing criticism. With both, there is a lot of internal negative rumination. There is, however, a major difference. *While feeling wounded has an overlay of being victimized by someone or something external, when we internalize the criticism, we become our own victimizer*. Like the elephant that no longer needs to be chained to the post to be held captive, we no longer need anyone external to criticize us. We have perfected the technique for ourselves. If you are the type of person who unmercifully criticizes yourself for even minor offenses, ask yourself the following questions:

- "Whose voice am I hearing inside my head?" "Is it someone who used to repeatedly criticize me as a child?" If so, use the laundry basket exercise above. See yourself taking off the "cloak of criticism," and throwing it in the other person's basket.
- "Is there a traumatic past experience of being shamed for something I swore I would never let myself experience again?" If so, getting in touch with that experience may help you unload the charge that current experiences are plugging into that re-traumatize you each time a new situations happens.
- "Have I set up a punitive inner environment that makes me afraid of making mistakes?" If so, you may benefit by practicing being kinder and more open-hearted toward yourself.
- "What strategies can I use to change self-criticism into self-evaluation?" By lessening the negative charge associated with criticism, you may feel less victimized by the feedback and find it easier to take in only the information that will be beneficial to your personal growth.

Answering these questions honestly can help you filter out internal criticism that is detrimental to your person growth. The exercise below may be helpful as well.

Exercise: Self-Criticism Log. For one day keep a self-criticism log. Each time you criticize yourself, write down the time and the words you hear yourself saying. Categorize the type of criticism that it represents. (See **Table 8.1** for an example.) At the end of the day, look for patterns in your criticism. Ask yourself when the pattern began. Working through some of the other exercises and questions in this chapter that may relate to your situation can help you get to the root cause of your self-criticism. Bringing it to awareness can reduce your internal negative rumination and help you shift your pattern so you are less hard on yourself.

Time	Criticism	Type of Criticism
7:30 a.m.	*Oh, no, I forgot to set the alarm! Now I'm late. I'm such a dope!*	*Intelligence*
8:00 a.m.	*These pants are too tight. I'm a big, fat slob.*	*Body image*
9:30 a.m.	*I don't have a clue what the boss just asked me to do. I'm so stupid.*	*Intelligence*
10:45 a.m.	*I hate this job and I hate myself for staying here! Why can't I figure out something worthwhile to do with my life?*	*Self-hatred, Lack of purpose and meaning*
12:30 p.m.	*I can't believe I just ate that whole pizza instead of taking half of it home for dinner. It's no wonder I look like a whale.*	*Body image*
5:30 p.m.	*I didn't get anything done today at work. I'm such a lousy employee.*	*Self-motivation, self-worth*

Table 8.1. Self-Criticism Log. For one day track each time you criticize yourself. Look for patterns to your criticism, examine the root cause, and then develop specific filtering strategies to discontinue your pattern.

- **Finding the corrective value and moving on.** At the crux of receiving criticism is our ability to deeply listen to feedback, determine its value, make any needed changes, and move on. Criticism is just criticism. It is the meaning we assign to it and how we process it that determines whether we are demoralized by it or use it to enhance our lives.

Each time we effectively deal with criticism, it becomes easier to forgive ourselves for our shortcomings. No longer are we held captive to our internal or external perception of who we "should be." We begin to relax into who we actually are and appreciate our individualized journey of becoming.

Donny Osmond's Champion Attitude

As a fan of *Dancing with the Stars*, I watch with fascination each week as the celebrities deal with criticism from the judges. Sometimes they argue with the judges. Sometimes they are personally wounded by the criticism and berate themselves so much that it negatively affects their performance the following week. Sometimes, like Season Nine star Donny Osmond, the celebrities listen intently for what they can change about their dancing in the corrective spirit it is given by the judges.

As a professional singer and former teen idol, Donny Osmond is used to being in the limelight, faults and all. One week on *Dancing with the Stars*, Donny acknowledged that his Quickstep dance was so bad it was "one of the worst moments of my life." Another week, Judge Len Goodman said Donny's 1980s themed Paso Doble was "the most scariest [sic], bizarre Paso Doble we've ever seen" and Donny's performance was awarded last place.

As the consummate performer, Donny thanked the judges for their feedback, took it back to the dance studio and made the suggested changes to improve his dancing. What he didn't do was let the judge's comments, or even his own assessment of his performance, affect his belief in himself or his perception of his value as a human being. He kept his energy focused on changing his techniques and practicing until those new techniques became second nature. Ultimately, Donny's hard work and perseverance paid off when he won the coveted mirror ball trophy and became the *Dancing with the Stars* Season Nine champion.

CHAPTER 9
RELEASE PERFECTIONISM

*"Perfectionism may be the ultimate self-defeating behavior.
It turns people into slaves of success—
but keeps them focused on failure..."*
—Hara Estroff Marano
Author and editor at large of *Psychology Today*

One of the particularly bad habits of thought that keeps us from forgiving ourselves, especially in Western culture, is the idea that we need to be perfect. Many people strive to be "super employees" *and* "super parents." We see this bad habit being trained into our children from an early age. More and more we see young people pressured to not only receive good grades to get into the right college, but also excel at multiple extracurricular activities, work on the weekends and devote any "extra" hours to public service. Some toddlers are even being pressured to read at earlier ages and finish potty training as soon as possible, so they can get into the "right" pre-school.

Feeling we have to be perfect makes it very hard for us to forgive ourselves when we make a mistake or fall short of our expectations. We often withhold self-love until we demonstrate that we are "worthy." Our failure to realize that we are innately worthy increases the pressure on ourselves for external proof of our worthiness. It also keeps us from experiencing unconditional self-love. (For an example of one person's experience related to unconditional self-love, see *Ellen's Story: A Mother's Lesson in Forgiving Her Imperfections* on pages 64-65.)

An additional problem with perfectionism and its companion, overachievement, is that they are not sustainable. They are like hungry beasts. No matter what we do, we can never *do* enough or *be* enough. We are continually trying to compensate for our fear of failure. We think we "should be" (more talented, better human beings, smarter, etc.) than we can possibly be.

If you feel this "should" of perfectionism creep into your consciousness, it may be an indication that there is an error in your thinking process that you would be well served to release. In her book, *Mindset: The New Psychology of Success,*[1] social psychologist Carol Dweck found in her research that there were generally two different kinds of mindsets, a *fixed mindset* and a *growth mindset.* With a *fixed mindset*, people have a rigid thinking process. They see their talents and abilities as fixed and unchangeable. Either they have certain capabilities or they don't. Through this filter, people often have a pessimistic or fatalistic perspective on life. They may avoid challenges, since trying to meet them might be a set up for failure. They also may feel stagnant or frustrated at the lack of personal fulfillment. Knowing internally that they are squelching their own potential, they may have a constant need to prove themselves. It is this mindset that is often more prone to perfectionism.

By contrast, people with a *growth mindset* have a more fluid thinking process. They see themselves as lifelong learners whose talents, intelligence and capabilities evolve over time. They see their world through the eyes of creativity, expansiveness and opportunity, which allows them to experience with awe the wonder of the world around them. As a result, they tend to be more optimistic, more willing to take risks, happier about how their lives are unfolding and, ultimately, more likely to be successful in life.

If you find your internal perfectionist making unrealistic demands, berating you for failing at a task, or telling you that you are worthless when you fall short of your goal, stop and ask yourself if you have slipped into a fixed mindset. If so, the following reminders might help shift your perspective toward a growth mindset:

- **Adopt a beginner's attitude**. Even though you may feel called to do something new, you may also be scared to actually make the change. Maybe it feels safer to remain where you are. Perhaps you don't want to give up the comfort of your current lifestyle or the prestige that comes from being an expert in your field. Whatever your reasons for maintaining the status quo, committing to a growth mindset can help you adopt a beginner's attitude. You look at situations with fresh eyes. You approach challenges with the curiosity of a child.

You also willingly open yourself to possibly feeling incompetent again. Having a beginner attitude makes it easier to step out of your comfort zone and minimizes the stress that often accompanies a change in mindset.

- **Recognize that learning takes effort.** Learning to tie our shoes, ride a bike, read a book, or drive a car, helps us know firsthand that learning takes effort. The learning process may be more time consuming than you would like it to be. It may also be more mentally, emotionally, or spiritually taxing than you anticipated. Giving yourself time to learn something new can reduce the pressure you put on yourself to instantly master it. Lessening the pressure may also reduce your fatigue and actually become an energizing force for your learning process.
- **Realize that it is okay to fail**. It is part of how you learn what works and doesn't work. Before Thomas Edison successfully invented the incandescent light bulb, he failed thousands of times. He also failed thousand of more times during the creation of his 1,092 other patented inventions, including the phonograph and the motion picture camera. As he said about failure, "I have not failed. I've just found 10,000 ways that won't work."[2] Being okay with failure reduces the frustration and unrealistic expectations you may be placing on yourself.
- **Chip away at tasks one by one to reach your goal.** Sometimes when you first see a vision of what you want, it may feel overwhelming because it seems so big or unattainable. You may initially feel frozen, not knowing where to start. But, if you pay close attention, you will often get an inkling of a task you need to do first. Once you do the first task, others often present themselves, sometimes in a specific order. Other times you may have to just pick one of the many tasks and begin working through the list one by one. Diligently applying yourself to the tasks at hand may feel tedious or slow, but over time you will be able to look back and see how far you have come toward accomplishing what you set out to achieve.

- **Be willing to let go of your small goals to get what you ultimately want.** Having clear goals and working diligently toward them can fuel your vision. However, there may be times when you find that you get blocked at every turn from making further progress in the direction you are currently headed. When this situation occurs, you may want to ask yourself if you have slipped into a fixed mindset by rigidly hanging onto a particular image of how your journey "should" unfold, rather than following a more unpredictable, but potentially more fruitful path. Just asking this question often opens your mind and sets you once again on the learning edge.

Ellen's[3] Story: A Mother's Lesson in Forgiving Her Imperfections

They say there is no other guilt like that of a mother. I would have to agree, and especially for someone like me whose sweetest dream in life has always been to be an exceptional, amazing mom to someone. I take mothering so seriously that I've been known to show up and briefly pull my four and five-year-olds out of class, so I can apologize to them if I was cranky that morning. I don't demand perfection of myself so sternly in any other area of my life, but when it comes to mothering, I expect myself to be on top of my game 100% of the time. Heck, I feel guilty if I go one night without reading to them or, (gasp!) feed them something not totally healthy and organic!

My greatest lesson so far related to self-forgiveness has come from my youngest and best teacher, and from the reality that no matter how hard I try, I cannot be a perfect mother. One of those mornings happened to be my oldest son's first day in pre-school. We had pumped him up about riding the bus all week and there he stood at the glass back door on his tiptoes dancing at the thought of that bus pulling up.

▶

The minutes rolled by as we assured him the bus would arrive any second. When the clock rolled past 8:00 a.m., I became worried, called the school and discovered that they could not pick him up on the bus until I brought in the signed paperwork they had given me a week before. I had simply forgotten about the paperwork. My heart dropped through the floor. I turned to my beautiful, blonde haired, crystal clear, blue eyed little boy, and I pulled him into my lap. With tears rolling down my cheeks I calmly told him that Mommy had goofed and because of that the bus wasn't coming.

He looked directly into my eyes, his eyes so brand new and sparkling, and his entire face transcended into the most beautiful smile. His little hand came up and gently touched my cheek. Without saying a word, his touch communicated, "It's okay Mom. No big deal. I forgive you."

Every time I find myself in that familiar place of wanting to tear myself down over the memories of my mistake-ridden past, I see my little boy's sparkling eyes forgiving me. I am reminded of the power and the sheer beauty of unconditional love. I realize that without showing *myself* that same kind of love, I put that very special connection and unconditional love I have with my children at risk. They need a healthy, happy mom, a mom that has *forgiven* herself and finds self-love in her heart as well. So I forgive myself as my gift to them, knowing that only by forgiving will I ever be able to give and receive the greatest gift of all: unconditional love.

CHAPTER 10
STOP COMPARING YOURSELF TO OTHERS

"To love is to stop comparing."
—Bernard Grasset
Contemporary French philosopher

Human beings are by nature relational creatures. You do yourself and others a great disservice, however, if you find yourself often feeling of less value than others, superior to others, jealous of someone else's accomplishments, prejudice, or wishing you were anyone other than yourself. This "one-up/one-down" perception of yourself and others is not simply an observation. It is a judgment that denies the unique value of each person. It keeps you from seeing the differences as positive attributes. It is also a time waster that diverts your attention away from fulfilling your heart's desires. (See related *Chapter 24: Give Your Authentic Gifts to the World.*)

Spending time judging yourself in relation to others leaves no room for self-forgiveness to thrive. This is especially true when your comparisons have become so habituated that you don't even realize consciously how often you are making them. (See *Dana's Story: My Comparison Habit* on pages 70-71.) Constant comparison may in fact amplify your shortcomings to the point of obsession. If you relate to any of these challenges, you may want to try the following exercise.

Exercise: Comparison Log. For one day, pay attention to each time you compare yourself to others, including when you feel jealous, superior to, or lesser than anyone else. Make a note of the type of thought you had at the moment you made the comparison. Did you feel up or down in relation to the other person? (See **Table 10.1** for an example.) At the end of the day, look at your list and see if there is a pattern to your comparisons. Are there certain people you compare yourself to repeatedly? If so, why? What emotions do they trigger in you? Do you compare yourself more at work or in a certain kind of social setting? Are your comparisons based on skills, innate traits, behaviors, outside circumstances, status, etc? What is your fear underlying the need to compare yourself to others?

Type of Comparison	Content of Comparison	Type of Comparison
☑ One-Up ☐ One-Down	*I am so much smarter than David. He is such an idiot.*	*Intelligence*
☐ One-Up ☑ One-Down	*I could never wear that dress the way Sally does. I am so fat.*	*Physical attribute*
☑ One-Up ☐ One-Down	*Why did they hire Jim? He is from the lower East Side.*	*Prejudice, worth as a person*
☐ One-Up ☑ One-Down	*Beverly is such an expert in this field. I do not know if I will ever be able to do the job as well as she does.*	*Skills*
☑ One-Up ☐ One-Down	*Robert is definitely not cool enough to be in our group.*	*Social acceptability*
☐ One-Up ☑ One-Down	*Helga is so gifted. She is a great pianist and poet. I just do not have any gifts like she does.*	*Innate value*

Table 10.1. Comparison Table. For one day pay attention to how often you compare yourself with others and make a note of the content of your thoughts and feelings to help you see any patterns. From this exercise, prime areas for self-forgiveness may become very clear to you.

This type of introspection can help you see areas that are prime for self-forgiveness and corrective action. You may also find how much of your time is actually spent comparing yourself to others. Once you stop wasting time with this bad habit of thought, you may find how much more time you have to fulfill who you uniquely are, which is ultimately what you really want!

Psychotherapist, leadership coach, and author Jane Shure found out this *Truth* for herself:

> In my earlier years, I held the misguided notion that if I wasn't smart in particular ways, then I wouldn't be liked by the people I wanted to be friends with. I don't recall when it was, but at some point in my adult life, long after I achieved a Masters and Ph.D. degree, years after

> becoming a wife and mother, a light bulb went off, flashing the message: why not simply value what you do well and stop giving so much importance to your shortcomings. What a concept![1]

When we focus instead on finding and developing our strengths, it changes our relation to not only ourselves, but also the people around us. In 1998, Donald O. Clifton, Ph.D., along with Tom Rath and a team of scientists at Gallup Research, created the online *StrengthsFinder* assessment tool.[2] In 2001, Donald Clifton collaborated with *New York Times* bestselling author, researcher and business consultant, Marcus Buckingham, on a book, *Now, Discover Your Strengths.*[3] The premise of this book is that by cultivating our strengths, rather than our weaknesses, we maximize our productivity and personal satisfaction. By ceasing to do what we don't like, we are more likely to thrive and be happy. Since then Marcus Buckingham has written several other books about how we can apply our strengths in daily life. These books and tools have helped millions discover their gifts and talents and learn how to lean into their strengths.

Developing what we do well rather than focusing on our shortcomings, goes a long way toward ending our need to compare ourselves to others. No longer do we see our value relative to others. We know our value is innate. Instead of spending energy placing ourselves in a pecking order in relation to others, we focus our attention on more fully developing our strengths and giving our unique gifts to the world as only we can do. This shift in focus helps us realize that there is no need for comparison. We each have strengths and gifts that complement one another. This awareness helps us develop a sense of reverence and awe for the unique role we each play in the grand scheme of life. It also often gives us the impetus we need to leverage our strengths for the betterment of humanity.

Dana's[4] Story: My Comparison Habit

I don't know when it started, maybe as early as elementary school when Laurie, the pretty new girl at school, wanted nothing more than to be a part of our group of friends. At ten I was already programmed to perceive a potential threat to my status. Feeling inferior to her caused me to behave in ways intended to diminish her, but just as likely resulted in alienating the people I was so diligently trying to hold on to. Of course, I didn't know that at the time. All I knew was that the thing I was most afraid of was happening. My friends were choosing her over me.

Then came Junior High. Don't even get me started! I went in with a very arrogant, superior attitude. After all, I'd been the bomb in elementary school, where I started the cheerleading squad and the school paper. I was part of the popular crowd.

So, how could it be possible that in Junior High I wasn't selected to be a cheerleader...or a pom pom girl...or get a lead in the school play? It was an incredible shock. Was it possible that I wasn't pretty or talented enough to have the things I wanted? I began to completely re-evaluate who I thought I was.

The wounding to my adolescent psyche has remained and caused me to be caught in the comparison trap for most of my life. Even now, I'm aware of sizing myself up when I meet someone new. Are they smarter than me? Prettier? More talented? Will they be liked/loved more than me because of their superiority? Ultimately, the question is: Will they get what I wanted—the guy, the part, the job, the recognition? I know it's insidious and ridiculous. But somehow, even in middle age in life, I haven't been able to shake the habit.

Having studied psychology, I understand self-fulfilling prophesies. I understand that our unconscious behavior very often creates the thing we are most afraid of, or at least our selective filters cause us to only see what we believe to be true.

Even knowing this, I haven't been able to turn off my comparison to others.

▶

The sad part is that the result of this type of thinking is so negative—from self-judgment and criticism to feelings of alienation. The hardest, and most ironic result is that it keeps me separate from others, exactly the opposite of what I say I want. I know I put this behavior in place as a protective mechanism. If I can figure out where I stand, I won't do the "wrong" thing and end up getting hurt. But this behavior is no longer useful. As long as I'm in comparison to others, perceiving myself as either superior or inferior, I can't appreciate who they truly are, or who I am. And the outcome of that thinking is that I don't have the type of deep, connected relationships I say I want to have.

CHAPTER 11
DITCH SELF-RIGHTEOUSNESS

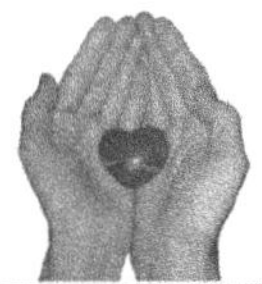

"...we may even be able to deceive ourselves in the belief of our obvious righteousness. But deep down, below the surface of the average [person's] conscience, he[/she] hears a voice whispering, "There is something not right," no matter how much his[/her] rightness is supported by public opinion or by the moral code."

—Carl G. Jung

Swiss psychiatrist and founder of analytical psychology

Self-righteousness is a particular form of comparison with others that keeps us from coming to terms with our personal flaws and prevents us from forgiving ourselves for our humanity. Without this vital connection to ourselves, we have a hard time connecting to others in a genuine and heart-felt way and difficulty forgiving them for their flaws and humanity.

Self-righteousness implies a moral superiority that breads arrogance. It can make us judgmental, condescending, and intolerant of the opinions and behaviors of others. When we are full of self-righteousness, others may experience us as detached, cold-hearted, or punitive.

People who are self-righteous sometimes confuse their stance with self-confidence. The two couldn't be more different, though. Self-righteousness is an external façade created by our ego to prop up the illusion that we are "better than others." But, this need to feel superior constantly needs to be reinforced. By contrast, self-confidence radiates from within. It is a quiet, peaceful assurance that needs no external validation.

Deciding to shed self-righteousness means we take ourselves off our own pedestal. In doing so, *we may find that the height of our pedestal is proportional to the depth of denial we have about our own shortcomings*. As we examine those shortcomings, we may discover that we are just as flawed as those we condemned with our smug superior attitude.

Releasing self-righteousness allows us to see ourselves and others in a more compassionate light. As we come to terms with our personal flaws and forgive ourselves for having them, we are more forgiving of those who are still blind to theirs. Instead of focusing on what separates us from others or what is wrong with them, we focus on what connects us in a heart-felt way to the underlying humanity we all have in common.

Marion's[1] Story: Exposing My Double Standard

One night about ten years ago I was watching a news program that showed an angry mob of people carrying signs and spewing venom toward a particular minority group. Some of the people interviewed professed to be religious as they self-righteously proclaimed that this minority group was an abomination to God and should have no rights. I became angry at how people, who professed to be religious, could be so intolerant. Then I realized something else. I was feeling very intolerant of intolerant, self-righteous people. I had to laugh at the irony!

Over the next several weeks my double standard kept bothering me. I wanted to believe that I had an inclusive, tolerant, "live and let live" attitude where all perspectives have value. The *Truth* was that I smugly thought of myself as more loving, more educated, more enlightened, and dare I say, more valuable as a human being than those I perceived as intolerant and self-righteous.

Right after I acknowledged this ugly *Truth* about my superior attitude, I attended a social work conference where I was presenting a workshop. The last day of the conference I participated in a workshop on the spread of fundamentalism around the world, including religious and political fundamentalism. In the discussion, I mentioned the double-standard I had been internally wrestling with for several weeks.

▶

In talking it out with this wise group of social workers, I realized that while I see it as a good and admirable quality to be inclusive of a variety of perspectives, many "intolerant" people, regardless of their religious or political affiliation, see inclusion as a threat to their defined way of life. By putting controls and laws in place to limit inclusion of other perspectives, they believe they are preserving a way of life from being eroded. Ultimately, even though the visions may differ drastically, both those who want inclusion and those who want exclusion have a desire to preserve a particular way of life. I realized my own fear was that my freedom could be taken away by those who oppose my perspective.

When I finally acknowledged my fear, I delved into it more deeply. If the worst case scenario happened and I was sentenced to live the rest of my life in a dank prison cell, would my freedom *truly* be taken away? The answer for me was that even if my body was imprisoned, "I" would always be free, since freedom is a state of mind. No one can take away my personal freedom without my consent. My superior attitude melted away since I no longer needed it to hide my deepest fear. At the moment that this realization really sunk in, I finally got a glimmer of what Martin Luther King, Mohandas Gandhi, Desmond Tutu, and other great leaders who had been imprisoned knew first hand and taught with so much eloquence and passion.

Does exposing the root of my double standard mean that I just lay down in the face of attempts to take away our freedom? Absolutely not! Do I still take political action based on my perspective? Absolutely! If anything, it makes the lessons of the great leaders mentioned above even more poignant. They all stressed taking action to stop perceived wrongs from occurring. The difference for me now is that operating from a deeper *Truth*, rather than fear, makes my actions less angry, more powerful and more clearly directed. Taking myself off my own pedestal takes away my arrogant edge, which makes it easier for me to be more present and really listen to the messages of *Truth* that underlie the rhetoric of those whose views are 180 degrees from my own.

CHAPTER 12
QUIT HOLDING YOURSELF HOSTAGE TO YOUR PAST

"The farther behind I leave the past,
the closer I am to forging my own character."
—Isabelle Eberhardt
Swiss writer and explorer in North Africa

As we shed what no longer serves us, we will inevitably encounter past experiences that we regret. While we may feel anger, disappointment, sorrow or remorse about what occurred (or did not occur), our sense of loss does not have to be debilitating. If you find yourself feeling like a dog unable to let go of a bone, it may be a sign that you are holding yourself hostage to your past. Reasons you may hold yourself hostage and are in need of self-forgiveness include:

- **Feeling you cannot disclose toxic secrets**. Sometimes there are situations in our past that are extremely embarrassing or shameful, which we do not want anyone to know, including ourselves. Other times we may have agreed consciously or unconsciously to hide what someone else did to us, such as incest, childhood physical abuse, or rape (as exemplified in *Sheila's Story: My Silent Shame* in *Chapter 5*, page 39). Regardless of the specific situation, we may fear the consequences that disclosing our secret will bring. We also may not want to risk being that vulnerable again or re-traumatize ourselves by reliving the experience. Yet, holding in secrets can be extremely toxic for us. Toxins may take the form of feeling ugly, stupid, worthless, inferior, flawed, unworthy, distrustful, humiliated, etc.

  To rid yourself of these toxins, sometimes you need to disclose your secrets to someone else like a trusted friend, counselor, or other person in authority. Sometimes the act of disclosure alone begins to rid toxins from your system. Whether or not you decide to actually divulge the information to anyone else, though, you can energetically release toxins. If the toxins relate to someone else, you may want to *visualize sending the energy back to its originator so you no longer hold it inside of you.* If the toxic secret originates from something you did (or did not do), one of the next three sections may help you shed the toxins.

- **Having unresolved pangs of conscience.** When we feel guilty for not adhering to our moral standards, we may feel a dynamic tension between who we believe ourselves to be and the behaviors we actually exhibit. To release ourselves from this internal tension, one solution is committing to change our future behavior to meet our moral standards. An example is having lied to someone and committing now to be truthful in the future. Another solution is to change our moral standards to meet our current behavior. An example is being raised in a strict spiritual tradition that prohibited mingling with those outside our sect and deciding that this perspective no longer fits our personal moral code. Once we resolve the dynamic tension, self-forgiveness often becomes a natural by-product.
- **Believing that you need to do penance**. While pangs of conscience generally relate to guilt over behaviors or actions, feeling a need to do penance relates to shame and may mean that we have a core belief that our flaws are evidence that we are innately bad or "sinful." Shifting this belief system may be more challenging than releasing pangs of conscience. Since it is rooted more deeply in our core perception of ourselves, we often cannot address the need to do penance at the psychological level alone. *Part 3* of this book will focus on how to reach more deeply within yourself to release this core issue, keep it from continuing to zap your life force, and help you forgive yourself in the process.
- **Punishing yourself for hurting others**. As we peel back the layers of our past, we may see the part we played through a different lens than we did at the time we were in the middle of a situation. Sometimes that shift in perspective reveals how we hurt others through our lack of awareness, self-centeredness, poor coping skills, etc. It can be extremely painful to face this reality and can result in feelings of profound guilt for our role

in hurting others. (See related example in *Leslie's Story: Releasing Self-Punishment for Not Protecting My Kids* on the next page.) If you find yourself burdened with this type of situation, you may want to try the following exercise:

Exercise: Releasing Self-Punishment. Feel the full weight of the burden of self-punishment you have been carrying.

1. Where in your body do you carry the load? Are you sore from carrying it?
2. Examine the burden. What does it look like? If it is like a bag, suitcase, backpack, etc., examine the contents. Take each piece out one by one and spread them on the ground so you can clearly see them. Do you notice any similarity about this group of items?
3. See yourself as a bystander passing by. Listen intently to the tale of woe from the part of you which is distraught from carrying the burden. As the detached bystander, what would you say to provide solace to this person who is so distraught? Are there any words of wisdom you can share that might be helpful? Can you offer any other assistance?
4. Shift your focus back to being the distraught one. What are the key nuggets of support given by this bystander that you have found most helpful? Can you now provide that support to yourself?
5. Visualize dropping the burden next to you where you stand. How do you feel in your body now? Anchor this feeling in your memory as you see yourself walking away and leaving the burden behind you.
6. Ask yourself if there are specific actions you can take to lighten your self-punishment load in other facets of your life? If so, make note of those actions and begin to implement them in your daily reality!

In *Chapter 1*, we discussed how forgiving ourselves takes the broken pieces of our lives, which were dismembered by tragedy and injustice, and "re-members" them into something whole. As long as an emotional part of you is stuck in the past, you will always feel fragmented. It is not until you *review the past with your present consciousness* that you can make room for a transformation of meaning to occur. It can actually help you *re-experience it* in a new way. In doing so, your past memory is no longer frozen in time. By rewriting your past it is united with the present moment, which erases your feeling of fragmentation. (For more information about how to re-experience your past in a new way, see *Chapter 19: Discover the Gifts of Your Shadow*.)

Leslie's[1] Story: Releasing Self-Punishment for Not Protecting My Kids

I entered my second marriage when my kids were only two and almost four years old. I thought my new husband, Frank, would be good to them. Their own father really did not seem to care much about them. Things started out well, but as the kids grew and began challenging authority, things spun out of control. Frank was physically and emotionally abusive to them. They started acting out and we were all afraid of Frank.

My pattern was to cower when he raged. I kept my mouth shut and prayed that nobody would get hurt. I kept hoping that time would elapse and somehow things would get better. I really didn't know what to do and I felt embarrassed about the whole situation.

My daughter turned seventeen and moved out. I felt sad, yet jealous. Several months later my son and I also moved out. I thought that leaving would upset the apple cart enough to save my marriage, but it didn't. We ended up divorcing. My son went to live with his father and since I was alone, I had a lot of time to think.

I realized that trying to hang onto my second marriage had resulted in great harm to my kids. I had put them into a horrible situation and did not protect them from their step-father. I knew that they were damaged and it was my fault. Their childhoods were ruined because of my choices. I felt so guilty for not protecting them from Frank.

▶

After my kids and I went our separate ways, we were not very close and seldom spoke on the phone. When we did, it was strained and stand-offish. I never intended it to be this way. I felt like a failure. Here I was a Christian woman who had been divorced twice and my daughter and son were a mess. My guilt was so heavy that it felt like a weight on my chest.

I prayed and cried out to God. I asked for forgiveness for the mess I had made of my kid's lives. I also told God I was sorry that I could not stay married to Frank.

I am not sure how it all works, but I saw in my spirit a very long table. I was on one end trying to carry it, but I could not do it by myself. I was being shown that I could not single-handedly make my marriage work, since it takes two to do that. I also heard in my spirit that I should no longer carry the burden of the damage that happened to my kids. It was now their journey.

It was at this point that I really forgave myself and acknowledged that my kids would have to work through the pain that had been inflicted on them. I called both to apologize and confess my part. That was the start of redefining our relationships and establishing a new intimacy. Still they had to choose what they would do with their own pain, but finally I was there for them. I understood that all of us have to work through the abuses of our past. Nobody can do that on our behalf.

Next I forgave myself for being divorced twice. I accepted that I was young and dumb and chose to give up the guilt. I accepted responsibility for the role I played in the failure of both marriages. As a result, I went from feeling like a victim to realizing I can change my behavior and make better choices. I now give myself permission to make mistakes.

My daughter says I grew a spine. She is right. I did!

CHAPTER 13
CLEAR THE PAST WITH FAMILY MEMBERS

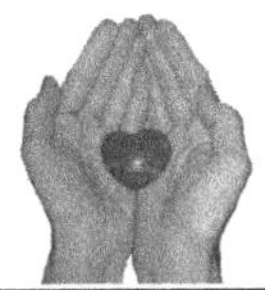

"If you want to see how enlightened you are, go spend a week with your family."
—Ram Dass
Spiritual teacher and author of *Be Here Now*

One of the specific challenges that many of us face about our past has to do with feelings that arise from our interactions with family members. Clearing the past with family members may be one of our biggest forgiveness and self-forgiveness challenges. It also may be an area we revisit repeatedly as we clear other areas of our life that no longer serve us.

Regardless of how well intentioned parents or spouses may be and no matter how angelic children can be, there are likely times when our family members have pushed our buttons and we have pushed theirs. Maybe we felt betrayed because they did not live up to our expectations. Perhaps we were severely hurt or deeply traumatized by their thoughtlessness, neglect or abusive behavior. Other times we may deeply regret how we lashed out in pain, anger, or ignorance toward them. And still other times we may feel profound guilt at how we treated our children or did not appropriately nurture and protect them such as in *Leslie's Story: Releasing Self-Punishment for Not Protecting My Kids* in *Chapter 12*, pages 80-81.

Even though we may logically know that we are all flawed human beings, we often have higher expectations of ourselves and those who are closest to us. We may find ourselves dwelling on how we or our family members "should" have been or "ought to" be different. By clearing these "shoulds" and "ought tos," we make room for "what is" and "what can be."

- **Release the fantasy.** Many of us have mental images, sometimes fueled by popular media, childhood stories, or cultural expectations, of what the "perfect" family or relationship should look like. Often those mental images are unrealistic and can be set ups for disappointment when the fantasies do not meet reality. Unlike the television show *Leave it to Beaver,* family dynamics are often messy. Parents may not have treated us how we feel we deserved to be treated. Traits we found charming in potential partners may grate on us once we are married. Children we longed for before conception, may act at times like little hellions, who make us prematurely gray.

When we fixate on relationships we "wish" we had, we may miss the relationships we are capable of actually having now and in the future. We may put enormous pressure on loved ones to be other than who they want to be or are capable of becoming. We may berate ourselves endlessly for situations that we cannot change. We may also keep ourselves in dysfunctional relationships much longer than necessary.

In *Chapter 9* we discussed how releasing perfectionism helps us forgive ourselves for our flaws. There is nothing like family dynamics to see how far we have come in releasing perfectionism and letting go of the flat image we have projected onto family members through our fantasy. Once we let go, it frees us to see them for their humanness. This is not to say we let ourselves or them off the hook for inappropriate behavior or an intolerable situation. To the contrary, once we see ourselves and others for the multi-dimensional people we actually are, we can *release the fantasy like letting go of a helium balloon.* Then we can finally address the reality of the situation and refocus our energy on what to do differently with this new insight.

- **Stop living in other people's "potential."** When we are close to family members, we may see them as "diamonds in the rough" with potential that has yet to be fulfilled. It can be supportive for those we care about to hold a vision for them and nurture their success. We have all seen spouses who put their careers on hold to help their partners establish their businesses or parents who worked two or three jobs so they could save enough money to send their children to college.

When taken to the extreme, however, trying to fulfill another person's potential can actually be counter-productive for that person's development. Sometimes it can divert the focus away from taking care of ourselves or fulfilling our own potential. An example of this is parents who push their children to fulfill the parents' unfilled dreams, even when their children have clearly expressed a desire to go a different direction in life. Another example is spouses who focus on "fixing" their partners rather than "fixing" themselves. Still another example is parents who continue to let their adult children live at home without contributing to the household or having a plan to be eventually on their own.

Some of the signs that you have crossed over the line and your "support" has become counter-productive include:

- Excessively doting on another person, whether it is a parent, child or partner,
- Living your life vicariously through other people,
- Continually pointing out other people's flaws under the guise of helping them become better human beings,
- Thinking that if you could just get another person to fix "this problem," your relationship with them would be perfect,
- Not holding others accountable for finding their own direction in life, and
- Neglecting your health or wellbeing over an extended time to take care of others.

If you have exhibited any of these signs, you may want to examine if you have focused too much attention on others at the expense of yourself. If so, it is yet another opportunity to forgive yourself and refocus your energy on better balancing your own wellbeing and personal development.

- **Quit being surprised by predictable behavior.** Sometimes when we are really close to family members, we may miss patterns in their behavior that are actually quite predictable and obvious to others. Examples of patterns include repeated bouts of anger followed by apologies, multiple requests for "loans" that are never paid back, manic activity that is followed by deep depression, or a continual state of trauma/drama that never seems to end.

Without seeing the pattern, we may be surprised each time the family member exhibits a particular behavior. We may react from our conditioning, rather than respond in a way that better serves the long term interests of that person and our relationship. We may get sucked into enabling bad behavior, rather than contributing to changing the family dynamics in positive ways.

Have you ever found yourself saying to friends, coworkers, or other family members, "I can't believe what he/she just did…"? If so, it may be helpful to understand that shock can prevent us from taking action. Next time you find yourself shocked, the following exercise may help you deal with the situation differently:

Exercise: Shed the Shock. Rather than repeat the story of the shocking incident, you may want to stop yourself.

1. Step back and observe this situation in light of the person's past history. Is this incident *really* a surprise?
2. Write down any trends you have observed in the person's behavior over time.
3. Acknowledge that, as painful as it is to see, *it is what it is* and you do not have control over whether the person chooses to change this pattern. *What you do have control over is your response to the situation.*
4. Ask yourself, "Next time another incident occurs, what will I do instead of being surprised?"

This exercise can help you shed the "shock" and replace it with discernment about the appropriate action you will take in the future. Going through this process also may provide yet another opportunity to forgive yourself for unwittingly enabling a negative pattern or reacting in a way that did not serve your own or the other person's personal development.

- **Stop thinking you can do the inner work for anyone else.** It can be difficult to watch people we love suffer. In our heart-felt connection to them, we may wish that we could take on their pain so they would not have to feel it. We may desperately want them to open their eyes and see what they are doing to hurt themselves and those closest to them. We may have so much remorse about what we did to others when we were less enlightened that we try to take back any negative effect we passed on to them.

  Whatever the reason we wish we could prevent other people's suffering, it is impossible to do their inner work for them. At some point we have to acknowledge the *Truth* of this, not just in our head, but in our heart, to free ourselves from trying. Below is an exercise that may help this *Truth* sink in at a deeper level:

  Exercise: **Release the Suffering of Others**. Ask yourself the following questions:

  - Do I spend an inordinate amount of time trying to figure out what else I can possibly do to help reduce a family member's anger, depression or sense of angst?
  - Do I put in a lot of effort into trying to get a family member to "see the light" about their behavior?
  - Am I consumed by the pain I caused a family member?

  If you answer **"yes"** to any of the questions above, ask yourself the following questions:

  - Has all of the energy I have spent in my effort to assist, really helped/changed this family member?
  - Has my effort actually been counter-productive in any way? If so, how?
  - Do I truly believe that this family member can choose, just as I did, when/if they do their inner work?
  - What has been my payoff for holding onto the *baton of responsibility,* rather than seeing it in the other person's hands?

  - Am I willing to move beyond the payoff, to free myself from the belief that it was ever my responsibility in the first place?

- **Quit taking on other people's negativity**. We have all encountered people who attack others unmercifully or spew vitriol toward anyone in their paths. When these people are family members their negativity can wreak havoc on the entire family. Their behavior may be particularly difficult to deal with or even feel abusive, if we are weaker or smaller than the other person, highly sensitive, or already have low self-esteem. Unfortunately, as children we may not have a lot of choice about being raised in such a negative environment. As adults, we do have choices.

  If you find yourself in situations with family members, or anybody else for that matter, who are being disrespectful or mean spirited, sometimes the action called for is to quit spending time with them. (For an example, see *Aurora's Story: Reparenting Myself* on the next page.) Other times the action called for may be to stand up to others. You may need to call them on their bad behavior and, with conviction, make it clear you will no longer tolerate that behavior. In this case you may need to be willing to remove yourself from the situation if they continue their negative pattern. This can be especially empowering for adults who were abused as children. The one caveat is if you are still living in an abusive environment, it may not be safe to confront your abuser. Instead, you may want to seek outside help.

  Even if it does not feel appropriate to leave a negative situation or confront others about their bad behavior, there are ways to stop taking on their negativity. See the exercise below for one idea.

Exercise: Hold the Mirror of Negativity. The next time someone spews negativity your direction, visualize yourself holding a mirror for the other person to speak into. Watch as the negativity deflects away from you and bounces back toward the sender. *Recognize that negative comments directed toward you are often a reflection of what is actually inside the other person.* Practicing this exercise may not result in others facing their personal issues. If they do, you may be able to become mirrors for one another and spiral each other upward in personal growth. Regardless of whether others are willing to face their personal issues, you have a choice about whether to take in their negativity or stop being a negativity magnet. Seeing the *Truth* of other people's behavior allows you to send love and compassion to the scared or hurt child that is likely hiding under the façade of bravado.

Aurora's[1] Story: Reparenting Myself

My father was an extreme fundamentalist Christian and a closeted gay man (who still lives in denial) and my mother was weak and in a loveless marriage with two young daughters who desperately needed her attention and love. My father was only present at dinner and on Sundays at church. The rest of the time he was at his printing company or sleeping.

Both of my parents were negligent and physically abusive. Spankings were regular and severe as was brutal pinching of the skin in our armpits, where the bruising wouldn't show. This all seemed normal to me as a child.

Once, when I was five, my mother left us with a babysitter at her friends' house where a teenage boy took me into a dark bedroom and raped me. When the adults returned I told them what happened. My mother did nothing to protect me or console me. She never told my dad or the authorities and it was never mentioned again.

The effect on me was that I felt unworthy of protection and love and that I did not matter. But I was tenacious. I was determined to matter to my parents, so I became a leader, a caregiver, a troubleshooter and a worrier about my parents' welfare. I spent the majority of my life under age forty listening to my mother's anxieties, while adoring her. I helped my father with his business to earn his love. ▶

Over and over again, instead of thanks and love, I received verbal abuse from both of my parents. I was told things like, "you should have never been born" , "we don't trust you" , "you're a liar and a thief, and we're changing our locks." I would agonize over why they intentionally hurt me.

With the help of therapy, I came to see my family dynamics clearly. I realized that I was not the problem, but I was creating problems for myself by trying to get love from people who were incapable of showing even basic caring, much less unconditional love.

Forgiving myself took longer. I blamed myself for wasting so much of my life while seeking my parents' love and attention. I felt like I had been a weakling and that I was too needy and foolish.

Now I've come to understand and accept that I could only work with the tools I had at that time. Over the course of my life I have learned to love and appreciate myself; my strength of character, my love for nature and humanity, my creativity and my resilience.

I see my parents occasionally. They are aging and ailing, but I do not feel responsible for them. They are human beings and I wish the best for them, but I do not feel that they are my family.

I have my own family with my life partner and I am re-parenting myself while parenting my daughters. I tell them every day how much I love them and how proud I am to be their mother. I am glad that I learned to forgive myself and walk away from people who intentionally hurt me.

- **Clear unhelpful patterns in dealing with your feelings.** As we clear the past with family members, one of the areas of personal growth is learning how to effectively deal with our feelings that arise as a result of challenging interactions with those close to us. Sometimes it is appropriate to clear the air by actually saying what is on our mind. Sometimes it may also be appropriate to internally process our feelings or discuss them with a trusted friend, therapist or someone else other than that family member.

  If you are someone who tends to avoid confrontation (e.g., "bite your tongue" for fear of saying something you will regret, hide behind a mask of niceness, bury your feelings, or deny that you even have feelings at all), it may be helpful to speak your *Truth* regardless of the consequences. If, on the other hand, you have a tendency to confront without considering the repercussions (e.g., speak before your brain engages, believe the best defense is an offense, react by lashing out when you are hurt, or assume the worst intensions in others), the action called for may be to process your feelings outside the presence of the family member with whom you have the issue. Later you can decide whether or not it is appropriate to share your feelings with that family member. (See *Gabrielle's Story: Letter to My Mother* on the next page for an example of how one person made amends for a past regretful incident.)

Regardless of whether you choose to speak to the other person or process a situation within, it can be helpful to step back for a moment before saying or doing anything and assess the situation from a different perspective than you may have done in the past. The following questions may help you in that assessment process. (See also *Appendix C: Resources for Effective Communication.*)

If you tend to avoid confrontation:

- What are my reasons for avoiding confrontation? Are these reasons fear-based or strength-based?
- Despite my tendency to withdraw, is there a strong urge within me to speak this time? If so, what makes this situation different from the past?
- Regardless of the outcome from the conversation, how do I want to feel about myself for having spoken out?
- When I am honest with myself, what is the action called for in this situation?

If confrontation comes easily to you:

- Is the issue with this person mine or theirs? If it is their issue, what is gained by saying anything? If it is my issue, what is gained from saying anything?
- Generally, when I speak my mind, do I later regret what I said? If so, is there a pattern to the regret I feel? (For example, I say hurtful things I do not really mean, the

words I say do not match the true feeling inside of me, etc.)

- If I were to process this issue internally, what would I learn from this process? What scares me about doing this?
- When I am honest with myself, what is the action called for in this situation?

As we clear the past with family members, we may find that the skills we acquire in dealing repeatedly with those closest to us also build our skills to more effectively deal with other areas of our lives. From a *Heroic Journey* perspective, where every experience contributes to our personal evolution, our family environment is one of our most cherished practice grounds. Our interactions with family members help us build character, develop unconditional love, and get to the root of issues that trigger us the most. The more we understand this, the more willing we are to face our challenges with family members, so we can learn these life changing lessons.

Gabrielle's[2] Story: Letter to My Mother

Saying goodnight at her door with the customary amount of distance, I could barely believe what I heard. My mother...this Spartan woman who had endured years of excruciating back pain, who always had to be in control ...softly asked from her bed, "Have you ever thought of suicide?" The tender sharing that followed led me to send her a letter asking for her forgiveness for some early behavior that still haunted me as an adult. Some months later, with the first ring of the late night call, I heard myself exclaim with a voice of knowing and shock, "My mother's dead!"

I am forever grateful that I seized the idea to write while she was still alive because I am now released from the gnawing guilt. Even though what I had done was a "stupid teenage put-down," it cut into me every time I remembered saying it to her. She never mentioned receiving my letter, probably because we were back to being New Englanders who did not discuss such matters. Yet once I sent the letter I was able to forgive myself. I was free of the angst that had been inside me for so long. I was free to love her easily. Here is my letter:

▶

Dearest Mother,
I was very touched by your bravery when you asked me if I had ever thought of suicide. For me, our ensuing conversation was the most intimate we have ever had. Being able to speak to each other honestly from our most vulnerable selves is a connection I have yearned for. It amazes me that the subject of suicide would be where we would meet in what I call Sacred Space.

So, first, let me tell you that I feel very honored to have your trust and I imagine I will carry this precious conversation in my heart the rest of my life. You must know it is bittersweet in its preciousness for the thought of losing you is hard to bear. Yet, somehow, perhaps in my New England stoicism and respect for you, my overriding thought was to be supportive and present.

Now, a few weeks later, after receiving your request for more specific information, I am feeling a certain hyper-alertness. Perhaps it is adrenalin. And, oddly enough, today in line at the grocery store, my eye caught a magazine article about the Hemlock Society. The Universe provides.

Secondly, I want you to know I have no arguments with you pondering this decision. I have been beyond sad to see you in such demoralizing pain for so long, seeing the restrictions it places on your enjoyment of being alive. I have no judgments, Mom. I imagine I could be pondering the same strategy if I were in your shoes. Actually, I admire how you have hung in there all this time. That said, I am hoping for two things as I send you information that will probably result in your transition along life's continuum.

First, will you let me know before you do this? This is not to interfere, but to be spiritually present with your choice. Second, would you be willing to hear a couple of things I am not proud of and wish I had done differently? I have carried them forever.

I am asking that you hear my love and my remorse: I remember a time when you came home radiating. You'd just gotten your hair highlighted and you were beaming! My teenage response of disgust was something like, "Oh…My…God!!!"

▶

When I think of saying it in that tone of voice, I imagine it pierced into your soul. I feel sick inside. I have such a deep sense of sorrow. I know you hardly ever spent money on yourself. I know you had a hard time living so far out in the country without much social life. I can imagine you intended to give yourself a giant boost of self-nurturing. I even imagine you thought we would all tell you how great you looked.

Now at age forty-five, I am still haunted with anguish and regret. I wish so much that I could go back and redo that moment. I wish I could have risen above my disgruntled attitude to celebrate your joy. I wish I could have wrapped my arms around you and danced in circles with you, which of course brings a deeper wish that we could have been a closer mother-daughter unit. I know I did not make it easy for you and I regret that as well. I remember you saying that I had broken your heart. While I am confident we both did the best we could, I mourn the lost years we might have had. You mourn them as well, don't you Mom? I've come to accept that you cannot access your voice for feelings and that's okay. And still, just in case, I want to ask, "How is it for you to hear my heart, even belatedly?"

I close hoping these words will heal us more deeply as you prepare to leave. You have loved me fiercely (and yes, sometimes I needed more room to be myself) AND please hear this: I will miss you more than I can know. I am grateful for your power, your strength and your deep feeling heart, even if you have never been able to express what is inside you. You are such a huge part of me. I will feel you "somewhere out there, beneath the pale blue skies" and I will do my best to take up the baton and be of service in the world.

Love, from your first-born daughter, who always loves you, even when trying to find her way differently than you may have wished. You have always been my Amazon trailblazer who inspires me to live courageously outside of the box.

Travel pain free with my Forever Love in your Heart.
Bon Voyage my Dearest Mother,
namaste... Gabrielle

CHAPTER 14
BREAK YOUR ADDICTION TO WORRY

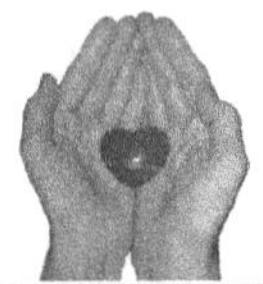

"It makes no sense to worry about things you have no control over because there's nothing you can do about them, and why worry *about things you do control? The activity of worrying keeps you immobilized."*
—Wayne Dyer
American self-help lecturer and
Author of *Change Your Thoughts – Change Your Life*

Holding ourselves hostage to the past can be a hard habit to break. So can worrying about the future. Both can rob us of the present moment, which is the only place we can truly *experience* self-forgiveness and anchor it firmly within ourselves, body, mind, and spirit.

Worry disturbs our peace of mind with anxious or uneasy thoughts, about something uncertain or that we perceive as potentially dangerous. We all worry from time to time as we think about the people we love or we work through scenarios and possible approaches for how to effectively deal with them. Some worry is healthy, such as worrying that if we do not fasten our seat belt and get in an accident, we may get hurt. But, for chronic worriers, worrying has become a negative habit. Like other bad habits, worrying has become addictive and interferes with their daily functioning. Some people spend an inordinate amount of time brooding about what is out of their control. As a result they waste precious time, may be paralyzed from taking action, or feel like their energy is totally depleted. With so much energy preoccupied with worry, the irony is that it becomes difficult for them to move into a future that has a different outcome other than what they fear. (See related story, *Give Up the "What if..." Mantra*, in this chapter on pages 98-99.)

Worry can escalate into anxiety that has negative physical consequences including heart palpitations, racing heart, shortness of breath, nausea, shaking, lower back pain, indigestion, grinding teeth, sleeping difficulties or loss of libido.[1] In some extreme cases worriers experience phobias, obsessive-compulsive disorder and flat-out panic attacks, which may be marked by feelings of terror.[2]

Some people realize that worry is not good for them, but they don't know how to stop themselves. It may become another way to punish themselves. It may also keep them so preoccupied that self-forgiveness becomes even more elusive. If you find yourself fretting incessantly over something without a clear solution presenting itself, you may find the following exercises helpful in stopping the worry habit:

Exercise 1: Write Down the Worst Case Scenario and Then Let it Go. Chronic worriers spend a lot of time and energy going over all the possible negative scenarios that "might" happen. Keeping all of these possibilities in their heads can perpetuate the ruminations. If you find yourself in this situation, write down all of the negative scenarios you can think of. Getting them out of your head often reduces the mental energy it takes to hold onto the negative. You may also want to take this exercise one step further. Assign a percentage to the likelihood that each scenario will occur. Doing this might help you realize how unlikely it is that your fears will actually come to fruition.

Exercise 2: Trust Your Ability to Handle What Comes Your Direction. Worriers tend to lack confidence in their ability to handle negative situations. In their minds they may exaggerate the consequences of their actions or the actions of others. They may think they (or their world) will fall apart, their wrong choice will destroy the life of someone they love, they will be unable to handle the pain from loss, etc. If you find yourself overwhelmed about your ability to handle a particular situation, you may want to try this exercise:

a. Using the negative scenario list from Exercise 1 above, say to yourself about each one you listed, *"Even if this specific scenario happens, I am capable of dealing with it."*

b. Think of at least three ways you could effectively deal with each scenario. (Examples include enlisting the assistance of others, breathing deeply to calm and center yourself before taking action, or breaking down a complex situation into smaller pieces to deal with them one at a time.)

By repeating the statement about your capability and seeing that you have options for coping with whatever occurs, you build resilience and confidence in your ability to work through difficult situations and handle whatever comes your way.

Exercise 3: Build Your Tolerance for Uncertainty. Many people feel uncomfortable with uncertainty. Worriers have an extremely low threshold. Sometimes their worry is focused on trying to tightly control their environment, so they can avoid any uncertainty. In these situations, worriers may feel like clocks wound too tight. This type of control only breeds more fear and anxiety. If you find yourself worrying about an uncertain future:

- Ask yourself if you are jumping to a negative conclusion without any real evidence that this will actually occur.
- Ask yourself what positive outcomes might come from the change. List as many positive scenarios as you can.
- If you cannot immediately think of anything positive, ask yourself, "If I could think of any positive scenarios, what would they be?" By shifting your focus to the positive, you open yourself to more possibilities and reduce your fixation on the negative.

Exercise 4: Give Yourself a Set Amount of Time to Worry. You can wean yourself off of worry by giving yourself a certain time (maybe one hour) to worry with your undivided attention. When your mind attempts to focus on your favorite topics of worry outside of that assigned time, stop yourself and redirect your focus to something else. You can then lessen your tolerance for worry by gradually shortening the worry time (to 45 minutes, then 30 minutes, etc.). After a while you will likely see how little time you actually need to worry. You also may find as you train your mind to worry less, you have a more positive outlook on life, you have more time and energy for life affirming endeavors, and you feel calmer and more centered throughout your day.

Exercise 5: Forgive Yourself for Worrying. As we discussed in the beginning of this chapter, worry can be habit forming. Like any addiction, it can take time to break the worry habit. If you find yourself slipping back into your old worrying ways, simply remind yourself, "I know I just forgot. Let's think about something else now." Being kind to yourself may actually speed up the change process as you instill a more heart-centered approach to your personal growth.

Worry and self-forgiveness are integrally intertwined. As we lessen our preoccupation with worry, we make room internally to forgive ourselves for why we developed the worry habit in the first place. We may find we are also more willing to honestly face our fears underlying worry that include fear of uncertainty and lack of control. As we forgive ourselves for our past worry habit, we strengthen our ability to live in the present moment and often ironically find we have much more energy to direct toward creating a more peaceful and fulfilling future.

Give Up the "What if…" Mantra

Human beings are constantly thinking. Dr. Dennis Gersten, a diplomate of the American Board of Psychiatry and Neurology points out that "the average person runs about 15,000 thoughts per day in which at least half of those are negative. And we know that our thoughts turn into our emotions and our emotions turn into physiology."[3] For worriers, the percentage of negative thoughts is even higher, which is no wonder that many times worriers have a higher incidence of associated negative emotional and physical consequences.

▶

Carole (not her real name) was depressed and had chronic fatigue syndrome. She sought counseling for her depression from Margaret Paul, Ph.D. As Dr. Paul describes:

> Carole was a constant worrier. Many words out of her mouth centered around her concerns that something bad might happen. "What if I never get well?" "What if my husband gets sick?" "What if I run out of money?" (Carole and her husband ran a very successful business and there was no indication that it would not go on being successful). "What if my son gets into drugs?" "What if my kids don't get into good colleges?" "What if someone breaks into the house?"
>
> Her worry was not only causing her depression, but was also contributing to her illness, if not actually causing it. Her worry caused so much stress in her body that her immune system could not do its job of keeping her well. Yet even the awareness that her worry was causing her depression and possibly even her illness did not stop Carole from worrying. She was addicted to it. She was unconsciously addicted to the sense of control that worry gave her.[4]

Worriers tend to believe that worrying gives them a sense of control over outcomes. Some worriers even believe that it is their worry that keeps grave consequences from happening. But, this sense of control is an illusion. The irony is that worry can keep us from making good choices in the moment that will actually affect better outcomes.

Mindfulness, which involves being attentive in the moment, can be a good counterbalance to the "what if..." mantra of worry. Many people practice mindfulness through meditation. By setting aside time each day to actively contemplate and reflect, we can train our mind to follow certain thoughts and turn our attention away from others.

One technique to do this is to see ourselves at a train station standing on a platform waiting for a train. Our thoughts are the trains that come and go through the station. As each train of thought comes to a stop in front of us, we look at our ticket and see if that is the train we have decided to take. If not, we let that train of thought pass on by and we turn our attention to the next train coming into the station. When the train arrives that we have agreed to take, we step onboard, knowing that this train of thought will take us to the destination of our choice.

❖

CHAPTER 15
EXTRACT YOURSELF FROM THOUGHT TRAPS

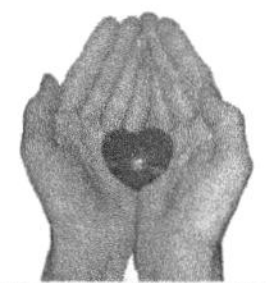

"Emancipate yourself from mental slavery,
none but ourselves can free our mind."
—**Bob Marley**
Reggae musician and songwriter

As we examine specific thoughts to determine whether they serve us or hinder us, it can be helpful to be on the lookout for thought traps that keep us stuck in self-perpetuating negativity or no win situations. As we have seen repeatedly, when we are in a negative state of mind it is virtually impossible to forgive ourselves and move on with our lives.

Sometimes thought traps originate from an "error loop" in our thinking process. Our minds are closed to new input, which tends to recycle negativity within us. With a closed negative loop in our thinking, we continually punish ourselves for the same shortcoming. To break free of thought traps, it may be helpful to think creatively about locating an exit point so we can escape.

Beware of particularly insidious thoughts that keep you trapped in the past or fixated on the future instead of living in the present moment. If you find yourself saying, "*if only*" it may be a sign that you are trapped in the past. If you find yourself saying, "*I will not be happy until ...*" it may be a sign that you are denying yourself happiness now in favor of chasing after an elusive carrot at the end of a stick.

When we are determined to trap ourselves, particularly when it comes to self-forgiveness, there is often a punitive quality to our thinking process. We look internally at ourselves with harsh eyes. To shift our thinking, the action called for may be to soften our approach. The very act of softening often reduces the pressure we put on ourselves just enough for new perspectives to emerge from inside out. (See *Elizabeth's Story: Gifts of My Brother* on pages 103-104 for an example of how self-forgiveness and self-love are helping one person extract herself from her thought trap.)

Sometimes the thought traps are so embedded in our psyches that we do not even realize that we have fallen into them. Like fish swimming in the ocean, we may be oblivious to the thinking within and around us. In cases like this it may be helpful to review some of the sample thought traps below that get in the way of self-forgiveness to see if you relate to any of them. (Refer to **Table 15.1**.) Take a systematic approach to shifting your thoughts, so you can leave the trap permanently behind.

Thought Trap	Shift in Thinking that Points to an Exit	Affirmation that May Help Complete the Shift in Thinking
I have done so much to hurt others, how can I ever forgive myself?	It is my lack of awareness that sometimes causes me to hurt others by my actions.	I forgive myself for being unaware and commit to being as conscious as possible for how my actions affect others.
I can never let my guard down by forgiving myself, otherwise I might repeat my wrongdoing.	It is possible to remember past wrong doings and change my future actions, without continually punishing myself for the past.	I forgive myself for confusing remembering with punishment. I choose to learn from past mistakes and move on.
I cannot have love *and* recognition. I do not want to pick between them, so I get neither.	I do not have to pick one over the other. I can have both love and recognition.	I forgive myself for thinking I had to choose between two options when actually I can give myself both.

Table 15.1. Examples of thought traps that prevent self-forgiveness and shifts in thinking that can help us escape them.

Extracting ourselves from thought traps can reduce the stress, tension, and angst that may have previously consumed much of our time and energy and prevented us from moving on with our lives. Self-forgiveness is a natural by-product of having less negativity coursing through our system. It also helps us replace the old error loop in our thinking process with a more affirming loop that positively influences our unfolding life story.

Elizabeth's[1] Story: Gifts of My Brother

How do I begin to forgive a self that so thoughtlessly threw away the gifts my beloved brother Phillip gave me? Once when we were young, my mother asked me to babysit him. I was fourteen, Phillip was ten. I resented having to babysit that night. When he came to my bedroom door, popcorn in hand (his white flag attempt), I slammed the door in his face.

What happened some years later feels a lot like that. I slammed the door on a life he wanted for me. A life he was losing as he lay dying of AIDS in 1992.

Phillip worked hard until his death at age thirty-seven. I struggled throughout my youth with finding my place in the world. Insecure, addicted to alcohol, and an impulsive spender, I was in recovery when Phillip told me in 1986 that he was HIV positive. A part of me died then. Six years later when he died in the upstairs bedroom of his beautiful, completely paid for townhouse that was to be mine, I died a little more. I isolated myself. I soon fell into my old ways of spending money and drinking alcohol. I did anything I could to dull the pain. My recovery was gone. I could no longer say, "But at least I am sober." I caved into a deep depression.

Then the money was gone. I had run up a large debt on the house payment, and, in 2001, I was diagnosed with breast cancer. This was my wake up call. I sold the townhouse to pay off my debt and took time off from work for my treatment. I bought a mobile home, which was already on site in a mobile home park. I began again in my recovery program and gained enough clarity to experience the full impact of just what I had done, what I had so recklessly thrown away, what I had lost. With this newfound clarity came much regret, much pain, and more depression.

▶

I sit here now writing this, ten years later, in my mobile home, just two blocks from the townhouse. I rarely drive in that direction and, if I must, I look straight ahead and speed by, never wanting, never able, to look at what could have still been mine. I pay the rent on my mobile home space and know that if Phillip is somewhere, anywhere, in the ethers of our vast Universe, if he is cognizant in any way, he has forgiven me ten times over. I am not quite as forgiving of myself. Yet sitting here today, I am grateful, sober, and conscious. I am aware of my many blessings.

I know that deep inside me there is a loving self, showering me with forgiveness, telling me, "You lost your brother, your best friend. You did the best you could with what you had. Phillip has forgiven you. I have forgiven you." I sit in my home now, and listen for that voice. When the shame comes, the regret, the recriminations, I hold still and listen for those words, "I forgive you." I can feel the peace and the serenity. As I think about this and realize that this is what Phillip had so long ago really wished for me in leaving me all he had, I am truly grateful.

CHAPTER 16
STOP BERATING YOUR BODY

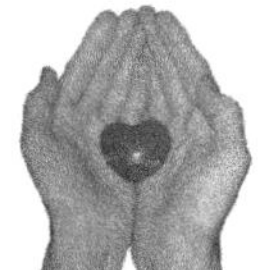

"Take care of your body.
It's the only place you have to live."
—Jim Rohn
American business philosopher
and author of *The Compound Effect*

For many of us, one of the most fertile areas related to self-forgiveness has to do with our relationship with our bodies. As the physical container that holds us in life, we cannot get away from our bodies as long as we are alive. This is not to say that many people do not try. There is a lot of denial, avoidance, abuse, addiction, self-loathing, and numbing out, which comes from not being at peace with our bodies. But, from a *Heroic Journey* perspective, our bodies have natural intelligence and are one of our prime vehicles for deepening our relationship to ourselves, building character, relating to the world in positive ways, and experiencing what it means to be fully alive!

When we befriend a part of our body that we have previously rejected, it may become one of our strongest heroic allies. Mirka Knaster, author of *Discovering the Body's Wisdom*, astutely observes, "When we establish an amicable relationship with our own bodies, they are sure to respond in kind— with comfort, pleasure, energy, strength, flexibility, ease…and wisdom." [1] Some of the aspects of our body related to self-forgiveness that may be most challenging to befriend are:

- **Innate traits you do not like.** Regardless of how others see us, many of us have at least some innate traits we wish were different. I was struck by what famous entertainer Cher said related to this, "I'm insecure about everything, because... I'm never going to look in the mirror and see this blond, blue-eyed girl. That is my idea of what I'd like to look like."[2] How often do we feel this same type of insecurity about ourselves?

  One of the great lessons related to your body may be to *learn to appreciate it and be at home in it, flaws and all*. This lesson is particularly important as it relates to self-forgiveness.

In *Chapter 10* we discussed the connection of self-forgiveness and comparing yourself to others. Constantly comparing yourself can amplify your shortcomings and keep you from focusing on your unique strengths. There is nothing like examining how comfortable you are in your own skin to drive home whether you have really mastered this lesson.

Another lesson may be to stop internal self-loathing chatter. This is when affirmations (discussed in *Chapter 6*) may help you break your negative habits of thought. Yet another lesson may be to celebrate the differences that are your unique signature. It is your special combination of traits that allows you to give to the world as only you can give. Learning to be at home in your body and seeing it as your sacred temple goes a long way toward forgiving and respecting yourself for being just who you are.

- **Weight and addictions.** Coming to grips with weight and addiction issues can be a powerful path to greater health and wellbeing. However, when you attempt and fail to shed excess pounds or relapse back into an old addiction, you may use the experience to further berate yourself. As a result you may feel even more emotionally battered, defeated or hopeless than when you began the process.

  Issues associated with weight and addictions are rarely related *only* to the physical aspects of your being. They are often complex and deeply rooted in underlying psychological and spiritual issues associated with misalignment between your inner and outer reality. The misalignment may be associated with your past, your relationship to yourself and others, your unmet needs, personal *Truths* you are avoiding, or any number of other disconnects between who you believe you are and how you portray yourself in the world. **List 16.1** has some of the common themes related to underlying weight or addiction issues. See if you relate to any of these themes or if they spark others not on the list.

Weight and Addiction Themes

- ☐ I immerse myself in thoughts of food/addictive substances to forget about other anxieties, tensions, or past traumas in my life.
- ☐ I use food/substance addictions to stuff what needs to be said, felt or released.
- ☐ My world is a frightening/unhappy place and I use food/addictive substances to temporarily be in a safe/hopeful/happy place.
- ☐ I am punishing myself with food/addictive substances for something bad I did/did not do in the past.
- ☐ Eating food (or taking a substance) that is not good for me is one of my only pleasures in this miserable existence.
- ☐ My weight/use of addictive substances allows me to keep a safe distance from my partner or hide my sexuality.
- ☐ I have no right to be thinner/healthier/happier than others in my family.
- ☐ My life is boring/filled with drudgery and I use food or addictive substances to spice it up.
- ☐ I use food/addictions as a cheap substitute for what really feeds my soul.
- ☐ ____
  ____

List 16.1. See if you relate to any of these themes or if they remind you of others.

Self-forgiveness can help you crack the code for the underlying reasons you struggle with weight or addictions. Self-forgiveness drops you into a heart space where you are less harsh on yourself. In this space you invite vulnerability and self-honesty and are more receptive to hearing what your weight or addiction is trying to get you to consciously acknowledge. To help you drop into a self-forgiving heart space, you may want to try this exercise. For any of the themes you checked in the list above, add a statement at the end, "…and I forgive myself for hurting myself in this way." By making this statement, you affirm that you are open to relating to your weight or addiction in a whole new way.

- **Disabilities and illnesses.** Several years ago, I started the year by breaking my foot. This was not exactly what I consciously had in mind for the New Year! It was only during the long course of my recovery and painful rehabilitation that I realized that I had been saying for quite a while that I really needed to "take a break." Realizing this impressed upon me the power of words and how literally I took the message I had been saying to myself! (I now say I need a *respite* rather than a *break.*)

  This experience gave me a tiny glimpse into how some people live their entire lives with serious disabilities and long-term or life-threatening illnesses. I am intrigued with how some people are able to tap into their *heroic reserves* in the midst of physically challenging and, sometimes excruciatingly painful situations to learn life altering lessons, act with kindness and respect toward others and themselves, give back to society and sometimes even exude a happy and joyful countenance through it all. *Now that is resilience and self-forgiveness in action*!

  Several people come to mind who have exemplify this kind of resilience and level of self-forgiveness. One is my friend Reverend Dr. Judith Larkin Reno, who has endured great physical pain and used it to her advantage. She is a counselor and spiritual guide, who has lived with a rare form of bone cancer for over thirteen years. She has rebounded numerous times from near death. Judith has repeatedly forgiven others as she has dealt with different facets of her illness, including health-care providers who have not known how to properly treat her. She has forgiven herself at many different levels, including the fact that she is no longer able to be as physically active as she once was.

  Despite her extended illness, Judith has maintained her clarity, sense of humor, and buoyancy of spirit. She has also continued her work as founder of Gateway University and she has written thirty books to share her wisdom with the world. (See *Appendix A: Skills to Tame Unruly Emotions* for some of Judith's philosophy.) Her book *Elephants in Your Tent,* [3] offers a guiding light to find gifts behind pain, true power under frailty, and an indestructible core beyond the impermanence of life.

Cameron Clapp[4] was an active and athletic fifteen year old, whose life changed overnight when he was drunk, passed out on a train track and was hit by a high speed freight train. Three days later he awoke in the hospital to find that both of his legs had been amputated above the knee and his right arm had been amputated just below the shoulder. Rather than wallow in self-pity, feel bitterness, or berate himself, Cameron faced the reality of the situation and felt lucky to be alive. He says, "I deserve the consequences of my actions… Getting hit by a train and living — you know, that right there is enough to be happy about."[5] He was determined to not only walk again, but compete as an athlete.

After leaving the hospital, he began swimming. In just five months of rehabilitation he was able to walk on state-of-the-art prosthetic legs. One day he astounded his doctors when he walked down steps without holding onto the railing! At that point there was no stopping Cameron. He learned how to drive, jump, and run and he went on to compete in athletic competitions for amputees, winning a gold medal in running one hundred meters and a silver medal in swimming.

Even with all that he has achieved, Cameron feels that his greatest accomplishment has been what he has given back to others from his experience. He counsels young amputees and soldiers returning from war with amputations about how to recover mainstream functionality. His message is that there are no limits and he encourages them to never give up. Since his twin brother died a few years ago from a drug overdose, Cameron has now embraced a new mission. He speaks to youth to encourage them not to make tragic mistakes like he and his brother did. When asked by a CBS news reporter if he could get his limbs back would he want them, Cameron said no. He feels that his metamorphosis happened that night on the railroad track. "My accident was a good thing in some ways; I wouldn't be the person that I am today. It's not what I'm left with; it's what I've done. I've just adapted."[6] Cameron's motto is, "Impossible is an opinion, not a fact." He says, "I don't live in pity or sorrow. I don't have regrets or remorse. There are lots of things people can take from my story, but the best is hope."[7]

Dr. Randy Pausch[8] was a professor of computer science at Carnegie Mellon University (CMU) and in the prime of his life when he was diagnosed with pancreatic cancer. After an unsuccessful procedure to halt the cancer, he was given a terminal diagnosis and told that he had three to six months of good health left. When he heard his diagnosis he said, "First came the shock, pain and tears."[9] Rather than focus on his sadness, he decided to make a plan to help his family cope with his death. He was determined to do what he could to make memories with his family.

Shortly after that Randy decided to give a CMU lecture to over 400 students and colleagues entitled, *"The Last Lecture: Really Achieving Your Childhood Dreams."* Even though he began the lecture by disclosing that he had pancreatic cancer, his talk was upbeat, full of wisecracks, and focused on his personal childhood dreams and life lessons. He said, "We can't change the cards that we were dealt, just how we play the hand." He discussed how he became a professor to enable the childhood dreams of others. At the end he disclosed that he had not done the talk for his audience, but for three people—his three young children. He explained that he thought it would help them remember him by seeing his lecture.

Randy's lecture was posted on *YouTube.*[10] It was so poignant and inspiring that it was viewed more than one million times in the first month. (To date it has received almost 14 million hits!) As a result of people seeing the video, Randy made many media appearances including on ABC and the *Oprah Winfrey Show*. He received an opportunity to write a book about his lecture that was on the *New York Times Best Seller* list for 85 weeks. He also made a public service announcement and testified before Congress to advocate for cancer research.

Throughout his very public process of dying, Randy was open about his challenges with forgiveness and self-forgiveness. Concerning forgiveness he said, “Cancer amplifies who people are and how they behave toward you. Nobody wants to make your life harder and nobody wants to be a jerk, but they don't know how to respond. As ironic as it sounds, you're going to have to gear up for forgiveness, or at least understanding.”[11] Related to self-forgiveness he had to deal with the awful realization that he would not grow old with his wife and not see his three young children grow up. He said, “It pains me to think that when they’re older they won’t have a father. When I cry in the shower, I’m not usually thinking ‘I won’t get to see them do this,’ or ‘I won’t get to see them do that.’ I am thinking about the kids not having a father. That’s what chews me up inside when I let it.”[12] Randy chose not to dwell on his regret, but instead focus on being as present in the moment and have fun with his family and friends as long as possible. Randy died eleven months after his terminal diagnosis, which was longer than originally expected. In playing the cards he was dealt, living with a forgiving heart, and having a zest for life, he made every day of his remaining time count. This is why his inspiration lives on and he continues to touch so many people’s lives.

Each of these people demonstrated what spiritual teacher Ram Dass (formerly known as Dr. Richard Alpert) called “fierce grace.”[13] They proved to themselves that they could bear the unbearable and transcend the limitations of their ego into a boundless state of being. While their stories are inspiring and speak to the resilience of the human spirit, sometimes the lessons that you learn from disabilities or illnesses may help you see what is important in life, clear the past, open your heart to others, make amends, or understand something profound about your personal nature or life in general.

Lee Atwater[14] was a Republican strategist, former chair of the Republican National Committee and the prime architect of George H. W. Bush’s successful 1988 Election campaign. He was skilled at attack politics. To those who revered him, he was known as an aggressive, but brilliant tactician and to those who despised him, he was known as the "Darth Vader" of the Republican Party for his manipulative and underhanded tactics. Lee was thirty-nine years old and at the peak of his career and political power when he was diagnosed with having a malignant brain tumor. The treatment for his tumor left him paralyzed on his left side and confined to a wheelchair.

As his illness progressed, Lee quietly sought spiritual guidance and later publically stated that he had made a conversion to Catholicism. In an attempt to repent for his past actions, he began to make phone calls and send letters of apology to political opponents for his past actions, including to Michael Dukakis for his "naked cruelty" in the 1988 campaign. Lee also apologized to Tom Turnipseed, a Democratic candidate for senate against Strom Thurmond in South Carolina in 1980. During that campaign, Lee made fun of Turnipseed for having electroshock treatment as a depressed sixteen year old, by saying Turnipseed "got hooked up to jumper cables." Lee wrote, "It is very important to me that I let you know that out of everything that has happened in my career, one of the low points remains the so called `jumper cable' episode."[15] In a *Life Magazine* interview, Lee said, "My illness helped me to see that what was missing in society is what was missing in me: a little heart, a lot of brotherhood."[16]

The disabilities and illnesses that the rest of us may face, will likely not be as high profile as someone in the public eye like Lee Atwater or some of the other people mentioned. Regardless of who we are, though, if we are faced with a disability or serious illness, we have a choice of whether or not we are receptive to learning the lessons of our bodies and how willing we are to forgive ourselves for what is happening. At times like these we may be challenged to embrace the idea that *it may take a disability or serious illness to get to the core of our being or strip away what no longer serves us, so we can heal our heart, psyche or relationships.* If the question, "Why is this happening to me?" comes to mind, as author and clinical psychologist, Beth Hedva points out, "How we answer a question like that brings either death, pain, and misery, or liberation."[17]

Sometimes we will experience mixed reactions as we work through what comes up for us in relation to disabilities and illness. It may be an iterative process as we examine our experience from different angles. As mentioned before, self-forgiveness is a process that occurs over time. One of our biggest self-forgiveness challenges may be to accept that we are a "work in self-forgiveness progress" as we dive deeper within ourselves to clear what no longer serves us. (For an example that illustrates this point see *Sara's Story: The Surgical Decision that Keeps on Giving* on the next page.)

If you find your psyche and soma at odds, this may be when you most need to flex your self-forgiveness muscles. It is a time to forgive yourself for your humanity and reach within for greater wisdom. As you do, you make space to listen to your body, your emotions, and the logic of your heart that may hold keys to why you are having the internal conflict or disconnect.

"Why not fall in love with the body
you've been sleeping with your whole life?"
—Stewart Emery
Author, executive coach and thought leader
in the Human Potential Movement

Sara's[18] Story: The Surgical Decision That Keeps on Giving

I haven't always been able to look at my body, especially not at the scarring and the void of tissue. It doesn't seem that long ago, but it's been almost fourteen years since my mastectomy. I did a lot of research beforehand. I looked at the slides from the biopsy. I got a second and third medical opinion. I talked to other women who had undergone various surgery modalities. I talked to friends who were fearful about me not having the mastectomy. They worried that if I only excised the lump with minimal surgery, the cancer would come back. I checked into the Gerson Therapy diet, which was touted as a natural treatment that uses the body's own healing mechanism to treat and cure chronic debilitating illness, including cancer.

With all this input, I dithered about whether to have the surgery or not. I was overwhelmed and couldn't hold all of this information. I didn't want the deprivation of the Gerson diet. I didn't have the energy to shop, chop, and juice veggies and drink them down, along with other special juices. I didn't want the continual focus on the negativity of disease and the need for ongoing treatment. I didn't have the courage. I didn't trust my support. I didn't trust myself to do it all. I just didn't trust. So, I decided to have the mastectomy.

I carried anger, no, make that rage, for years about my decision. Why didn't I stop at a lumpectomy? Who will ever love me now? How can I ever think of myself as a whole person again? Who would ever want me as a sexual partner? How can I ever love myself again? What did I do wrong to deserve this?

With all of the questions, self-recriminations, guilt, and lack of trust, when do I stop? When do I say ENOUGH? When do I forgive myself for not saying no? When do I forgive myself for choosing the mother I did, who also had breast cancer? When do I forgive myself for not listening to my spiritual teacher who said, "You want to be a little girl, so you can be taken care of. That's why you want to have the mastectomy."

How do I live with all the physical, mental, emotional, and, yes, spiritual changes? When do I forgive myself for all of this? When do I stop denying myself the pleasure?

▶

When? Now. Every day that I look in the mirror and say, “I love you.” Every day when I say, “I'm so sorry for the decision I made that had such a drastic effect on my life.” Every day when I say “I forgive you.” And I have to say these statements often. I also have a partner who loves me, who has helped me admit that I wasn’t able at the time to hold the belief needed to do alternative therapies instead of going ahead with the Western medicine.

Have I forgiven myself completely? I don't think so. I am, however, developing a greater trusting relationship with a forgiving, loving God. I still struggle with a question of whether my beliefs will carry me through to an ongoing creation of health, not cancer. I struggle with lapses into fear of “is this symptom indicative of more cancer?”

I read that we create our own reality, and I study how to do that. Even though much of me believes this to be true, there is still that little piece that is fearful, unforgiving, and unloving. I'd like to say I'm strong, powerful, confident, healthy, and no longer struggling 100% of the time. I can't, truthfully say that I always feel that way, though. I still have my doubts. Regardless of my doubts, though, have I done enough? Will I stay cancer free? Will I lose the weight I've gained for protection, as a way to swallow the myriad of feelings I have? I don't know, yet. But, I do know that every day I say to myself, “I forgive you and I'm sorry for the past,” changes me and allows me to create more self-love.

PART 3
ARRIVE AT THE CENTER OF YOURSELF: CLAIM YOUR INNER WISDOM

Composite with Graphic Time Travel/Photos.com

"On our way home, we may follow for a while paths that take us away from ourselves, but the center we have experienced becomes a lodestar drawing us back–to confront the Minotaurs of our fears, to overcome our doubts and to prevail over all real or imagined threats that lurk in the labyrinth's shadows."

—Arianna Huffington
Co-founder of the *Huffington Post*
and author of *The Fourth Instinct*

In the *Introduction* to *Part 2*, we discussed how the self-forgiveness challenges we face in the shedding process may seem painfully slow, tedious, or threatening at first. It can feel like there are an overwhelming number of areas of our lives that need to be addressed. The more we shed, however, the easier the process becomes. This may be because each challenge we face helps us achieve a level of heroic maturity not possible earlier in our personal development. Each new skill we master helps us grow beyond our previous limitations and increases our ability to learn more rapidly. As we "learn how to learn" we build our strength, confidence, and resilience.

While the shedding process will no doubt continue for the rest of our lives, for those of us who remain steadfastly committed to our personal growth, there comes a point in our self-forgiveness journey when a shift occurs. While the first phase of winding inward involved cracking through the thick shell of our ego resistance and lack of awareness, the second phase of claiming the wisdom at the center of ourselves is often more subtle and nuanced. It involves, however, going to a deeper level within ourselves than was required in the first phase. Where before we may have spent what seemed like an inordinate amount of time gnashing over each new challenge, in the second phase, we begin to take new challenges in stride. We know we will eventually master them, even though we may not yet know the exact mechanism of that mastery.

This second phase is the part in our heroic story of self-forgiveness in which *illumination* occurs. It is as if a light bulb of personal awareness has suddenly been turned on. Something that has been hidden is brought to light, so it can be transformed to reflect our true nature. In this process there is a resolution to the internal dynamic tension, which may have previously consumed so much of our conscious and unconscious energy.

Illumination is considered by many cultures to be the highest form of knowing. It bypasses our intellect and connects us directly with the collective wellspring of knowledge. Accessing this level of knowledge lightens our mind and spirit, and gives us, what author and educator Michael Schneider describes as a "deep sacred center"[1] where there is "stillness, with no mental, emotional, or desire ripples disturbing the quiet 'pond' of awareness within us..."[2]

When we shine light on a shadow, the shadow instantly disappears. This is what illumination can do to the "Minotaur of our fears." As we discussed in *Chapter 2*, the Minotaur is often depicted as a fierce monster at the center of the labyrinth, but when faced, it becomes our most cherished symbol of wholeness. Illumination shines the light of awareness on our internal Minotaur, so it can never again completely hide in the shadows of unconsciousness. (See more about the Minotaur in *Chapter 2: Follow Your Heroic Path of Transformation*, pages 14-15.)

Modern psychology often calls the part represented by the Minotaur the "shadow self." The Swiss psychiatrist and founder of Analytical Psychology, Carl Jung, explored this part of the human psyche extensively. In her book, *The Path of Transformation*, Shakti Gawain also describes the shadow, "A shadow self is simply any part of us that we have not recognized and accepted. Since that self is a part of us, it can't go away just because it has been rejected. So it follows us through life like our shadow, until we notice and acknowledge it."[3] The shadow self represents not only the parts of ourselves that we do not like, but also the parts that we want to become and have not yet owned.

It has been said that what we fear most can become our greatest gift. Illumination can give us the wisdom to see the shadow self's gifts buried under our fears. We choose whether we ignore the gifts and continue to be frightened or embrace the gifts and allow our shadow self to be transformed and integrated into who we are.

Jungian therapist and author, James Hollis talks about the importance of doing shadow work:

> Shadow work requires a heroic willingness to take responsibility for oneself, to grow up, and therefore be less demanding and expectant of our [relationships]."[4] "Most of all, Shadow work in the context of relationship asks that we see that what is wrong in the world is wrong in us, as well. We are less likely to wound our partner, despise our neighbor, or hate our enemy when we recognize that we share a common condition, a common set of aspirations, and a common fallibility.[5]

When we experience our life as a *Heroic Journey*, each self-forgiveness challenge becomes a personal Minotaur. It invites us to go deeper within and illuminate a part of ourselves that has been lurking in the shadows of our fear. Framing self-forgiveness challenges in this way, gives us a gentle process for facing the scary aspects of ourselves that we will inevitably encounter in this phase of our journey. It also helps us learn from inside out that we can, in fact, transform each personal Minotaur into a valuable ally, who can support us on the remainder of our *Heroic Journey*.

CHAPTER 17
LISTEN TO YOUR INNER WHISPERINGS

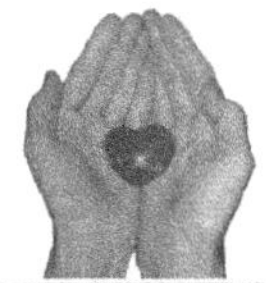

"None of us will ever accomplish anything excellent or commanding except when he[/she] listens to this whisper which is heard by him[/her] alone."
—**Thomas Carlyle**
Scottish historian, teacher and author of
On Heroes, Hero-Worship, and the Heroic in History

Most of us live in environments flooded with sights, sounds, constant activity, and in some cases overwhelming chaos or negativity. With our senses and emotions bombarded by so much staccato and fragmenting energy, it can be difficult to hear ourselves think, much less tune into the more subtle whisperings from the core of our being.

As we move into the second phase of our journey of self-forgiveness, we are called to develop the skills to actively listen to the subtle whisperings of our inner voice. We need a strong inner voice to have the wisdom to face and integrate our shadow self. In fact, *it is virtually impossible to fully forgive ourselves without well developed inner listening skills. It is our ability to intently listen to our shadow self that holds the keys to the deepest levels of self-forgiveness.*

Our inner voice is our most "inspired and ingenious self."[1] It is a quiet, but clear voice that is connected to our inner *Truth*. It is through the whisperings of our inner voice that our personal wisdom communicates clearly with us and sheds light on what is most difficult for us to face. If we don't have access to this part of ourselves, our ability to forgive ourselves will likely remain at a superficial level, with an undercurrent of unforgiving harshness lurking just under the surface of our conscious awareness.

The whisperings of our inner voice point the way home to our authentic self, where self-forgiveness is our natural state of being. These inner whisperings hold the keys to the freedom we seek from the self-imposed prison of our mind and emotions. They may help us release past conditioning that has locked us into a mindset of self-punishment. They may encourage us to take risks to grow beyond fear and paralysis that have kept us from taking action. They may warn us to avoid potentially dangerous or painful situations that would compromise our wellbeing. They may encourage us to make different choices that, if taken, will set us on a new more positive trajectory in our life. (See related story, *Override Limiting Beliefs with Inner Listening*, on page 125.)

Inner whisperings may urge us to address something in our heart that feels incomplete. Maybe we try to convince ourselves that we have finished old business with our family of origin, but an inner whispering tells us otherwise. Maybe we try to convince ourselves that we don't want to complicate our life with a relationship, while our heart silently aches to do the dance of partnership. Maybe we have a laundry list of reasons why life will be easier not to have children, yet a nagging desire urges us to jump with both feet into parenthood.

At the core of our being resides a genius that is just waiting to be activated. Tuning into our inner whisperings can help bring our genius to the surface, so it can become an active player in our life. Our genius may take a myriad of forms, including artistic or musical creativity, being a math or science whiz, having an uncanny ability to read people, possessing an entrepreneurial knack for starting new businesses, etc. Whatever form our personal genius takes, it may lay dormant within us until we heed the call of our inner voice that whisperings what we need to do to bring our unique gifts into physical form.

Listening to our inner voice may also help us let go of something that we are trying to force ourselves to do that is not what we are are personally called to do or does not play to our strengths. It may help us release an old "should" about what we feel we ought to do. It may also help us move beyond the feeling that we are like a square peg trying to fit into a round hole.

It may take practice to listen to our inner voice. Just like exercising our muscles, we may need to exercise our inner listening skills to recognize the subtle cues from the depth of our being. When we begin to actively listen, it may be difficult at first to discern our true inner voice. We may confuse it with the voice of our emotions.

We may have a hard time distinguishing our personal voice from the voice we internalized from others who influenced our formative development. We may rely so heavily on our "voice of reason" that, even when we hear our inner voice whisper something different, we automatically override it.

Wisdom requires us to "empty" and "quiet" our minds. It is in this space that wisdom flourishes. It is also in this space that our wisdom gives us the subtle, but powerful cues that help us distinguish between our inner voice and imposters. Through trial and error, we learn the resonance of our inner voice that distinguishes it from all of the others competing for our attention. The more we synchronize to our inner voice, the stronger it becomes and the easier it is to ignore extraneous internal and external distractions.

Many people find setting time aside for meditation each day a helpful structure for inner listening. The following exercise may also help you practice becoming more receptive to inner listening.

Exercise: Take Notes with a Grateful Heart.[2] Gratitude can be a powerful tool to help us open to inner listening. When we focus on gratitude we shift our focus from the activities of the outer world to the inner world of our heart space, where wisdom and our inner voice play a more prominent role in our awareness. It is also in this open heart space that we are more receptive to messages we need to hear related to self-forgiveness. For purposes of this exercise, set aside at least 20 minutes in a quiet place with a pen and paper nearby.

1. Breathe deeply for at least twenty breaths, while you visualize filling your lungs with clean fresh air and breathing out the stress of the day.
2. If you find yourself having difficulty releasing a particular thought from the day, use the skills you learned in the mindfulness exercise in *Chapter 14* of seeing yourself on a train platform choosing which train of thought to take. (See more detail in the last paragraph of *"Give Up the 'What if...' Mantra,"* page 99.)
3. As you continue to breathe, think about something or someone you are truly grateful for in your life.

4. Expand your thoughts of gratitude, by thinking about what else you are grateful for.
5. Continue being grateful until you feel yourself drop fully into your heart space and feel yourself soften and full of love.
6. In this loving heart space, ask your inner voice for words of wisdom or guidance, such as, "Inner voice what do I need to do to forgive myself more fully? Do you have a message for me?"
7. Continue to sit receptively in gratitude until a message comes to you.
8. Write down the message, so you will remember it later and can act on it in your daily life.
9. If a message does not readily come, repeat steps 4-7 and continue to practice gratitude. By doing so, you open your heart more fully and demonstrate to your inner voice that it is safe to come forth and share its wisdom. You also open yourself to a deeper level of self-forgiveness than your conscious awareness can help you attain.
10. Gradually expand the time you set aside in gratitude for inner listening. As you do, you may find yourself looking forward to this time to communicate with this wise and peaceful part of yourself. You may find yourself relying on it more for subtle cues on how to forgive yourself more fully. You also may find that after a while you no longer need to set aside special time for this exercise, since your inner voice has a stronger and clearer presence in your day-to-day life.

Allowing our inner voice to play a more prominent role in our life is at the heart of our heroic story of self-forgiveness. Our inner voice helps us root out the strands of unforgiving harshness that remains deeply embedded within us. It helps us override old conditioning that keeps us stuck in an old story we have outgrown. It also helps us retrain our mind to listen to our inner source of authority rather than rely on others who may or may not have our best interest at heart.

As we learn to trust our inner voice more fully, it can change how our heroic story unfolds. Our story may become richer and more textured, deeper and more meaningful. In remainder of this book we will see how vital our inner voice is in successfully navigating the inner and outer terrain on the rest of our self-forgiveness journey.

Override Limiting Beliefs with Inner Listening

When Catherine Pratt was in 4th grade she excitedly told her teacher, "I'm going to be a writer when I grow up." She expected him to mirror back her enthusiasm with "great," or "way to go." Instead, he replied, "There's no money in that. You'll end up starving." Catherine said, "It was like a huge pin being stuck in my birthday balloon. I was instantly deflated. What I'd been so excited about accomplishing with my life was now a waste of time and not only that I'd end up penniless and starving in the street. Hmmm, my young mind thought. Maybe it wasn't such a good idea after all. Even though my inner voice said it was wrong, I decided I'd have to do something else with my life as writing was obviously a mistake. It was a huge disappointment for me, but I knew my instructor wouldn't lie to me…It's only recently that I realized that I was letting a limiting belief be placed upon me. I was letting this myth I'd heard all my life become true in my mind.[3]

Like Catherine, many of us grew up with limiting beliefs that we have carried into adulthood. One of the challenges of adulthood is questioning our beliefs to see if they now have validity. There are several signs that help us determine if we are operating from limiting beliefs. One clear sign is that we make decisions from fear rather than strength. Another is seeing ourselves as having few or no choices. Another is feeling anxious or confused. Yet another is experiencing anxiety in our body, such as difficulty breathing, constriction in our throat, or uncontrollable shaking.

Practicing inner listening can stop limiting thoughts in their tracks. No longer are we at the mercy of past conditioning or the limitations placed on us by other people. We trust our own wise counsel to guide our thoughts and actions and help us create a life full of options and possibilities.

❖

CHAPTER 18
OWN YOUR SHADOW

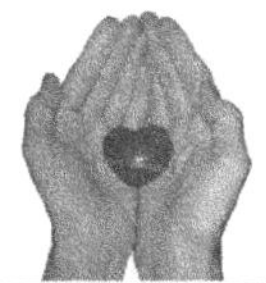

"As we move through our shadow, we reclaim our light."
—Debbie Ford
From *The Shadow Effect: Illuminating the Hidden Power of Your True Self*

Self-forgiveness challenges can be very scary to face. If they were easy, the suffering we experience from the lack of self-forgiveness wouldn't be such a prevalent part of the human condition. In *Part 2*, we discussed many of the challenges with self-forgiveness that lurk in the shadows of our awareness. As we shed what no longer serves us, we inevitably come face-to-face with our shadow self, that part of us that we most resist forgiving. It is how we deal with the shadow self that helps determine whether we are able to successfully move through our deepest, darkest self-forgiveness challenges or they remain stuck inside of us to be dealt with (or not) at a later time.

The shadow self by its very nature is dark, secretive, and hidden in the recesses of our awareness. It represents the aspects of us that we are uncomfortable with owning. The shadow contains the parts of us that we are blind to, embarrassed about, thoroughly repulsed by, or scared to acknowledge. It contains the parts we feel we have no right to claim, are afraid we will misuse, or worry we will be ridiculed for exhibiting. The shadow also contains the parts that are there to help us, but we have not yet acknowledged we possess, such as courage, personal authority, or a specific talent. Mythologist Joseph Campbell pointed out, "The shadow is the landfill of the self. Yet it is a sort of vault: it holds, great, unrealized potentialities within you."[1]

So, why do we keep the shadow so tightly locked away from our conscious awareness? The answer in short is because it is a threat to our ego. Our ego is the conscious part of us that helps us navigate our day-to-day existence of survival and social functioning. It focuses our energy in the here and now, helps engage our mental and linguistic faculties, and brings intentionality to our actions. Our ego believes it sits at the apex of awareness and holds all the keys to who we are. It thrives on control, consistency, and continuity.

The shadow by definition is hidden from us and, therefore, not in our conscious control. It is unpredictable and untamed. It is a direct affront to our ego that thinks it is all knowing, all seeing, and in charge of our existence.

For those of us dedicated to claiming our wisdom, the shadow is a great compliment to our ego, when we allow it to be. Jungian therapist and author, James Hollis describes the importance of the shadow to our personal evolution, "The shadow can play a positive role in our individuation process."[2] "It is less adapted and therefore more honest; it is less acclimated and therefore more original; it is less conventional and consensual and therefore more nearly expressive of the whole person we are meant to share with others."[3]

Recognizing that our shadow has innate value can make it less scary to our ego. It helps our ego approach this wild and untamed vault of potential with curiosity. Curiosity opens a path to explore the deepest, most hidden, and uncontrollable parts of ourselves. By embracing a mindset of curiosity, we greet our shadow with openness. Openness leads to understanding, which in turn leads to acceptance and eventual integration into conscious awareness this previously fractured part of us.

When we do not acknowledge or recognize the shadow self's presence and value, it can wreak havoc in our lives. The more we deny it, the more our shadow pops up in our lives in the form of nightmares, unhealthy relationships, and a skewed perception of the world.

Depression is an effort to "de-press" what is inside of us. It is the opposite of "express." Depression is often caused by trying to press down our shadow self to keep it from coming to the surface to be faced. But, the more we attempt to press it down, the louder the shadow becomes to get us to pay attention to it. We can try to suppress the shadow by numbing ourselves with prescription medications or illicit drugs. We can temporarily divert our attention away from our shadow by keeping ourselves busy with endless "to do" lists or working non-stop. We can avoid listening to our shadow by zoning out in front of the television, spending time gossiping, texting incessantly, or bombarding ourselves with loud music. No matter how hard we try, though, we cannot get away from our shadow self, since it is an integral part of us.

Failure to acknowledge and deal with our shadow self, despite the mounting evidence of the need to face it, can lead to developing a rigid outer shell to protect our ego from self-knowledge. This rigidity is not only evident in our psyche, but it also affects our body and how we relate to the world. (See related *Chapter 25: Align with Your Body's Wisdom*.)

When we are not busy denying or repressing our shadow self, we may be *projecting* it outward. This outward projection may be experienced as the needy childlike part within who shouts "look at me!" It then does everything possible, including acting out, to get its needs met.

Our projection may represent a part of us that we would ideally like to be, but does not match how we really feel, such as when we project confidence, even though we actually feel terrified. It may take the form of acting like an upstanding citizen in public, even though we privately act in despicable ways with the people closest to us.

If we find ourselves strongly attracted to famous people like movie stars, sports heroes, royalty or even infamous criminals, it may be because we are projecting onto them a disowned part of us that desperately wants to be seen and acknowledged. It may be helpful to have these projections as ideals to aspire to and incorporate more fully into ourselves. If, however, we find ourselves placing others on a pedestal or worshiping them as the pure embodiment of these traits, chances are we are not seeing them as real people. It may be a set up for disappointment when they show their humanness. It also may indicate that we are not doing the inner work necessary to embody the traits that we admire in others.

One very common projection is when we project our personal negative shadow traits onto others. How many times have you left one relationship, thinking the problems were behind you, only to enter a new relationship and find that you have the same problems? People who do not take responsibility for their projections may feel persecuted, think others are purposefully "baiting them" or "out to get them." One of the tests of whether or not we are projecting our shadow self onto others is described by philosopher and author, Ken Wilber, "If we look at something in our environment as a point of information or interest, we are probably not projecting. If something affects us, we are pointing our finger, objecting, or we are plugged in, chances are we are a victim of our own projection."[4]

Projections can manifest in a *collective* positive way in the form of ideals such as peace, justice, beauty, kindness, etc. These ideals may be what we strive to achieve as a culture, even though the collective reality may fall far short of the ideal. At its best, the projected ideal becomes a vision to help us bridge the gap between who we are now and the most positive aspects of who we are capable of becoming as a society.

At its worst, when the reality of the gap is collectively denied or issues are not addressed or even actively subverted, we can become deluded. As best-selling author and authority in body healing, Deepak Chopra describes it, "The collective shadow manifests as evil, as war, as terrorism, as social injustice, as radical inequities in our economic status…The ones who show the most self-righteousness are often the ones with the deepest, darkest shadow side."[5]

If we see people as "enemies" it often points to the fact that we have a deeply denied shadow self. As noted author, professor and philosopher Sam Keen astutely observes, "…the radical commandment 'Love your enemy as yourself' points the way toward both self-knowledge and peace. We do, in fact, love or hate our enemies to the same degree that we love or hate ourselves. In the image of the enemy, we will find the mirror in which we may see our own face most clearly."[6]

We have seen the great harm repeatedly perpetrated on others by collectively projecting our shadow onto them. One of those repeated patterns is the false belief that a particular group of human beings have more value than another. This "master race" delusion was used to justify slavery in the early American South and the systematic and scientific annihilation of more than six million Jews by the Nazis.

Whether our shadow self is hidden or projected, acknowledging that we have individual and collective shadows is a bold step toward freedom from our self-imposed prison and taking personal responsibility for our perceptions. It is also a profound step toward changing our personal and collective story and forgiving ourselves for being deluded for so long. (See related story, *Marion's Story: How I Used My Shadow to Grow Beyond Myself*, on the next page.)

Taking the step of owning our shadow may shake us down to our very core! It is not just admitting that we have a minor flaw. It is a recognition that we are fundamentally not who we thought we were. We can no longer claim naiveté about the purity of our nature. As Rodney Smith, former Buddhist monk, social worker, and director of a hospice center in Seattle stated:

> When we define ourselves as being on a path of purification, we create a shadow that expects us to be superhuman. The results are shame, guilt, and an unforgiving mind…The more we pressure ourselves with our morality, the greater our self-condemnation…We are usually unable to forgive ourselves and allow ourselves to be fallible human beings. Because of this harshness, we are not good at forgiving others. We have little room in our hearts for self-acceptance, much less for forgiveness of others.[7]

We are not purely good or evil, but rather an eclectic mix of both positive and negative traits. It takes heroism to face this painful realty about our true nature. *The heroic path of self-forgiveness is not a quest for purity within, but rather a quest for growth and maturity as the imperfect human beings that we are.* Coming to terms with our shadow self can actually accelerate the process of self-forgiveness. Rather than wasting time wishing for what was or searching for purity that does not exist, we can refocus our attention on living as best we can in the here and now.

With less fear of our shadow self, we can finally relax, come to terms with this part of us, and eventually open to the gifts it brings us. Having worked through our own issues related to our shadow self, we understand how difficult this process can be for other people. As a result we often become less judgmental, kinder and more compassionate about the specific challenges others face on their personal journeys.

The contribution we make by doing shadow work cannot be underestimated. Each time we make a personal shift, we lessen the negativity of the collective shadow. When enough of us change the collective shadow, we will live in a significantly different world!

Marion's[8] Story: How I Used My Shadow to Grow Beyond Myself

Many years ago, when I was just beginning my personal growth work, I joined a women's therapy group. It was very instructive to listen to the stories of other women as they struggled to come to terms with their personal issues. I remember one particular woman I'll call Sandra, who came to the group week after week whining about how her married boyfriend wouldn't leave his wife to marry her. Each week she asked the therapist the same question, "Why am I like this?" When the therapist began to speak or confront her, Sandra zoned out. It was clear that she was not willing to look within. She was more married to her victim story than she would ever be to her boyfriend!

Seeing how dedicated Sandra was to her denial was eye opening. It helped me make a commitment to myself to push beyond my own denial and look within, no matter how difficult it was or what horrible parts of myself I discovered. I intuitively knew this was important to my personal growth.

▶

Several weeks later when I was in a private therapy session with the same therapist, I did some inner work concerning a knot I was feeling in my stomach. My therapist suggested that I visualize the knot sitting opposite me in a chair. She asked me to describe it. I saw the knot as a quivering mass of flesh with muscle like petals at the top clamped tightly shut to keep something inside from escaping. My therapist asked me to slowly open the petals and describe what I saw. At first I felt myself clamp down even tighter around the mysterious mass within. But, eventually I mustered the courage to relax the petals and let them open slightly. As I did, in my mind's eye, I saw what appeared to be threatening apparitions fly around the room, much like in the movie, *Ghost Busters*.

At first I felt like I had unleashed pure evil from the core of my being. I regretted my decision to let out these apparitions and I was terrified of them. The more they flew around me and stared menacingly in my face, though, the more I realized that these angry apparitions were all bluster and bluff. They were not really harming me or anyone else. Within a few minutes the intensity of their energy dissipated and the apparitions faded into oblivion. After they disappeared, I no longer had the knot in my stomach. I realized I also no longer had the feeling that I had to keep my gut instincts tightly controlled to prevent them from harming others and myself.

After this inner work, I began to more readily trust my gut instincts. Now when my stomach knots up, I ask myself if there is something my gut is trying to tell me and I rely on it to help me in my decision-making. Although this first major piece of inner work was very scary at the time, now I think back on it my liberation from my self-imposed prison that kept me trembling in fear of what my gut instincts knew beyond the realm of my conscious understanding.

CHAPTER 19
DISCOVER THE GIFTS OF YOUR SHADOW

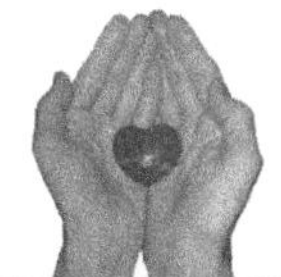

"The cave you fear to enter holds the treasure you seek."
—Joseph Campbell
Great mythologist and
author of *Hero with a Thousand Faces*

In the previous chapter we discussed the shadow self as a single entity. In actuality, it represents a group of "selves," or different aspects of our personality that we have not yet acknowledged and claimed. If you have ever felt like you had a *Harsh Critic* that is merciless when you make a mistake and a *Vulnerable Child* that feels hurt by the criticism, you understand the group nature of the shadow self. If you have sometimes felt inundated with so much internal chatter that it is difficult to get anything done, you have probably experienced what has sometimes been called the "monkey mind," which is another example of the shadow self's group nature.

We all have internal parts of ourselves that want to be heard. When there are multiple parts of us that have not yet acknowledged and forgiven ourselves for perceived past transgressions or self-critical abuse, the internal negative chatter may be deafening. We may not even realize how pervasive the chatter is or that we have the power to stop it, since it may have been ingrained in us since childhood. Without fully understanding what is going on internally, it may feel like a superhuman task to quiet this level of negativity. This is especially true, the closer we get to the root of an issue that may have caused a part of us to splinter and retreat into the shadow in the first place.

In the early 1900's an Italian psychiatrist, Roberto Assagioli, recognized these distinct "sub-personalities" in his development of *Psychosynthesis*. Sub-personalities are structures of consciousness in the form of an entity that influences a person's perception of themselves, how they feel, and how they interact with their external environment. Central to Psychosynthesis is the perspective that the ultimate *Truth* of a person is not rooted in the sub-personalities, but rather transcends these ego created structures and is connected to a deeper source of being that is part of all that is. By becoming more self-aware of our sub-personalities and making an *empathetic connection* to them, the sub-personalities are more likely to be more honest with us, so we can understand them, [1] forgive them, and clear past difficulties we may have had with them.

Voice Dialogue is a technique developed in the early 1970's by Drs. Hal and Sidra Stone that built on the foundations of Psychosynthesis.[2] Voice Dialogue identifies the different "sub-personalities" and gives voice to them. By openly dialoguing with our sub-personalities, we are more likely to develop an empathtic connection to them. This empathy helps us better understand their perspective and appreciate the value they bring to our lives. When our sub-personalities feel more acceptance, they are less defensive and more open to changing their perceptions and behaviors, so they can operate in more functional ways in our lives. By working with our sub-personalities instead of at odds, we are better able to access our untapped potential that lies hidden in our shadow.

Voice Dialogue takes the form of an interview with the sub-personalities. Each sub-personality is treated as a separate character, complete with its own perspective, needs and desires. By giving voice to each sub-personality, interesting insights can come to light about the sub-personality's values and rules it lives by. We can learn what it wants from us and why it is acting in a certain way that is sometimes counter to what we consciously say we want. After completing a conversation with one of your sub-personalities, as Hal and Sidra Stone say, you may have "a sense of having more 'breathing space' as though you have separated a part of your personality out of the mass of selves who are usually crowded together and there is now more space for 'you' to emerge."[3]

Some sub-personalities are more publicly acceptable than others. (**Table 19.1** provides examples.) Recognizing and owning the previously unclaimed aspects of ourselves can help us develop more self-compassion, be more forgiving of ourselves for previous regrettable behavior, and ultimately begin the process of making peace with those particular parts of ourselves. When we make peace with enough aspects of ourselves, the cacophony of chatter inside our head may also begin to dissipate.

Examples of Publicly Accepted Sub-Personalities	Examples of Disowned Sub-Personalities
• Responsible Parent	• Harsh Critic
• Conscientious Worker	• Vulnerable Child
• Likable One	• Lazy One
• Strong Leader	• Scapegoat
• Good Team Member	• Airhead
• Driven Achiever	• Procrastinator
• Winner	• Manipulative Whiner
• Playful Jester	• Controlling One
• Caregiver	• Inner Saboteur
• Upstanding Citizen	• The Addict
• The Calm One	• Defiant Teen
• The Teacher	• Long Suffering One
• Visionary	• Angry Hothead

Table 19.1. Examples of publically accepted and often disowned sub-personalities.

One of the best gifts of Voice Dialogue is that it can help you become the director of your own life play. As the director you are detached from the characters that each sub-personality represents and you recognize each character's value to the play as a whole. You see the play from a big picture perspective and do what it takes to make it a success. You do this in part by helping all of the characters play their role to the best of their ability. Sometimes particular characters feel strongly that they want to play their part in a different way than you feel will make the play successful. You listen to them, help them understand the big picture, and negotiate possible changes to the script. When the characters feel heard, they are less likely to act out in counter-productive ways. Ultimately, though, as the director, it is your responsibility to provide the leadership necessary to make sure that no one character takes over and ruins the play.

From a Voice Dialogue perspective, the real "you," whom I call *the Wise One, is the director of your life*. This internal aspect of you is innately connected to all the wisdom of humanity. It stands apart from the other sub-personalities as a detached, non-judgmental, but loving and compassionate observer. Getting in touch with the *Wise One*, allows you to become less identified with your sub-personalities. For instance, rather than feeling like *you* are a victim, you identify the *victim part of yourself.* As the *Wise One* you stand between the different aspects of yourself from the place of a detached wise witness. This stance helps you mediate between the various parts of yourself and develop the wisdom to respond to your environment in a different way.

You may also find that as your *Wise One* becomes a better director, it begins to have a stronger voice in your life and your sub-personalities are more comfortable with and trusting of your *Wise One* taking the lead. The more prominent your *Wise One* becomes, the less reactive and freer you are to choose responses that arise from a place of authenticity, self-love and a genuine appreciation for all facets of who you are. (For more information see *Appendix D: Voice Dialogue Resources.*)

When your sub-personalities operate at their optimal capacity, they become strong members of your *Internal Dream Team.* The mission of this team is to help you succeed in life, be all you can be, and fulfill your dreams. With your *Wise One* directing a well functioning *Internal Dream Team*, you become an unstoppable positive force in the world!

The following exercise is designed to help you use the basic framework of Voice Dialogue to delve deeper within yourself and discover the gifts of each of your sub-personalities. Once you do, you may be amazed at how easy it is to integrate them into your conscious awareness. You may find that in their transformed state your sub-personalities are eager to make a positive contribution to your *Internal Dream Team* and become trusted allies to support you on the remainder of your self-forgiveness journey.

Exercise: Transform Your Shadow's Sub-Personalities into Trusted Allies. This exercise is intended to be done over a period of time, since it takes deep contemplation and a willingness to be truthful with yourself to fully integrate each shadow sub-personality and transform it into a positive force in your life. In fact, as additional sub-personalities emerge into awareness, this integration technique may become less of an exercise and more of a way of processing new information that accelerates self-forgiveness and your personal evolution.

The first time you do this exercise, though, it may be helpful to set aside at least 20 minutes per day for one week to complete all of the steps in the exercise. Have a pen and paper close by and designate a quiet place so you can focus your full attention on each step.

Be aware that in working through the steps in this exercise, strong feelings that may have been buried below your conscious awareness are likely to come to the surface. This is one of the values of this exercise. When this occurs, however, if your pattern has been to bury strong feelings when they surface, I encourage you to change your pattern by working through the entire exercise to the end. By doing so, you are more likely to experience the transformational value of completing the exercise. *If you have difficulty working through all of the steps, you feel overwhelmed for an extended period of time, or you experience extreme distress or anxiety, you may want to seek professional therapeutic assistance to help you with this process.*

Regardless of how far you get with the exercise, remember to be gentle with yourself. Applaud your courage and your willingness to go deeply within. Remind yourself that this journey is not for the faint of heart or everyone would have already done it. You are among the very few who are willing to heroically press forward to gain the reward of finding the hidden treasures at your core.

Step 1: Make a list of your sub-personalities. Without thinking too deeply about it, make a list of the different characters you are aware of at this moment in your internal play. You may want to refer back to **Table 19.1** for examples to get your creative juices flowing.

a. Put a star by any of them that make your life more difficult or that you wish would go away.
b. Of the sub-personalities that you have put a star by, select the one that most calls out to you to work with throughout the remainder of this exercise. Remember as you work through the next steps that you cannot ever eliminate a sub-personality. It is part of you and thus it can only be listened to, acknowledged, negotiated with, and hopefully transformed.

Step 2: Create a *Voice Dialogue Log*. (Refer to **Table 19.2** on the next page for an example.)

a. **Column 1**: On the first row, record the sub-personality from step 1 that you are going to work with at this time. Populate the rows below with each of the other sub-personalities you put a star by in step 1, so you can work through the rest of the exercise with each of them at a later time.
b. **Column 2**: For the sub-personality you are working with in this exercise describe the overt behavior that it exhibits in your daily life.

Column 1 Character that the Sub-Personality Represents	Column 2 Overt Behavior	Column 3 The Gift (The contribution of this sub-personality to your *Internal Dream Team*	Column 4 New Identity	Column 5 Change in Behavior to Better Serve Your *Internal Dream Team*
Example 1: *Harsh Critic*	*Relent-lessly berates me when I make mistakes*	*The one who is there to help me succeed*	*Coach*	*Discernment of when to push and when to gently provide encourage-ment*
Example 2: *Saboteur*	*Under-mines my ability to move forward to fulfill my goals and dreams*	*The one who slows me down to keep me from acting rashly*	*Advocate of Reason*	*Rather than stymie progress, helps evaluate actions to determine if they are the best course to pursue*
Example 3: *Whiny Child*	*Nagging complainer, who demands my attention when I am working*	*The one who keeps my workaholic from totally taking over my life*	*Playful Child*	*Rather than nag and complain, simply reminds me that it is time to take a break, kick back, and enjoy life*

Table 19.2. Example of a Voice Dialogue Log. Record distinct sub-personalities that you observe. Identify each of the associated items in each category to help you shift the contribution that the sub-personality makes to your *Internal Dream Team*.

c. **Column 3**: Record how your selected sub-personality has served you in some way, even if that service may have been misguided. If you look at each sub-personality as being one member of your whole team of sub-personalities, it can help you see how each one contributes to making you the unique and gifted individual that you are. As an example, your *Harsh Critic* wants to help you succeed. It thinks that berating you pushes you to improve. In its misguided belief, your *Harsh Critic* thinks that berating you fulfills its mission as a member of your *Internal Dream Team.*

   Recognizing the logic of the *Harsh Critic* can help you better understand why it is so relentless in belittling you. Knowing this can help you more effectively communicate with this aspect of yourself and give you greater compassion for why it developed this behavior toward you. Acknowledging the underlying gift that the *Harsh Critic* contributes goes a long way toward bringing the *Harsh Critic* out of the shadows, softening its stance, and inviting it to become a more functional and collaborative participant on your *Internal Dream Team.*

d. **Column 4**: Shift the sub-personality's self-identified role to better serve your *Internal Dream Team.* In the example of the *Harsh Critic*, it thinks that being harsh pushes you to improve. Have a brainstorming session with other members of your *Internal Dream Team* to help your *Harsh Critic* see if there are other strategies that can better fulfill its mission. In this discussion one team member points out that being harsh shuts down the *Creative One.* Another member of the team suggests that changing tactics from being harsh to being more gently encouraging, might get better results. Yet another team member suggests that good coaches have the discernment to know when to push and when to more gently encourage. This kind of group dialogue can help your *Harsh Critic* see that even though it originally thought being harsh was the only way to achieve its mission, redefining its role as a *Coach* provides more options that may ultimately prove more successful. Write down the new role and see how it fits. If it is a good match, your *Harsh Critic* will likely feel excited about this new role and actively embrace it. Have the other *Internal Dream Team* members affirm this new role and join in the excitement. This group acknowledgement reinforces the new role and makes this sub-personality more open to feedback about other ways it can contribute in a positive way to the wellbeing of your entire committee of selves.

e. **Column 5**: Write down the new behavior that your sub-personality commits to contribute to the *Internal Dream Team* in its newly defined role. In the example of the *Harsh Critic*, turned *Coach*, the new behavior is to "discern when to push and when to gently provide encouragement." Making a written statement reinforces your internal *Coach's* commitment to the new behavior.

<u>Step 3</u>: **Have your sub-personality create a new contract with the *Internal Dream Team* that memorializes the change in behavior it is agreeing to make.** While the above type of dialogue is still fresh in your mind, write down the old role and behaviors as well as the changes that the sub-personality is agreeing to make. Then have your sub-personality (e.g., *Harsh Critic*, *Saboteur*, *Whiny Child*, etc.) sign the contract. Creating a written document provides a physical reminder that you can look at later if your sub-personality slips back into its old ways. Having your *Wise One* witness the contract on behalf of your *Internal Dream Team* helps

memorialize the change. Much like having witnesses at a marriage ceremony deepens the new commitment, having your *Internal Dream Team* witness this commitment acts as a sacred rite of passage in releasing the old ways of behaving and embracing the new. Even if you cognitively do not think this step is necessary, do not underestimate its value until you try it. You might be surprised at the subconscious power that this simple exercise has in shifting long held behaviors that no longer serve you and helping you embrace new ones with a minimum amount of effort. (See an example of a Voice Dialogue Sub-Personality "Role Change" Contract on the next page.)

Once you complete this exercise with one sub-personality, you may want to select another one to work with that you identified in step 1. Each time you work through this exercise to completion with a new sub-personality, you develop a greater sense of wholeness and appreciation for all facets of who you are. Appreciation goes a long way toward creating a self-forgiving environment that encourages each sub-personality to come out of the shadow and take its rightful place on your *Internal Dream Team*. Don't be surprised if over time additional sub-personalities come to light requesting to be the next one you work with, since deep down they recognize the transformational power of this exercise.

Voice Dialogue Sub-Personality "Role Change" Contract Example Samantha's Contract

This contract is between Samantha's *Harsh Critic* and her *Internal Dream Team*. The intent of this contract is to:

1. Change the role of Samantha's *Harsh Critic*,
2. Discontinue behaviors that, although well intentioned, have sabotaged Samantha's ability to feel good about herself, and
3. Adopt new behaviors that help Samantha better fulfill her dreams and make her happy.

From this time forward, the *Harsh Critic* agrees to relinquish this outmoded role and adopt instead the new more fulfilling role of *Coach*. In this new capacity, **the *Coach* will discern when to push and when to gently provide encouragement to Samantha**. In doing so, the *Coach* will build a relationship of trust with Samantha that supports her to be more authentic, live more joyfully, and naturally evolve into her best self.

Specifically, the behaviors that the *Harsh Critic* used to do that the *Coach* now agrees to relinquish are:

- Picking on Samantha for her faults, even when they are minor,
- Harping on Samantha relentlessly when her performance is less than perfect,
- Finding fault with Samantha's looks, including telling her she is ugly and that she will never measure up to others,
- Name calling that is designed to put Samantha down, including names like "loser," "fat pig," "dumb blond," "worthless bitch," and any other derogatory terms not specifically enumerated in this contract, and
- Berating Samantha at bedtime for everything she did wrong during the day, making it difficult for Samantha to get to sleep or have deep rest.

▶

Specifically, the behaviors that the *Coach* agrees to adopt are:

- Focusing on Samantha's strengths, rather than her faults,
- Praising Samantha when she does something well,
- Encouraging Samantha to keep trying when she is frustrated with her performance,
- Reminding Samantha how smart and talented she is if she forgets,
- Pointing out to Samantha her inner and outer beauty,
- Finding affirming words to describe Samantha that are uplifting and can build her confidence, and
- Other creative strategies that boost Samantha's morale, draw out her passions, encourage her to dream big, and support her to take the actions that bring greater meaning and happiness to her life!

____________________________ ____________________________

Signature: *Coach*
(formerly *Harsh Critic*)

Date:

In witnessing this contract, the undersigned agree to: 1) support the *Coach* in her new role, 2) remind the *Coach* if she slips back into old, outmoded behaviors, and 3) encourage the *Coach* to be an active participant on Samantha's *Internal Dream Team*, including, but not limited to coaching each of the *Internal Dream Team* members as needed on how they can better serve Samantha in her quest to be the best she can be.

____________________________ ____________________________

Signature: *The Wise One*
(on behalf of Samantha's
Internal Dream Team)

Date:

❖

CHAPTER 20

GET TO THE ROOT OF YOUR CORE PAIN

"It takes courage to endure change in our lives, because of the pain that often comes with the process. In biology, in order to release what's inside, a seed's shell must split wide open and break. Sometimes life does that to us, too—splitting us wide open at our most vulnerable points—and it's painful. But, it's often at the point of pain when the transformation begins and the seed begins to grow."

—Sasha Vukelja

Oncologist, cancer survivor and author of *Seeds: A Memoir*

Whether we use Voice Dialogue, or another process to integrate the various aspects of ourselves into a unified whole, we may notice that something else takes place within us. A repeated pattern of pain might emerge in our conscious awareness. This *core pain* is a deeply hurtful theme that plays out over and over in our perceptions as well as outside experiences throughout life. There may be an associated sensation in our body such as heartache, a blow to our gut, a gnawing hunger, a deep, deep longing, or any number of other sensations. Whatever form the pain takes, it often surfaces when we least expect it or in situations that catch us off guard.

As we discussed in *Part 2,* when we first began the self-forgiveness journey, much of the shedding process revolved around peeling away layers of pain to get to the center of ourselves. In this portion of the journey, with our internal *Wise One* at our side, we now have the personal guidance, loving support, and active encouragement we need to *look straight into the face of pain itself.* We now have the internal fortitude to root out the source of the pain and transform it into a trusted ally and valued member of our *Internal Dream Team.* With our eyes wide open we see the original cause of our core pain. We understand what caused our ego to pull the layers of protection around us in the first place. We are more likely to forgive our ego for the depth of the pain that drove it to do whatever it felt was necessary to hide our most cherished jewels in the shadows to protect them from harm.

From this new more compassionate perspective, we see how profoundly our core pain has fueled the past stories we told ourselves and influenced the ways we interacted with the world. Getting in touch with our core pain can fundamentally change the stories that we tell ourselves from this point forward. It also makes self-forgiveness easier now that we realize how universally challenging it is to clear pain that is so deeply buried within. (See **Table 20.1** for some of the common themes of core pain.)

Common Core Pain Themes That Fuel Stories We Tell Ourselves	
❑ I do not feel wanted/loved	❑ My life is all about suffering
❑ I regret not being born the opposite sex	❑ I continually find myself in the role of scapegoat
❑ I feel like an orphan/continually abandoned	❑ I cannot depend on anyone but myself
❑ I am repeatedly betrayed by those I love	❑ No matter how much I do, I am neverrewarded/recognized/loved
❑ I am a burden to others	❑ I feel shame for surviving when others around me died/suffered
❑ I am unworthy of love	❑ It is unsafe to speak out
❑ I am continually hurt by cruel people	❑ If I say what I want, it will be withheld from me
❑ I am so lonely/all alone in the world	❑ I feel shame for wanting to give my unique gifts to the world
❑ No matter what I do, it is never good enough	❑ I must obey or I will suffer dire consequences
❑ I am not as important as others	❑ I cannot do what I want unless I get external approval
❑ It is not okay for me to be financially secure/well compensated, wealthy, etc.)	❑ Others will be jealous of me/hurtful if I am powerful, successful, happy, etc.
❑ If I am myself, it will be a disappointment to those whose love I want	❑ I am constantly being oppressed by _____ (e.g. men, the system, other races, etc.)

Table 20.1. Have you experienced any of these themes of core pain? What others have you experienced that are not on the list?

The first reaction that most of us have when we experience core pain is to quickly bury the feeling again or busy ourselves to avoid dealing with it. Another common reaction is to feel victimized. Yet another is to make a rigid decision, such as "I will never go there again."

All of these reactions to avoid pain, though, can actually stunt our emotional growth. In our effort to keep from feeling hurt, we may be like automatons going through the motions in life. We may create rigid barriers between us and other people instead of permeable membranes that allow us to experience true intimacy. Avoidance may also make us hyper-vigilant as we attempt to keep our core pain at bay. Unfortunately, the more the pain is repressed, the stronger this shadow part of us becomes and the more of a toll it takes on our wellbeing until we are willing to fully feel it.

It takes courage to dive into core pain and feel the associated feelings, when all we want to do is run from it. As spiritual practitioner Elizabeth Hamilton says, "What do we find when we open the vault? A misery deposit, consisting of the painful physical, mental and emotional components that have been festering during years of neglect."[1] The action called for when core pain rears its ugly head is not to turn away from it or judge it, but rather *dive into it* and feel the feeling fully and deeply!

Curiosity, which is the antithesis of avoidance, can help you with this process. For example, if you are hurt by something someone says to you, you may first feel a tightening in your body. This tightening then sets off alarms throughout the rest of your system. At this point you can ignore the alarm. You can deny the alarm. You can attack and blame the one who touched off the alarm. You can use your sub-personality *Abuser* to hurt yourself. All of these choices only give you the illusion that you retain some control over your pain, without actually helping you deal with it.

By contrast, you can use your curiosity to change your reactive pattern and learn more about yourself in the process. When you first feel alarmed and threatened, you can activate your curiosity and ask it to non-judgmentally investigate what is really going on internally. You can call on your *Wise One* to assist you and be there for support. The first step is to acknowledge that the other person has a right to their feelings and you have a right to yours, which may differ from what the other person feels. The second step is to ask yourself if there is *Truth* to what is being said or if you are just part of the other person's projection. The third step is to pay attention to your internal whisperings—feelings in your body, gut feelings, etc.—that may reveal the *Truth* to you.

Once you separate your *Truth* from the other person's projection, it can help transform the pain into compassion for yourself and empathy for the other person. *This separation also can help you transform the original alarm into a clarion call for self-knowing.* Over time, as you accept this invitation to self-knowing, you may find that long standing triggers and reactive patterns have dissipated. You feel calmer, more peaceful, and better able to listen to what others have to say from a less reactive and more open-hearted place.

Remaining aware during this process may actually lessen the intensity and duration of the pain and create a space for insights to emerge that have been long buried under the pain. As you stay with the process, you may begin to see the part you played in the past to perpetuate your misery. *This does not excuse what you or someone else may have done that originally hurt you, but rather you own that you now have a choice about whether the pain still holds you captive.* Maybe you have been hanging onto a belief about life, formed as a child, that no longer serves you. Maybe you falsely assume that others are acting in a certain way because they are intentionally being cruel. Or maybe you are exhibiting a risky behavior that draws to you the very type of situations or people who will repeatedly hurt you. Whatever you have been perpetuating that causes you repeated pain can be changed, sometimes in an instant, once you willingly own the part you play in keeping the pattern of pain alive within you.

It is from this new place of awareness that you can more clearly see how important self-forgiveness work is to your everyday reality. As Charles Richards, author and psychotherapist states so clearly, "*You need to forgive yourself for taking your pain to such a deep place that it shut you down.*"[2] [emphasis added] Self-forgiveness and self-compassion redirect your energy, which was previously so preoccupied with burying your pain. Instead you can now focus your energy toward living your life to the best of your ability.

There is a spiraling nature in dealing with core pain. You may find yourself repeatedly coming back to the same issue. This is the reason it is called *core pain.* It doesn't mean that you didn't get to the root of your pain, but rather that the core pain may have spread tendrils into your system that also need to be cleared. It also may mean that this core pain spread to your sub-personalities, since you did not have your *Wise One* there in the past to guide you through the transformational process. (See *Elaine's Story: Lean into the Pain* below for how one person used her personal wisdom to guide her through her transformational process.)

The core pain may always be with you. It does not have to be debilitating, though. In fact, with your *Wise One* in the lead, you may find that you willingly and excitedly dive deeper than you ever were able to before, since you now know that under the overlay of pain is a place of greater peace and freedom just waiting to be tapped and brought to the surface.

Elaine's[3] Story: Leaning into the Pain

I felt myself coming close to the edge of something. I felt the danger of life coming to its end, so close I could touch it. How easy it would be for this pain to end. But, how hard it would be to actually cause my own end. And what would I leave behind? As much of a relief as it would be to have the burden of the heart lifted from my soul, I knew it wouldn't be fair to others.

It would be an act of selfish indulgence to leave behind remnants of a life and a body, a grave or ashes and grief for others to bear. I would pass my sorrow onto others. I listened with all of my attention to the voice inside of me, the *Wise Managing Self* (WMS) as I came to call this part of me. This is the one who sees beyond the defensive guarding. The WMS had an insight: "Whatever courage it would take to end your burden, why not take that same courage and give yourself another chance?" It made sense. I could see the power in this insight.

▶

Then I knew what I had to do. I had to negotiate with the part of me that wanted the pain to end at any cost, including suicide if that was all I had left. I named it logically, *End the Pain* (EP). The *Wise Managing Self* could then strike a negotiation and make a deal with *End the Pain*:

WMS: You can always kill yourself. There will be a time when your life comes to an end anyway. What if you wait and, while you wait, what if you can then heal the pain?

EP: I've already tried that and it doesn't work. Nothing works. I'm tired of the pain, it seems hopeless to go on. No one really cares anyway.

WMS: You know to end your life now would take courage to complete but, in the end it would only be a cowardly act. You know others do care, so why don't you care enough about yourself to use courage for self-healing?

EP: I do care about myself. That is why I don't want to go through any more pain. I just don't know what else I can do.

WMS: Then I will ask you. Will you step aside and let me lead you through this? If so, will you give it your all? If it still doesn't work in a year, you can always end your life then. But in the meantime will you let me lead you and will you give me the year to do it? I must warn you, however. It will get worse before it gets better. You must be willing to go to the depths of hell. You must walk through the pain and let it overtake you. Resist the urge to avoid the pain. Feel it, go to it, let it envelope you. Let it take you over and see where it goes. Why not try something different? What if you could make pain your friend? Let it help you heal. It is your last chance.

▶

EP How can it help me to feel this misery? I am scared I will die from tortured pain rather than a quick painless end.

WMS You have tried avoiding pain, but what if that was the mistake you have been making? What if the answer is the usual ironic twist of the rule of life: *Face that which you avoid to give you the freedom you seek.* I will call for the *Great Spirit* and *Compassion* to help us through this journey. It is the best way. It might not work. But give me the year and that is all we can do. Give yourself this one last unwanted gift.

EP: I see what you are saying. I am ready to make a commitment to focus. Instead of moving away from the pain, I will allow the pain to come forward. Even though it may feel as though my flesh will burn in agony, I will continue to focus towards the very thing I have avoided. I know it will take all of my effort to hold my feet to the fire. But, nothing else has worked. Why not give myself one more chance and try something different?

The burning did happen and I did not die from the pain. It was a kind of death and the rebirthing was even more painful than I imagined. In the end came something I had never thought possible. Out of this hellish journey, I was washed clean of my old patterns. To my surprise, it was not so much the harm I had done to others, but the harm that had been originally done to me from a lack of consciousness. What was worse, though, was the harm I had continued to do to myself from the same unconscious source. In the end this death when complete was what allowed my *Naked Soul* to return to its original glory. The very pain I had avoided became the track that led me through to the greatest transformation I believe a human can hope to experience.

❖

CHAPTER 21

LOVE YOURSELF – SHADOW, PAIN, AND ALL

"Love is, above all, the gift of oneself."
—Jean Anouilh
Popular French playwright

Exploring the uncharted territory of our inner self is no picnic in the park. It takes profound courage. As we confront the darkness within us and feel the pain fully, something interesting often begins to happen. We find that we love ourselves *unconditionally*, shadow, pain, and all.

Unconditional love means we love ourselves without reservation. Our love is not conditioned on the innate traits we possess. We do not withhold self-love based on our behavior or actions. From a stance of unconditional love, we look at ourselves with kind eyes. We recognize that as human beings we are always a work in progress. We open-heartedly support ourselves through the highs and lows of our journey. We comfort ourselves when we are in pain, reassure ourselves when we have doubts, cheer ourselves on when we try something new that is scary, and soothe ourselves with the salve of self-forgiveness when we are disappointed with ourselves.

It is ironic that we can rarely experience unconditional love until we get to this phase of our journey, even though this is exactly what we all want as sentient human beings. As long as we are preoccupied with keeping our dark and painful experiences at bay, we can only conditionally love ourselves. We are likely telling ourselves consciously or subconsciously, messages such as:

- "If you are *good*, I will love you."
- "If you do _____ you will be unlovable."
- "If you look like _____ you will be desired and worthy."
- "You had better not (think, feel, or say _____) or I will reject you."

It is no wonder we do not know how to unconditionally love ourselves. Many of us were not taught what it is or how to do it. We were loved conditionally by parents who learned how to love from their parents, who didn't experience unconditional love either.

As we clean out the cobwebs of our inner being, we no longer have to be manipulative to get love. We no longer have to project a false representation of ourselves, since we already know the *Truth* of who we are. We no longer have to hide from ourselves what we most fear, since we have already thoroughly explored that terrain.

Courageously facing our deepest challenges of self-forgiveness frees us to experience unconditional self-love. One by-product may be a peace of mind that permeates our entire being. Another may be the emergence of genuine self respect that strengthens our resolve to complete the remainder of our *Heroic Journey* to the best of our ability.

At the point we began our inward voyage of self-forgiveness, we were likely operating on blind faith that the journey would actually lead us in a positive direction. We had to willingly step into a place of "unknowing." Even though we may have trembled in fear at what lurked in the shadows and shuddered at the thought of dredging up painful experiences, we courageously forged on.

As we learn how to access and trust our inner wisdom, we no longer have to act on blind faith and the place of "unknowing" is no longer a scary place to be. It is instead our place of *inner solace*. It is where we actively choose to go to listen to the whisperings of our inner wisdom.

When we are guided by our internal *Wise One*, we acknowledge that the darkness within us is there to teach us something. The darker and more repulsive the parts of us seem, the more profound the lessons to be learned. If we are open to what they have to teach us, they can be transformed into harbingers of personal freedom. In their transformed state, they become beacons of light, calling us back to the center of ourselves in all that we do.

Our labyrinth of personal experiences provides a variety of situations that test how well our external character is aligned with the core of who we are. The more we trust our wisdom to guide us through these experiences, the more confidently we move to the next phase of our heroic story.

"Wisdom is the reward you get for a lifetime of listening when you'd have preferred to talk."
—**Doug Larson**
Popular Wisconsin columnist

Marion's[1] Story: Making Peace with My Inner Abuser

One aspect of myself, my *Inner Abuser*, had been a shadow deeply embedded within me for as long as I could remember. Even though I had longed for it to stop hurting me, I did not know how to make it go away. My relationship to this part of myself literally changed overnight as a result of using the Voice Dialogue technique I developed during the writing of this book. I was able to get to the root cause of my pain and change it, so I no longer needed to continually look over my shoulder in fear waiting for the next blow to come.

One night, I was dealing with yet another issue around a common theme for me, which was why a part of me seemed to take such great pleasure in my pain and suffering. This time instead of turning away from the pain and cringing in fear as was my usual pattern, I decided to face this part of myself. As I did, I clearly saw the maniacal smile of my *Inner Abuser*, a look that was all too familiar to me. What was different this time, though, was that I had no fear. I felt the strong presence of my internal *Wise One* with me, which gave me strength and clarity. With the soft eyes of compassion, I asked my *Inner Abuser*, "Oh, honey, why do you want to hurt me so much?"

My *Inner Abuser* was shocked that I did not respond with my normal pattern of fear. She was so taken aback that she responded honestly without censoring herself, "Because I am terrified of your inner knowing. If I hurt you, I can divert your focus away from seeing how ugly I am."

▶

In that moment of *Truth*, I was able to see my *Inner Abuser* in a different light. She was not dominant over me, but rather a scared child who believed that the best defense was an offense. I said with both compassion and confidence, "You have nothing to fear from me. Don't you know that we are both one? My inner knowing is your inner knowing. You are not ugly, only misguided. I see who you are and I love you unconditionally."

My *Inner Abuser* was surprised to know that I actually saw who she was and loved her anyway. She dissolved into tears as she understood for the first time that I would not reject her, even after seeing the ugly *Truth* of why she behaved the way she did toward me. After a few minutes of intense crying and deeply taking in the love, she felt cleaned out.

With a sense of completion from this deep inner process, I knew it was time to go to bed. As I walked to the bedroom, I felt my *Inner Abuser* standing beside me for the first time instead of lurking in the shadows behind me. I realized in that moment that this part of me had been forever transformed into my *Internal Partner*! We could not stop smiling at one another and happily walked arm-in-arm to bed.

That night I slept very deeply and had a vivid dream, which I will always remember. In the dream, I was a child and our family was gathered around our Christmas tree. The decorating was complete except for the star on top. My family turned to me and I knew it was my task to put the star on the tree. As I reached for the glistening star encased in a beautifully, elaborately decorated box next to me, my new *Internal Partner* reached for the star, too. We smiled knowingly at each other. Together we gently lifted the star from its case, took it in our hands, and walked to the top of a wide step ladder to place the star on the pinnacle of the tree.

I awoke from the dream, knowing I had fully integrated this major part of my shadow. I also knew that we would no longer work at odds, but together, to accomplish my dreams and goals. Ever since then I have had a sense of internal peace, freedom, and joy like I had never experienced before! I no longer spend energy being vigilant, waiting for my *Inner Abuser* to attack me. I feel less fear in general and am able to more fully take in the sweetness of life. I also now feel more internally supported to fulfill my life purpose, knowing that I will always have my loving *Internal Partner* at my side.

❖

PART 4
WIND OUTWARD:
HONE YOUR AUTHENTICITY

Fingerprint/photos.com

"[This phase] invites us, empowers us, even pushes us to be more authentic. It gives us the confidence to take risks as we manifest our gifts in the world."

—Lauren Artress

From *Walking a Sacred Path: Rediscovering the Labyrinth as a Spiritual Practice*

Winding *outward* is the third and final phase of our heroic story of synthesis. It is the part of the story in which our inner illumination meets the outer world. Having been transformed in a powerful way in the previous phase, we are, as author Lauren Artress says, "literally ushered back out into the world in a strengthened condition."[1] Authors Marilyn Mandala Schlitz, Cassandra Vieten, and Tina Amorok believe, "…the convergence of life and practice is about the hero's return—in which you bring the fruits of your journey of self-discovery back home, into your life, your family, and your community. Embodying transformation is a process of continual exploration."[2]

When we first stepped inside our labyrinth of experiences, we may have been more easily distracted, confused, or sidetracked. But now that we operate from the center of ourselves, our attention and energy are anchored from within. Winding outward hones our ability to deal with all kinds of situations from the core of who we are.

This phase of heroic development is where the "rubber meets the road." Being authentically ourselves is key to mastering this phase. Author and leadership teacher, Lance Secretan observes, "When we are authentic, we align our hearts and our mouths and our minds and our feet…When we are authentic, we feel, we say, we think, and we do what we mean."[3] Because we are aligned with our hearts, our desires for authenticity are tempered with empathy and compassion for ourselves and others. Otherwise, we could become selfish or destructive under the guise of being true to ourselves. (For more information about how to become more authentic, refer to *Appendix E: Authenticity Resources*.)

One of the main challenges in this phase is to simultaneously be as authentic as possible and *forgive ourselves for being human when we miss the mark*. There will inevitably be people who push your buttons, causing you to revert to old patterns you thought you had shed long ago. Do you still lash out in retaliation toward people when they hurt you deeply? Are you able to remain true to your values when your job is on the line? Does your old pattern of jealousy get triggered when a friend attains a level of success that you want for yourself? If you find yourself being triggered by others, it may be an indication that you are now being called to clear this particular issue and forgive yourself at a deeper level than was possible in *Phase 1* of your journey. You may find it helpful to review pertinent chapters in *Part 2* and *Appendix A: Skills to Tame Unruly Emotions.* For issues related to your work environment, you may also want to read a booklet in my "Workplace Heroism Series," *Messengers of Wisdom: Ten Ways the People You Work with Can Help Evolve Your Heroic Character*.[4]

There will likely be repeated scenarios that trigger your core pain. Do you continue to feel that no matter how hard you try, you just can't get ahead? Do you have a clear idea about where you want to go in life, only to retreat in fear when presented with an actual opportunity? Do you feel on top of the world as long as everything is going well, and in the depths of despair the first time you encounter a major setback? If you find that certain types of situations make you feel like a child again or take you to an old, dark, and painful place, you may want to review *Part 3*, and particularly *Chapter 20: Get to the Root of Your Core Pain.*

There will undoubtedly be disconnects associated with living in your finite physical body while accessing your wisdom that resides in the infinite. Are you able to love yourself fully in spite of physical imperfections or limitations? When faced with extreme or long term physical pain, are you able to deal with it gracefully and grow from the experience? How do you reconcile living life fully now with the fact that eventually you will die? If you find yourself faced with any of these types of body related issues, *Chapter 25: Align with Your Body's Wisdom* and *Chapter 26: Embrace Aging as Life's Ultimate Lesson* in this part of the book may be particularly helpful. You may also want to review *Chapter 16: Stop Berating Your Body.*

Each time a new situation arises that challenges your inner and outer alignment, it may be a sign that you need to lean more fully on your inner wisdom to get to the root of why you are not authentic. It is also an opportunity to understand at a deeper level that as a human being it is unrealistic for you to be authentic 100% of the time. Each time you move this knowledge from your head to your heart it becomes easier to forgive yourself for your lack of authenticity. It also helps you more quickly refocus your energy on doing what it takes in the here and now to be more authentically yourself.

We all instinctively know when we lack authenticity. We may be able to fool others, but not ourselves. Deep down we feel misaligned. This misalignment can cause us to respond in a variety of ways. We may mask the *Truth* from ourselves or numb to the fact to pretend the misalignment does not exist. We may become spacey and check out of our bodies to avoid dealing with the material world. We may retreat behind a thick protective barrier to hide our misalignment. We may overcompensate by projecting cockiness or striving unnecessarily as we try to make ourselves appear more authentic than we actually are. No matter how we respond to the misalignment, we may experience an acute sense of angst as we struggle to bridge the gap between our internal and external realms. Until we have reconciled the two, it will likely be difficult to dissipate our underlying agitation.

When we are authentic, the convergence point of our inner and outer realities is clear and unequivocal. It may feel like tumblers aligning in a lock. We may experience it as an energetic release, like we have let go of a rope in a tug of war with ourselves. Our body may spontaneously relax. We may feel expansive from no longer trying to suppress an aspect of ourselves from coming forth.

Being authentic is a completely natural feeling that takes much less energy than being inauthentic. As best-selling personal and professional development author Brian Tracy said, "Just as your car runs more smoothly and requires less energy to go faster and farther when the wheels are in perfect alignment, you perform better when your thoughts, feelings, emotions, goals, and values are in balance."[5]

Committing to authenticity does not mean we have to dwell on it twenty four hours a day. The act of making the commitment is often all it takes at a conscious level. Once the commitment is made an invisible force often takes over to help us keep this commitment when we forget or temporarily stray from it. When we began our journey inward by shedding what did not serve us, there may have been a deep chasm between our internal self and our external persona. Now that we have access to our inner wisdom to guide us, though, we receive clearer signals when we are not authentic. Like Olympic gymnasts on a balance beam, we are aware of the subtleties when we begin to get out of balance.

The more comfortable we are with being authentically ourselves, the easier it is to forgive ourselves for our human foibles as we deal with the world around us. By our very nature we are learning creatures, who cannot possibly know everything there is to know. Being authentic means we willingly accept the individualized curriculum that we are on earth to learn. We view mistakes as simply signs of what not to do on our continuing course of self-correction.

Forgiving ourselves takes away the sting and emotional charge from having made a mistake. It also allows us to more quickly recover and refocus our attention on following our personalized lesson plan, knowing that each incremental growth step we make gets us closer to fulfilling our heroic quest and enjoying the process more along the way.

"[When you bring] into alignment your beliefs
and the way you live then, and only then,
can you begin to find inner peace."
—**Peace Pilgrim**
American pacifist and peace activist

CHAPTER 22
LEARN TO LIVE IN THE PRESENT MOMENT

"You must live in the present, launch yourself on every wave, find your eternity in each moment."
—Henry David Thoreau
American philosopher and author of *Walden*

In *Part 2* we discussed the importance of re-experiencing the past and the future from our present consciousness. As we integrate old memories into the here and now, they are no longer frozen in time, but instead become important elements in our unfolding life story. As we worry less about our future, we tend to be less anxious and, therefore, have more energy to actually create the peaceful and fulfilling future life we want. Pulling our past and future into the present moment helps erase our feeling of fragmentation and allows us to relax more fully into authentically being ourselves.

As we also discussed in *Part 2*, the only place we can truly experience self-forgiveness is in the present moment. I have found like others who have reached this phase of their journey, that less and less of my time now is spent gnashing over my past or fretting about whether I am making the right decisions about my future. As soon as pain about my past or fear of the future arise, many times I can now bypass all the struggle and anguish and go straight to telling myself the *Truth* about the situation. When I'm not able to figure it out myself, a short conversation with a trusted friend who knows my personal challenges often helps me get to the *Truth*. Whether I figure it out for myself or receive help to see the *Truth*, once I understand why I punished myself in the past and withheld self-acceptance or why I am so fearful about the future, I can quickly bring those feelings into the present moment. As a result, I now am able to more quickly experience self-love, forgive myself, and if necessary make amends with others for my previous lack of awareness. I have more energy to devote to authentic, heart-felt relationships. I am also able to authentically be present with others and better support those who are not as far along on their own self-forgiveness journeys. (For an example of how one person's self-forgiveness journey helped her become more authentically present in her life, see *Lee's Story: Living in the Present* on pages 168-169.)

In the beginning, your ability to live in the present moment may be a skill you need to actively cultivate. It might take a lot of active intention and attention to train your mind to come back into the here and now rather than race in an unproductive direction. It might take a great deal of effort to center yourself when you feel off kilter. You might have to practice calming yourself to keep your emotions from holding you captive from some past regret or perceived future threat to being happy. With practice, though, living in the present moment will become more natural and feel like a place you call home. The following exercises are designed to help you train your mind to live in the present moment.

Exercise 1: Live on the Stage of Now. For purposes of this exercise, see yourself as an actor standing on a stage facing the audience. The stage represents the now of your life. As any good actor knows you need to be mindful of where you are standing to remain actively in the play. If you move too far back on the stage (living in your past) you can get caught in the back curtains or run into the scenery and props behind the stage. If you move too far forward (living in your future) you can fall off the stage into the orchestra pit. For one day, keep the image of this stage in your mind as you go about your daily tasks. Each time you dwell for more than a few minutes on your past, see yourself getting caught in the back curtains and pull yourself back toward the center of the stage. Each time you worry about your future, see yourself stepping too close to the orchestra pit and pull yourself back more toward the center of the stage. Practicing this type of mindfulness, trains you to be more fully in the now and activates your *Wise One* to help you remember where you are mentally when you forget.

Exercise 2: Breathe into the Present Moment. If you have ever watched a baby who is asleep, you may have noticed how naturally they breathe from deep within their bellies. As we grow up, though, we discover that when we feel emotional or stressed, if we hold our breath or breathe shallowly we can reduce the pain we experience. If you find yourself feeling very emotional about something from your past or having stress or anxiety about what the future holds, this short deep breathing exercise may help bring your energy and attention back to the present moment even when you have a limited amount of time between other activities.

1. Wherever you are, whether laying down, sitting, or even standing, take one full breath of as much air as you can take in and hold it for 5 full seconds.
2. Exhale slowly and completely over another 5 full seconds.
3. Without taking another breath, hold the void of air for a full 5 seconds.
4. Repeat steps 1-3 about 10 -20 times or as long as you have and you may notice that you feel calmer, more centered, and ready to take on the next activity from a place of more presence and awareness.

Exercise 3: Extract Yourself from the Whirlwind of Emotions. As we discussed in *Chapter 4*, emotions act as a sophisticated inner guidance system that alerts us to potential danger, assists us with decision making, helps us gauge personal happiness, and allows us to communicate with and connect deeply to one another as human beings. Sometimes, though, our emotional guidance system gets stuck in overdrive, which creates a vortex that grabs hold of our mind and whips us into an emotional frenzy of pain and fear. For purposes of this exercise, see your *Wise One* standing calmly in the center of this vortex, untouched by your emotions. Visualize your *Wise One* reaching out and offering a hand to your mental self to step into this calm center. Once your mental self sees it has a logical choice of where to be out of the chaotic energy of the emotional whirlwind, it is an easy decision to move to the center. Now see your mental self and your *Wise One* together reaching out and offering their hands to your emotional self to invite it into the center, too. With the help of both the *Wise One* and your mental self beckoning your emotional self to join them, your emotional self can feel the support it needs to calm down and hit its own reset button.

As you master the ability to be authentically present in the moment, it is worth pausing to celebrate how far you have come in successfully connecting your interior and external worlds. With this mastery may come the recognition that there was actually no separation between the two realms, despite the stubborn illusion to the contrary. As you fully take in the irony of this insight, you may have yet another opportunity to forgive yourself for your previous lack of awareness. Peeling the layers of your self-forgiveness onion will likely be a lifelong task. But, it becomes easier each time to undertake when you are whole-heartedly living in the here and now.

"Doing the best at this moment puts
you in the best place for the next moment."
—Oprah Winfrey
American talk show host,
media owner and philanthropist

Lee's[1] Story: Living in the Present

After my son and daughter were on their own, I would lay awake each night going over my failings as a parent. Night after night I recalled events and situations I should have prevented or handled differently. The mental self-flagellation went on and on.

Eventually, I accepted the fact I could do nothing to change the past. Next, I shifted my focus to the present and acted when I saw opportunities to help my kids. As they began to thrive, I knew I was on the right track.

▶

One good action I took was keeping the lines of communication open. When reminded of a past painful event, I fully accepted my failure and validated their feelings. My focus was on healing them. This was not the time for justifying what I did or did not do as a mom. It took many years, but today they are both leading healthy and successful lives.

Simultaneously, my life began to change and then totally transformed. Within a few years I remarried my wonderful husband. In 2006 we sold our house in San Diego, CA and bought our sailboat, *La Vita*, which means "The Life" in Italian. We have been in Mexican waters ever since. We plan to continue our voyage south, go through the Panama Canal, and sail across the Atlantic to the Mediterranean.

Just like in life, when I'm at the helm of *La Vita*, I must pay close attention to where we are going. I must constantly watch for possible hazards, such as commercial vessels, small fishing boats, fishnets, debris, and rocks. The only way to steer and bring *La Vita* and crew to safety is to focus on what's happening in the moment.

This lifestyle is filled with challenges and rewards. Each port-of-call requires communicating in a foreign language and learning the bus system. We also have to locate a bank, grocery store, fresh water, fuel, and marine services. Rewards include seeing sea life up close, forming friendships with the local people, and the feeling of success as we overcome life's challenges.

During our two-day passage from Mazatlan to Puerto Vallarta, my husband experienced difficulty breathing and loss of strength. In early 2011, we sailed into Marina La Cruz, near Puerto Vallarta, México. Within six weeks my husband experienced two near-death medical emergencies. Recovery required three hospitalizations. His job was to regain his health. My job was to take care of the boat, communicate with the Spanish speaking medical staff, and make sure the $50,000 (USD) medical bill was paid. Both of us succeeded with our self-assigned responsibilities because we stayed in the present and dealt with each challenge one at a time.

Through this experience we have developed a much deeper appreciation for each other. We laugh more easily and take more time for ourselves. My husband is taking guitar lessons and I'm learning Spanish.

By living in the present, my life continues to unfold and flourish beyond my wildest dreams!

❖

CHAPTER 23
STRENGTHEN YOUR PATIENCE

"Patience and perseverance have a magical effect before which difficulties disappear and obstacles vanish."
—John Quincy Adams
Great American Diplomat, Secretary of State, and Sixth President of the U.S.

Many years ago I was frustrated that it was taking so long to complete a project I had been working on for several years. I was very hard on myself about how difficult it was for me to synthesize the information. I was getting whiny with friends about it and relentless in chastising myself. I questioned whether I was being too much of a perfectionist on my work product and wondered whether I would be better served to just put out *something*, even if it wasn't as good as I would have liked.

Right after I began this line of self-questioning, a series of synchronicities (meaningful coincidences) occurred in rapid succession. One night after my meal at a Chinese restaurant, I opened a fortune cookie that said, "Patience comes to those who wait." I was in a group gathering soon after that where we were each offered an inspirational "Angel Card" from a basket of cards. The one I selected said, "The virtue of patience is patience." I was at home one evening shortly after that and decided to draw a *rune* from the bag of ancient Viking oracle stones to give me guidance about my project. The one I drew was *Harvest*. One of the statements of counsel for this rune in *The Book of Runes*[1] had particular meaning to me, "There is no way to push the river; equally you cannot hasten the harvest. Be mindful that patience is essential for the recognition of your own process, which in its season, leads to the harvest of the self." My first reaction was to toss the rune across the room in rejection. Instead I decided to draw from the bag again to get a different message. I put *Harvest* back in the bag, mixed up the 25 runes, and drew the same rune! Now I was more than a little agitated and said angrily to myself, "I'm tired of being patient!"My internal *Wise One* laughed at this immature part of me, knowing that I had received exactly the message I needed.

Patience is still one of my biggest personal challenges. Conceptualizing is so much easier than execution, whether it is related to a project, doing inner work, or responding differently to others who trigger me. There is nothing like writing books, especially ones about the introspective journey of coming to know ourselves, that has given me lots of opportunities to practice patience!

I now realize that there is little else that can put a damper on my enjoyment of being in the moment more than being impatient with myself. It shows me the remaining pockets of inner work I need to do on self-trust. Now when I feel impatient, I question why I doubt that my inner wisdom is leading me in the right direction. I also look at this inner challenge as yet another opportunity to forgive myself for being a human who is still figuring out what life is all about. (For an example of how another person's years of inner work, patience with herself, and self-forgiveness are now bearing fruit see *Rita's Story: Checking the Map* on page 177.)

Your challenges related to patience may be different than what I've experienced, but the need for patience seems to be universal. Philosophical perspectives and spiritual traditions throughout history have included patience as a major tenet. As human beings when we are given a choice, we have a tendency to choose short term rewards over those that are long term, even when there are greater benefits associated with what awaits us in the long run. Patience helps us consciously overcome this tendency. In the face of delay, difficulty, stress, strain, pain, annoyance, and anger, patience helps us persevere, so we can reap the rewards that better serves us.

From a *HeroicJourney* perspective, patience is a reflection of our personal maturity. Maturity comes from patiently following our inner guidance that leads us toward the long term rewards, even while our ego and the unconscious parts of us urge us to take a shortcut to instant gratification. Patience helps us endure the challenges put before us, knowing that each experience helps us grow in wisdom, so we can better fulfill what we came to earth to do.

As we become more mature, wise, and patient human beings it is easier to forgive ourselves for our previous impatient reactions to life. We know that those reactions resulted from being less conscious and lacking the insight and skills that we now have incorporated into our way of being. Since we are more self-forgiving about our own impatience, we tend to be more patient with others. We may even radiate a calm presence that is contagious to be around.

It is worth remembering that the journey to patience is about becoming *authentically* patient, not pretending to be patient when you are not. Being inauthentic only drives your impatience into the shadows, which as we now know can leak out in subversive and possibly destructive ways. The key to becoming more patient is to get to the root of your impatience, accept it, and transform it. As you do, your patience self grows along side of you and becomes one of your most trusted heroic allies.

As you face daily life you are sure to tap into pockets of impatience. Each time this happens, if you approach it as an opportunity to further develop your heroic maturity, you affirm your commitment to the long term reward and you increase the odds that you will fulfill your personal journey. When you find yourself feeling impatient, here are some reminders to help you become more patient and self-forgiving in the process:

- **Approach impatience with curiosity**. Impatience, like other shadow traits, can provide important clues for what is going on inside of you at an unconscious level. When you approach it with curiosity, you invite the unconscious parts of yourself to be truthful about what is really going on. Next time you feel impatient, it may be helpful to assess what you are experiencing in that moment with an inquisitive attitude and a genuine, heartfelt interest in exploring this facet of your internal terrain. Impatience may naturally melt away as you accept it and then deal with the underlying reason you originally created the external overlay of impatience.
- **Come to terms with "magical thinking."** Most of us can't just pick up a musical instrument and instantly know how to play it without instruction and years of practice. As we grow up we learn that even though we want instant gratification, we don't always get it. Although we know this consciously, the childlike part of us that still believes in magical thinking, persists in believing it "should be" otherwise. The more prominent this childlike aspect is in our persona, the more

impatient we may be with ourselves and others. If you find yourself frustrated at not being able to instantly master something, ask yourself if you are feeling that you "should" know how to do it. If so, it may be a sign that you are operating from magical thinking. Just recognizing this can help you come to terms with this childlike part of yourself, forgive it for having such an unreasonable expectation, and show it how to develop the patience skills necessary for long term mastery.

- **Experiencing small pains and irritations helps develop patience to endure greater adversity**. We all want to be comfortable in life. Anyone who has trained for a marathon, though, knows the importance of pushing through pain to build endurance in advance of actually running the race. Law enforcement officers, firefighters, and medical personnel, who train for all kinds of catastrophic situations, purposefully put themselves into stressful situations, so they can develop the skills and patience to handle an actual emergency. As we each endure the hard knocks of life, we may rebel when we experience hardships and tell ourselves that they are intolerable. If you find yourself saying that a situation is intolerable, ask yourself, "Is this truly intolerable or just uncomfortable?" Asking this question gives you more discernment about what are truly intolerable situations, so you can take action to remove yourself from them. For most other situations that are merely uncomfortable, you can decide if the action called for is to lean into the discomfort, so you can learn and grow from it. Building tolerance for discomfort, strengthens your patience and gives you the endurance necessary to effectively deal with truly adverse situations.
- **Advancement happens one step at a time**. Many people create long "to do" lists with the unrealistic expectation that they have to do everything on their list in the same day. When they fall short of finishing everything, they berate themselves for their failure. It is important to learn how to pace yourself and chunk off time in realistic increments. By putting less pressure on yourself and slowing down, you may actually

achieve more with better results. Thinking through details one step at a time helps reduces the time you spend doing busy work and assures that if you complete all of the tasks on your list they will actually take you in the direction you want to go. Next time you find yourself being impatient or too hard on yourself for not getting everything done on your "to do" list, you also may want to add *having fun* to your list, so you can get more enjoyment out of the process along the way.

- **Disentangle achievement from happiness**. In Western society we place an inordinate emphasis on achievement. For many people their identity and happiness are totally wrapped up with what they have accomplished. Until they have achieved their goals they withhold happiness, which demonstrates only conditional self-acceptance. As a result, they may create perpetual disappointment and impatience with themselves. One of the greatest areas of personal growth related to patience comes from truly understanding that your identity and your happiness are not integrally tied to your achievements. If they were everyone who has achieved external success in their lives would be the happiest people on earth. No matter what your external circumstances or where you are in your process of achievement, there is nothing but yourself preventing you from unconditionally loving yourself and being happy right now! If you are feeling unhappy, it may be a good reminder that you are a "human being" and not a "human doing." You also may want to examine why your happiness is conditional on your circumstances. What part of you is withholding self-love and happiness? What messages did you hear as a child about happiness? Is your happiness living in the past or future instead of the present moment? What part of yourself have you not yet fully accepted? As you delve into these questions, you may find that the part of you that had a stranglehold on your happiness lets go. As a result you may feel happier, more relaxed, more loving toward yourself and more patient with exactly where you are in your unfolding journey.

- **Upgrade your patience storyline**. There are some people who love to regale anyone who will listen with their stories of impatience. Some repeatedly express irritation with their partner or kids. Others roll their eyes as they describe their lack of tolerance for yet another "stupid" person at work. Others repeatedly pick on themselves for the latest personal shortcoming they just cannot bear that they have. If you find your conversations repeatedly focused on impatience, either with yourself or others, you may be wearing your impatience like a badge of honor, which further ingrains it in your psyche. If you want to stop this bad habit of thought and change your storyline, you may find it helpful to retell your story of impatience in the past tense and affirm a new story using the following structure:

> "I used to be impatient about _______,
> however, I now realize that the underlying cause of my impatience was __________. This former impatient part of me is now one of my strongest allies and has transformed me in the following way in my daily life __________."

As people committed to becoming more authentic, we can use impatience as a tool to help us better align our inner and outer realities. Just realizing that this is an option can change the lens through which we view impatience. Seeing it in this new way can reduce our frustration with ourselves and create a more loving and forgiving environment, which is one of the prime long term benefits we seek on our heroic path.

"Be patient with yourself. Self-growth is tender;
it's holy ground. There is no greater investment."
—Stephen Covey
Author of the best-selling book,
The Seven Habits of Highly Effective People

Rita's[2] Story: Checking the Map

After years of therapy, retreats, meditation, self-help books and workshops, as well as hours of talking with my best friend, I am now at a place where I feel those efforts have borne fruit. In midlife, I feel more secure about who I am. I realize that there are some parts of my personality that will always have a bit of a limp, and have forgiven myself for that. For example, I am not an optimistic person. After years of beating myself up because I don't have a "can do" attitude, I realize that my natural concern about the things that can possibly go wrong make me a great partner for people who forge ahead with less concern for consequences. They provide the energy to move forward, but I provide the skilled navigation so we don't run into the rocks.

Now when I bump into one of my unhealed places I am more apt to stop and get curious about why I am reacting that way rather than simply acting out. It is somewhat easier to forgive myself for my negative reactions . Not always. Sometimes my husband has to remind me when I'm being harsh or stubborn. After a long series of distancing and hypercritical boyfriends, the man who became my second husband is a great partner. He is well aware of my warts, but instead of berating me, he gently teases me, we both laugh, I apologize, and we move on.

Now when I find myself in unfamiliar emotional territory (or unpleasantly familiar emotional territory), I take some time to do what I call "checking the map." I write in my journal, talk with a close friend or my husband, or schedule a session with my therapist, as a way to remind myself of where I am in my journey. Sometimes when my work or my life gets really hectic, and I start to lose my sense of self, I try to take a couple of hours for a "wander" just to walk aimlessly and clear my head so I can focus on what I'm feeling and thinking. Instead of weeks in a dark funk, my emotional lows can be resolved fairly quickly, because now I have tools to help me re-center myself, including forgiving myself and others for being human.

This is the reward of doing inner work: a deep sense of self, comfort in who I am and deep gratitude for the people and the process that brought me here.

❖

CHAPTER 24
GIVE YOUR AUTHENTIC GIFTS TO THE WORLD

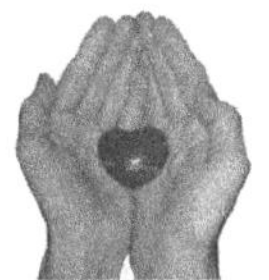

"Each person comes into this world with a specific destiny—he[/she] has something to fulfill, some message has to be delivered, some work has to be completed. You are not here accidentally—you are here meaningfully. The whole intends to do something through you."

—Osho

Indian mystic, spiritual teacher and professor of philosophy

Within each of us there is a heroic mandate to give our authentic gifts to the world. We all want to live our lives with a sense of meaning, passion, and purpose. From a heroic perspective this means that in some unique way our life exists not only for ourselves, but to contribute to the world in a significant way.

Some people know from the time they are tiny tots what their gifts are and what they want to do with those gifts when they grow up. From an early age they are driven to accomplish their internal calling. For most of the rest of us, though, the quest to find our unique place in the world takes time, dedication, and most of all *patience* to discover. It is more of an uncovering process as we try on new experiences to see which ones bring fulfillment to our lives and which ones are not a good fit. We know when we have hit the mark because our energy is boundless, even when we are dealing with specific tasks we may dislike doing.

Since this uncovering process can take an enormous amount of effort and can be very challenging, many people do not dedicate themselves to this level of self-discovery. Instead they settle for what they already know, what others expect of them, or what is good enough to get by. The problem with doing this is that their authentic self may be screaming to be let out of its self-imposed prison of mediocrity. Without breaking out of the prison, they do not feel truly authentic and they will have an internal sense that their journey of heroism is incomplete. As mythologist Joseph Campbell said, "We must be willing to get rid of the life we've planned, so as to have the life that is waiting for us."[1]

This may be a time when self-forgiveness is an extremely helpful tool for breaking through the remaining blocks that stand between us and the life that is waiting for us. Maybe we need to forgive ourselves for being scared of being ourselves for fear of rejection by our family or community. Maybe we need to forgive ourselves for taking so long to figure out our internal calling. Maybe we need to forgive ourselves for being fuzzy on the specifics of how to fulfill our personal mission.

This may also be a time when shadow work can facilitate the self-forgiveness process and help us recover our personal authority. As Jungian therapist and author, James Hollis points out:

> The recovery of [personal] authority is critical to the examined life, critical to the recovery of one's proper journey, and is only possible by the reclamation of whatever has been consigned to our Shadow[2]...Shadow work thus requires discerning what wishes to be expressed through us and mobilizing the energy, courage, and commitment to sustain it, even amid conditions unfavorable to its expression[3]...Not answering the call is not only a personal Shadow issue, but an abrogation of our obligation to others.[4]

In the earlier phases of our *Heroic Journey*, we may be able to follow the example of others who have undertaken their own journey of authenticity. But, at some point in our quest, we will be called to blaze our own trail. Following our unique path requires the courage to rely on our own inner *Truth* and listen to our personal wisdom, even when it differs from those we have previously turned to for wise counsel.

The more comfortable we are in our own skin, the more willing we are to risk being hurt, make mistakes, or look foolish to get to a new level of self-understanding and fulfillment. Even though it may be a scary proposition to continue forward, we know in our heart that the rewards outweigh the risks. Like salmon spawning upstream, we are determined to achieve whatever we are called to undertake, even when it is not something we consciously chose to do. (See related article *Stumbling Into Your Life Purpose* pages 184-185.)

Although we each have to do our inner work to figure out our personal heroic calling, here are some exercises that may help bring your calling to light.

Exercise 1: Unleash the Fire Within. We each have a passionate fire within that is our inner calling just waiting to be unleashed. Many of us have learned from an early age, though, that we need to squelch that fire. When you were growing up maybe your passion felt too overwhelming to others and they told you either verbally or non-verbally, "Who do you think you are to want this?" or "You are acting too big for your britches." Maybe you got the fear-based message that you had to play small to keep from being hurt. Or maybe when you felt most comfortable with yourself, you were considered weird among your peers. Whatever the reason that you suppressed your fire within, you can unleash it now and rekindle your passion so you can heed your inner calling from this point forward.

1. When you were a child and you felt truly passionate about something, think about the messages that you received either overtly or subtly. Was it OK to express that passion? If not, do you remember what age you were when you hid it?
2. If you received messages that squelched your passion, whose voice was it that you internalized? (Hint: It is often an external authority figure that you relied on as a child for validation.) If someone specifically comes to mind, see yourself handing the "passion squelching message" back to that person, so you no longer have to carry it within you from this day forward.
3. Now, see glowing embers at your core that represent your passion. Visualize blowing on the embers until they catch fire and burn brightly with white hot heat. See the light from the fire permeate every cell of your being. Visualize

the light spreading outward until your body can no longer contain it and it radiates into the world around you.

4. Ask your *Wise One*, as the observer of this intense passion, to introduce you to your *Personal Authority*, the member of your *Internal Dream Team* who is the keeper of your passion.
5. Greet your *Personal Authority* with an open heart and ask what form your passion is to take and how you can help bring it forth in the world. If you don't get an immediate answer, just sit patiently with the questions. In this receptive and supportive mode you invite your *Personal Authority* to formulate the individualized message that you need to receive right now to unleash your passionate inner calling.

Exercise 2: Take Baby Steps. Years ago when it first became clear to me that one of my heroic callings was to "help others discover how they can gain wisdom and insight from every situation and person encountered," the task felt overwhelming to me. I didn't know where to start. Over the next few weeks, though, as I sat with this message, I felt guided to offer a free class at my local library entitled, "Turn Your Gullibility into Wisdom." The class was well attended and several people said afterward that it was helpful to them. This gave me the confidence to offer other classes and workshops. Taking the first baby step of picking up the phone and calling my local library to schedule a class, was what launched me on a new phase of my personal *Heroic Journey*.

If you find yourself feeling overwhelmed by your heroic calling or the tasks ahead feel daunting, commit to taking just one baby step toward your goal. Then take another step and another. Each step you take, even if small, affirms your commitment to following your calling and builds the confidence and skills you need to meet future challenges and fulfill your vision.

Exercise 3: Clear the Fog. Sometimes you may just have an inkling of your heroic calling, but the form it will take seems shrouded in fog. If you have experienced this foggy feeling, the following visualization may be helpful:

1. See yourself standing facing the fog bank that separates you from clarity about your inner calling.
2. Take a step forward into the fog and let it fully envelope you. As you do, breathe deeply and exhale any stress, strain, or fear associated with being in the fog.
3. As you stand in the fog breathing in and out, see the mist of the fog bank dissipate until you are standing in a clearing.
4. Describe the clearing. You may want to close your eyes and sense it with your inner vision. Pay attention to subtleties in this new environment. What feels particularly good and natural about being here? What is surprising to you about this place? Take in those feelings and anchor them deeply within your conscious awareness. Pay attention to any symbols or words that come to mind that may help you better anchor the experience.
5. When you are ready to return to the here and now, bring the vision of the clearing back into your present reality. Make note of the experience, so next time you feel foggy you can more easily return to this place of clarity.

American poet, essayist, and playwright Edward Estlin Cummings (popularly known as e. e. cummings) once said, "It takes courage to grow up and turn out to be who you really are."[5] Whatever the challenges of this phase, self-forgiveness, shadow work, visioning, and dedication to uncovering your passion can help you remove the remaining resistances that keep you from completing what you came here to do and leaving your personal legacy for future generations.

"Most people never run far enough on their first wind to find out they've got a second one. Give your dreams all you've got and you'll be amazed at the energy that comes out of you."
—William James
Pioneering American
psychologist and philosopher

Stumbling into Your Life Purpose

Before his death in 2011, Steve Jobs was widely recognized as a pioneer in the personal computing revolution. He was the co-founder and chief executive officer of both Apple Computer and Pixar Animation Studios. Steve took an unconventional route to get there. He never graduated from college. He dropped out of Reed College after the first six months. As he said in his commencement address at Stanford in 2005, "I had no idea what I wanted to do with my life and no idea how college was going to help me figure it out."[6] Instead he began to "drop in" to just the classes that interested him. This decision wasn't easy and he struggled financially during this time of his life. However, what he stumbled into by following his curiosity and intuition turned out to be priceless later on.[7] One of the classes he took was in calligraphy. At the time he took it, he didn't think there were any practical applications for what he was learning.

►

After his college experience, Steve worked as a technician at Atari, Inc. and he went to India in search of enlightenment before starting Apple Computers in his parent's garage with Steve Wozniak and Ronald Wayne. During the design of the Macintosh computer, information Steve Jobs learned about typography in his calligraphy class ten years earlier came flooding back to him. He was able to incorporate his knowledge into the design of the Macintosh, which became the first computer to have beautiful typography with multiple typefaces and proportionally spaced fonts. Soon after the Macintosh was released for sale, Windows copied the Macintosh typography. If Steve hadn't taken that calligraphy class, personal computers might not have the wonderful typography that they do now. Steve said, "You can't connect the dots looking forward; you can only connect them looking backwards. So you have to trust that the dots will somehow connect in your future. You have to trust in something - your gut, destiny, life, karma, whatever. This approach has never let me down, and it has made all the difference in my life."[8]

Like Steve Jobs, many of us may take unconventional routes with our career or stumble into our life purpose through serendipity. At the time we are making decisions about what to do next we may not fully understand consciously why we made certain decisions, what we unconsciously agreed to do, or where those choices will lead us. When we are faced with decision points, though, our heroic task is to grab hold of our passion and follow wherever it leads. Once we do, a magical process unfolds that helps us overcome personal doubts and external obstacles to achieve our goals. It may only be when we look back at an incident that we understand how significant it was as a catalyst for creating such a meaningful, purpose filled life. (For more information about how to successfully move through your personalized journey, especially as it relates to work, see *Work as a Heroic Journey*.)[9]

Even if you now see that you missed taking action when one of these serendipitous moments occurred in the past, do not despair. It is never too late to rededicate yourself to your true passion. Pick yourself up, forgive yourself, and open your eyes. Once you do, you will see the opportunities that exist in your midst right now as possible first steps on your path toward personal fulfillment.

CHAPTER 25
ALIGN WITH YOUR BODY'S WISDOM

"It is difficult to dislike your body
or a specific part of your body and still like yourself."
—Linda Tschirhart Sandford and Mary Ellen Donovan
Authors of *Women and Self-Esteem*

In *Chapter 16* we discussed the importance of no longer berating our body to shedding what no longer serves us. By peeling away denial, avoidance, abuse, addiction, self-loathing, and numbing out, we take away major barriers that keep us from being at peace with our body. This is an important first step toward self-forgiveness as it relates to our body.

In addition to housing the physical components that allow us to exist, our body stores the memories of our thoughts, emotions and psyche. The body continually sends overt and subtle signals about what is going on within us. To be more fully comfortable in our own skin and authentically ourselves, the task of this third phase of our *Heroic Journey* is to really listen to our body's natural intelligence and heed its wisdom. When we do, we have access to a deeper level of self-forgiveness than is otherwise possible. We also see more clearly how our bodily imperfections and physical challenges help us evolve as human beings and their contributions to our unique life story. (To learn more about the language of your body, see *Appendix F: Body Wisdom Resources.*)

When we are oblivious to our body wisdom or attempt to deny it, our body has a way of attempting to get our attention. Just as the shadow aspects of us may make themselves known in covert or destructive ways, our body uses whatever means available to communicate with us. Once we stop and really listen to our body, though, not only do we learn a tremendous amount about ourselves. We also are more likely to forgive ourselves for resisting this self-knowledge earlier in our personal development.

Many people see their body, mind, emotions, and psyches as distinctly separate aspects of themselves. All of these aspects, however, are intimately intertwined. Our bodies do not lie. They hold the stories of our personal emotional history. What we attempt to mentally conceal from ourselves and hide deep within our psyche often comes out in our body.

As children we learn early how to energetically regulate our emotions. As we discussed in *Chapter 22*, we discover that if we hold our breath or breathe shallowly we can reduce the pain we experience. If we "keep our chin up" it can suppress crying and prevents us from expressing sadness. When we are stressed, we instinctively tense our shoulders to carry the psychological burdens that weigh us down.

Emotions are stored in our body until we release them. If we hold in emotions for long periods of time, the unreleased emotions may sink into our unconscious and become chronically locked into our bodies. It then may become difficult to even feel pain or sadness, much less express these feelings. We may not realize there is an underlying emotional reason we have become perpetually tensed, have difficulty breathing deeply, have migraine headaches, experience intense jaw pain or TMJ (temporomandibular joint) disorder, or have a host of other physical symptoms.

Internationally acclaimed psychotherapist Alexander Lowen understood this mind/body connection well when he developed *Bioenergetic Analysis*.[1] He taught therapists and individuals how the body's expressions, including our postures, patterns of muscular holding, and energy blocks, help tell our personal emotional history. By reading the language of the body, he helped bridge the mind/body split and clarify what was going on deep within our psyches.[2]

Louise Hay, American new thought leader and author of the 1984 book, *You Can Heal Your Life,*[3] helped further our understanding of the mind/body connection. She popularized the idea that by learning to tap into our body's innate intelligence, we have a mechanism to get to the unconscious realm where the emotions are rooted. In her book, *Heal Your Body A-Z: The Mental Causes for Physical Illness and the Way to Overcome Them*, she provides clues for possible causes of physical symptoms and the affirmations that may help tap into our unconscious realm and change our thought pattern. For example, when we have allergies it might be an indication that we would benefit by examining who we are allergic to and whether we are denying our own power.[4] Stiffness in our body may be a sign we have rigid or stiff thinking.[5] When we have laryngitis it may be because we are so mad we can't speak, we have a fear of speaking up, or we resent authority.[6] Stuttering may result from insecurity, lack of self-expression, or not being allowed to cry.[7] The causes Louise Hay lists may or may not apply to our specific physical symptoms. However, we can use these clues as a starting point to search for the specific message our unconscious is attempting to communicate through our body. Once we know the *Truth* of our personalized message, the emotional charge and the particular symptom associated with the emotion may immediately disappear, even when a specific symptom has been a pattern in our body for years.

I personally know the power of listening to the wisdom of my body. I have used it often through the years to do what I call "spelunking" or "exploring the cave of my unconscious." In one instance many years ago, I realized I had experienced a stuffy nose since I was a child. I decided to look at what Louise Hay's *Heal Your Body* book said about stuffy nose. It said, "Not recognizing the self-worth."[8] The statement jumped out at me. I felt the *Truth* of it immediately. The associated affirmation to create the new thought pattern said, "I love and appreciate myself."[9] As I sat in meditation thinking about the statement and the affirmation, the stuffiness in my nose instantly disappeared. For the first time in my life that I was aware of, I was able to breathe through both nostrils at the same time! At first the sensation of having my nasal passages filled with this much air felt uncomfortable. As I continued to breathe and take in this new sensation, I had a flash of recognition. Until that moment I had denied myself the full breath of life, since a shadow part of me didn't believe I deserved to be alive! I immediately showered love over this part of me that felt so undeserving. I also forgave it for thinking I didn't deserve to be here. Since identifying the root cause of my stuffy nose, I've had only occasional stuffiness since them. My breathing has been deeper and more relaxed. Also, I am more appreciative of being alive, knowing that I really do deserve to be here.

Learning the language of your body can help you get in touch with deeply buried sub-plots of your emotional story that have been living out below your conscious awareness. With this new awareness you have a better chance of forgiving yourself for your previous lack of awareness. You also have the opportunity to shift your story, so you can move forward in more positive, productive, and fulfilling ways.

Abigianna's[10] Story: Mirror, Mirror on the Wall

I sat across from Dean Wilson—feeling alone and paralyzed in the seat as I patiently watched him read through my resume and application. Fragments of fear and doubt floated into my mind like pieces of brittle, jagged wood drifting down a calm stream. So, I distracted myself by focusing on the man in front of me. I noticed his wrinkled khaki trousers; ancient argyle sweater; classic professorial tweed jacket; and faded, worn out sneakers—topped off with this straggly, unpretentious Einstein-esque hairstyle. Yet, despite his frumpy appearance, I heard compassion, kindness, and respect in his voice.

"Thank you for your interest in our counseling vacancy." Then, he hesitated before completing his thought, "Although you have great credentials, honestly, I can't hire you at this time."

Unable to speak, I mustered an unenthusiastic but appreciative nod as I stood up, shook his hand, and headed for the door. Exasperated, I gained my composure, turned around, faced him, and said "Dean Wilson, I've been job hunting for over nine months—always with the same results. Would you mind sharing your reason for not hiring me?"

Sure," he graciously replied, "Your credentials are great but your level of obesity indicates that you have emotional issues that will diminish your effectiveness as a counselor."

Although his words felt like glass splinters in my heart, his empathetic candor left no lingering doubt—my obesity overshadowed my employability. When I returned home, I located the dusty scale that I had conveniently pushed into the back corner of my closet; I stepped on it thinking that I probably weighed about 200 pounds. As the dial on the scale teetered to its final resting number, the figure jumped up and slapped me in the face—298 pounds—two pounds short of 300!

▶

Denial crept into my mind as I thought, "This scale is old. It must be wrong!"

Luckily, I fought the urge to buy a replacement scale and decided instead to take an honest look at myself in the mirror. I gasped for breath as I suddenly realized I had been looking at myself through jaded eyes—never actually acknowledging the obese woman who now stared back at me.

I wondered, "Why had I forsaken her, ignored her emotional needs, and disavowed her very existence?" Now, she stood before me naked, damaged, and vulnerable like Venus de Milo and in dire need of serious repair.

For several days my thoughts meandered like a restless wind across the open plain; they tumbled blindly—eventually making their way into shocking, life-changing awareness: I was addicted to food! Sadly, I had given control of my life over to food making it my emotional escape. As I swallowed a particular food, I literally swallowed and ignored healthy human emotions, stress, and even depression. The more I ate, the more I buried those emotions creating my dependence on and obsession with food.

Despite my new-found awareness I felt confused, ashamed, and angry—mostly angry. Even though my training taught me that anger erroneously seeks to blame, I still wanted to blame someone—anyone—for my current dilemma. I quickly decided to blame my mother, for she too was obese and, therefore, solely responsible for teaching me poor eating habits and modeling inappropriate coping strategies that resulted in my emotional dependence on food.

Initially, blaming her felt good—a way of venting my anger, avoiding the *Truth*, and side-stepping my own personal responsibility. Sometimes I shudder when I think of just how easily I could've continued victimizing myself in the never-ending blame-shifting game. However, my mother lived 2,000 miles from me.

So at some point I asked myself, "What can she do in the present to make my situation 'right'?" Thankfully, I soon realized that blame-shifting accomplished nothing, but render me powerless to create the change I so passionately wanted.

▶

So, I quickly turned my anger and shame onto myself—igniting the self-loathing, blame flame. The heat of the fire burned fiercely, consumed me leaving me ineffective until I realized that blaming myself without forgiving myself was just as futile and destructive as blaming my mother. In the beginning I didn't realize just how powerful and crucial self-forgiveness was to winning my losing battle. Somehow, though, I instinctively knew that self-forgiveness meant loving me enough to break my dependence on food.

Breaking this dependence also required diligence, for the process was slow, arduous, and painful both physically and emotionally. I counted calories and walked—initially only for 15 minutes at a time, for my arms and legs rubbed together, chaffed, bled, and then scabbed. In 24 months, I also learned to distinguish the difference between true physical hunger and emotional hunger as I grasped an important lesson: If I wasn't physically hungry, eating wasn't a solution. The solution was, however, embracing my fears and becoming vulnerable long enough to examine my emotional triggers—those catalysts that could easily put me back on the compulsive-addictive cycle of dependence.

During my two-year journey, I lost 165 pounds. I gained a deeper, healthier appreciation of the value of forgiveness. Forgiveness minimized my fears—relinquishing their control over me. In that sense, forgiveness eventually led to understanding, understanding led to freedom, freedom led to remedy, and remedy led to hope.

Hope keeps me strong as I look in the mirror and admit to myself, "I'm Abigianna and I'm a food addict." Saying this statement is a gentle reminder of who I am, where I've been, and what I could easily revert back to if I didn't remain mindful of the many lessons I learned during my *Heroic Journey*.

CHAPTER 26

EMBRACE AGING AS LIFE'S ULTIMATE LESSON

"Life can be compared to a piece of embroidered material of which, everyone in the first half of his[/her] time, comes to see the top side, but in the second half, the reverse side. The latter is not so beautiful, but it is more instructive because it enables one to see how the threads are connected together."

—Arthur Schopenhauer
Influential German philosopher
known for his philosophical clarity

When I was a young child I remember riding my bike in the neighborhood with a friend when she said she had to go home because her family was having a birthday party for her mother, who was turning forty years old. I stopped in my tracks and said, "Forty years old?!? Your mother is the oldest mother I know!" That was the first time I had thought about how old a person had to be to be considered "old." Now in midlife I consider "old age" to be over 90 years old. I sometimes wonder what I'll consider old when I am 90. Age is definitely relative!

Regardless of what age we think of as old, each stage of the aging process takes us a step closer to learning our ultimate lesson, which is to face the existential terror that comes from having to let go of this physical realm and embrace the fact that we will eventually have to shed our earthly body. As much as we would love to believe that we can personally escape this fate, at some point we will each be faced with the *Truth* that we are no different from anyone else and we are going to die to this human form.

In many ways, practicing other facets of the shedding process, claiming our wisdom, and honing our authenticity discussed in the previous chapters, prepares us for this ultimate lesson. *As we forgive ourselves for other aspects of our humanity, we take ourselves closer to forgiving ourselves for our mortality.* If we have done our job well along the way, by the time we let go of this existence, it will be like stepping out of a garment that no longer fits and into a realm that better suits our expanded consciousness.

In our society, more so than some other cultures, we are caught up in the material side of existence. Rather than see ourselves as part of the continuity of life, we see this as all there is to life. It is no wonder there is so much focus on maintaining our youth as long as possible.

This is not to say that there is anything wrong with wanting to maintain our vibrant physical health and vigor. Many centenarians, those who have reached one hundred years of age, can show us the way to living a long, vibrant and happy life. Dr. Leonard W. Poon, Ph.D., director of the Gerontology Center and professor of psychology at the University of Georgia, is at the forefront of current scientific research regarding centenarians. He says that the traits that centenarians have in common, which seem to contribute to their longevity, are optimism, engagement or commitment to something they are interested in, activity or mobility, and the ability to adapt to loss."[1] (**Table 26.1** contains additional traits that many centenarians have in common.)

Resilience		
Fortitude	Determination	Steadfastness
Courage	Optimism	Openness
Buoyancy	Sense of Humor	Appreciation
Spunk		
Persistence	Enthusiasm	Ingenuity
Dedication	Zest for Life	Adventurousness
Cleverness	Good sense	Eagerness
Connection to Others		
Loving	Loyal/Committed	Good Natured
Sociable	Playful	Giving
Romantic	Kind	Strong Social Conscience
Inner Strength		
Dignity	Peaceful	Clear Sense of Self
Keen Perception	Intuitive	Lightness of Being
Belief or Faith in Something Greater than Self	Awareness	Serenity

Table 26.1. Traits that can help us adopt the "Centenarian Spirit."[2]

These are traits that we can all adopt to help us age well, no matter what our current age. You will probably recognize from reading previous chapters that many of these traits are intimately intertwined with our ability to forgive ourselves and others. There is an ease in living and lightness of being when we exhibit these traits, which is not possible before we jettisoned internal baggage that weighed us down. We are better able to flow through life without the resistance that causes struggle and strife. We are more buoyant and able to adopt the "centenarian spirit" when we are no longer looking backward with regret or fear. If we have practiced the "centenarian spirit" throughout our life, by the time we reach the pinnacle of our existence, these traits will be second nature and add richness and meaning to our remaining years.

One of the paradoxes of aging is that we are charged with doing all we can to maintain the vibrancy of our physical body, mental faculties, and emotional psyche, while simultaneously coming to terms with the inevitability of our death. Knowing that we are not our body goes a long way toward helping us deal with this ultimate paradox. Shortly before mythologist Joseph Campbell's death when he was in his eighties, journalist Bill Moyers taped a series of conversations with Campbell about what mythology had taught him about life. These conversations were later turned into a very popular book and video series, *The Power of Myth.*[3] In the course of the conversation Campbell said about aging:

> One of the psychological problems in growing old is the fear of death. People resist the door of death. But, this body is a vehicle of consciousness, and if you can identify with the consciousness, you can watch this body go like an old car. There goes the fender, there goes the tire, one thing after another—but, it's predictable. And then, gradually, the whole thing drops off, and consciousness rejoins consciousness.[4]

This is a very different perception of aging than what most of us have been taught. *Rather than approach death with fear and resist, we can dance with it as both active witness and engaged participant.* This shift in perspective can help us release the dread associated with death. It can help us more effectively manage pain, lessen the misery associated with loss, and reduce anxiety about the future.

Dancing with death can accelerate the forgiveness and self-forgiveness process. It can make us less resistant to and fearful of shedding the remaining aspects of our life that no longer serves us. Earlier in life when we were more attached to the physical world and our old ways of being, the shedding process may have been slow, tedious, and stressful. When faced with our mortality, however, our preoccupation with petty annoyances and earthly concerns often naturally falls away. We may find ourselves reflecting on what is most important to us, making heart connections that eluded us earlier, and as Lee Atwater did before his death, make amends for our past.

(See pages 111-112.) Each piece of our past that we clear unburdens us and frees our spirit to step into a more peaceful existence for the remainder of our life.

Spiritual teacher Ram Dass learned first-hand the power of this ultimate lesson in letting go. In the process of writing his book about aging, *Still Here*,[5] he was having trouble finding an ending to the book, when he had a massive stroke that paralyzed one side of his body and left him in a wheelchair. It also affected his ability to speak. This formerly vibrant and active sixty nine year old, who lectured all over the world, suddenly found himself helpless and in need of people to care for him. In typical Ram Dass fashion, he took this turn of events as a challenge to go deeper into himself and learn the lessons of his stroke. He said:

> Recently, a friend said to me, "You're more human since the stroke than you were before." This touched me profoundly. What a gift the stroke has given me, to finally learn that I don't have to renounce my humanity in order to be spiritual—that I can be both witness and participant, both eternal spirit and aging body…The stroke has given me a new perspective to share about aging, a perspective that says, "Don't be a wise elder, be an incarnation of wisdom." That changes the whole nature of the game. That's not just a new role, it's a new state of being. It's the real thing. At nearly seventy, surrounded by people who care for and love me, I'm still learning to be here now.[6]

Ram Dass has found, as so many others have through their own aging process, that aging is not only a time to continue learning, but it is also a time to reflect and embody the wisdom that we have gained from our many experiences throughout life. Wisdom, however, has not been as valued in our culture as it is in other cultures. In India, China, indigenous cultures, and many other cultures throughout the world, people believe that as they grow older, they also grow in wisdom. Wisdom is revered. It is considered a cultural asset that adds to the richness of society and provides the continuity between generations.

In our scientific and technologically-based society we place more value on amassing information than we do on gaining wisdom. This might be one reason why older people, whose information becomes obsolete over time, are often considered obsolete themselves. With the aging of the baby boomers, though, there is hope that "the sheer weight of numbers to become a major force for change"[7] will help our society recognize the value that wisdom can bring to our cultural fabric.

While learning information requires us to "busily fill up" our minds with data, facts, figures and details, wisdom requires us to "empty" and "quiet" our minds. In the space created, a profound process occurs that allows us to discern what is valuable in life, synthesize our experiences into meaningful new wholes, and transform our perspective into new understandings of reality.

It is our wisdom, not our mental "information processing" faculties, that guides us on our *Heroic Journey* of self-forgiveness. We don't need to feel shame about the fact that "thinking about" self-forgiveness never substitutes for "experiencing" self-forgiveness. Experiencing self-forgiveness occurs in our heart and soul, where our wisdom flourishes.

While other aspects of our life diminish with age, as Ram Dass points out, *"[W]isdom is one of the few things in human life that does not diminish.* While everything else falls away, wisdom alone increases until death if we live examined lives, opening ourselves out to life's many lessons, rather than shrinking [away.]"[8] Seeing ourselves as "sage-ing"[9] rather than just aging, helps us heroically reframe the challenges of aging and ferret out the residual pockets of fear and remorse that remain to be cleared. (See **Table 26.2** for examples.)

Aging Challenge	Heroic Reframing
Grieving lost youth	Focus on the valuable part you play right now in the continuity of life and lovingly pass your baton of wisdom to the next generation.
Missing your former role in society (e.g. mother, business person, civic leader, etc.)	Shift identification with your ego's "power mask" and instead identify with your real power that lies at the heart of your being.
Regret for not having a fulfilling life	It is never too late to give to others, even in small ways. Connecting from your heart can melt away regret.
Dependency/loss of independence	A time to be on the receiving end of the flow of "give and take." When you graciously receive, you allow others to experience the joy of giving. There is *interdependence* in this exchange.
Loneliness	A time to *partner with your inner self.* Even though you may be alone, you are not lonely when you dance with your inner self.
Not having enough to do	Enjoy being and experience the wonder of small things you may have overlooked when you were busier.
Rigidly clinging to past living arrangements that no longer fit the current situation	Chance to break out of your cocoon, meet new people, and gain a new support network.
Fear of the future	Face the unknown with curiosity and excitement about what each new phase can teach you about your relationship to yourself and the world.

Table 26.2. Examples of challenges you may face with aging and possible ways you can reframe your experience to forgive yourself and make the most of this time of life.

Drawing on your life experience and personal wisdom in this way, helps to more fully integrate forgiveness and self-forgiveness into your way of being in the world. It also allows you to experience the grace that can come from having internal peace at this time of life. The next section of this book is designed to help you, no matter what your current age, to put your self-forgiveness challenges into a life affirming perspective and positive heroic storyline to bring more meaning and joy to the remainder of your personal journey.

PART 5
RECONSTRUCT YOUR STORY FROM INSIDE OUT

Composite created from Microsoft Gallery graphics

"What lies behind you and what lies in front of you, pales in comparison to what lies inside of you."
—Ralph Waldo Emerson
American lecturer, essayist, poet and leader of the Transcendentalist movement of the mid-19th century

Many people float from one situation to the next, without really examining their lives. They are unaware of the patterns that their thoughts, feelings and actions contribute to creating their personal stories. They also do not realize that they can make different choices, which could radically change the trajectory of their lives so they could unfold in a positive way.

By our very nature, human beings are "storytelling" and "meaning making" creatures. The more conscious our personal stories, the more likely they are to take us in a rich and meaningful direction. Writing our stories down in the form of a narrative, especially when those stories may have involved negative experiences, can be very beneficial. This type of writing may improve our physical and psychological health, including reducing the number of sick days taken, improving immune functioning, and decreasing anxiety.[1] Professor Shelley Carson, with the Harvard Department of Psychology, explains why narrative writing may be so powerful, "...by writing a narrative about our lives, we are transformed from victims of uncontrollable events into well-informed authors, and our life stories become meaningful works of art...[T]hrough narrative writing we can gain control over painful events by exploring and reframing them in a purposeful way."[2]

One of the great values of experiencing our personal story as a *Heroic Journey* is that it shows us the route to take to restructure our lives from inside out. Although we do not have control over all of the circumstances in our lives, we do have control over the meaning we assign to our experiences. We can choose to construct a life story that, at the end of our existence, takes our breath away with awe. From this vantage point, we are amazed at what we created and feel immense satisfaction for a life well lived. We are proud of the courage we exhibited. We feel a sense of triumph from picking ourselves up after falling and transforming our lives for the positive from the experience. We feel fulfilled from living a life of service that lovingly touched other people along the way.

The three previous parts of the book describe the process to create a story from inside out so we can have these feelings, not just at the end of our lives, but at every phase along the way! Winding *inward* helps us deconstruct our old story to make room for a change in perspective. Arriving at the *center* helps us develop a new storyline based on internal wisdom, which we may not have trusted in the past or even known we possessed. Winding *outward* integrates our new found wisdom into an authentic and loving plot in a world still fraught with fear, pain, struggle, and strife.

The heroic path of self-forgiveness is a daring journey that can accelerate the momentum in creating the amazing life story we long to experience! As author and clinical psychologist Robert Karen points out, "…forgiveness should be thought of not as a discrete event, but also as a way of being."[3] The more we integrate forgiveness of ourselves and others into our way of being, the easier it becomes to let go of stories that no longer serve us and focus our energy instead on realigning our thoughts, feelings, and actions with the core of who we are capable of becoming!

CHAPTER 27
BUILD A STRONG HEROIC CONTEXT

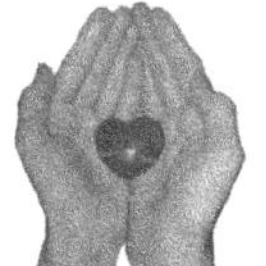

"For me context is the key—from that comes the understanding of everything."
—Kenneth Noland
American abstract painter

Most objects, organisms, and entities in the material world need a structure to keep them intact, whether it is a building with its foundation and steel beams, a bacteria's cell wall, or a snowflake's unique crystalline lattice. There are outer structures (exoskeletons) such as the hard shells of insects, crustaceans, or mollusks and there are inner structures (endoskeletons) such as those of vertebrate animals and human beings.

Sometimes a structure is visible and tangible, such as the examples mentioned above. Other times the structures are intangible, such as the force of gravity, the power of love, or the social patterns that groups of people exhibit when they interact. The *Heroic Journey* provides both an external structure, in the form of the story we live by, and an internal structure in the form of the *context* we use to bring cohesion and meaning to our experiences.

In *Part 1*, we discussed how experiencing our lives as a *Heroic Journey* can provide a context for transformational change, which brings together our "experience fragments" into a meaningful plot in our unfolding story. Meaning is not created in a vacuum. To construct a meaningful context, we need something to *anchor our experiences to internally* so they make sense to us.

Context is especially important as it relates to the process of self-forgiveness. Prior to experiencing our lives as a *Heroic Journey*, our unforgiving thoughts may have felt random and unrelated to one another. Within the contemplative context of our *Heroic Journey*, though, we look for meaningful connections between these "unforgiving strands." We examine how they may relate to any previously unrecognized patterns within us. Examples of patterns include a belief that we are stupid, a feeling that we don't have a right to succeed, shame about having needs and desires, a perception that no matter what we do, it will never be good enough, etc. These patterns may also relate to our core pain.

Once we clearly see our pattern, we may realize that a context we inherited from our past powerfully influenced the creation of this particular pattern within us. Perhaps we saw the same pattern played out in our family of origin or we learned it by osmosis from the culture in which we were immersed.

Many contexts from our past are valuable and help us function effectively in the world. Others do not. Part of shedding what no longer serves us is reexamining our existing context to determine if it still fits who we are now. If not, our heroic task is to delve deeper within to clear space for a new context.

As we do this inner clearing and bring the many facets of our shadow self into the light, our *heroic context* naturally emerges and fills our internal space. With this new heroic context firmly embedded in the core of our being, we are no longer dependent on an exoskeleton of external circumstances to make us feel strong and whole. We know from inside out that we have a strong, yet flexible endoskeleton that we can take with us wherever we go.

With this new infrastructure firmly at our core, as we wind outward on our heroic path, we have the internal strength of character to meet new challenges. Like a willow that is able to bend without breaking, we have the resilience to more effectively handle change. We are able to approach new situations with more clarity, creativity, and confidence. Because we have a clearer sense of self, we also waste less energy agonizing about how to proceed on our journey.

I mentioned earlier about how some contexts are tangible and other are intangible, such as gravity, love, and group patterns of social interactions. The heroic context is an intangible force around which the rest of our being coalesces. While it may be intangible, we know when it is present and fully functioning in our life. It is the most natural part of us that makes us feel authentically at home within ourselves. We don't have to will it to come forth. We exude it without even trying.

Having a heroic infrastructure changes the nature of our interactions with others. People instinctively know that there is something different about us, even though they may not consciously be aware of it. Maybe it is because we radiate a peaceful and calm demeanor. Maybe it is because while others fight to take up space in the room, we have no need to compete. We just quietly radiate a powerful presence. Since our interactions are less forced, we have no need to manipulate others to be with us. People around us feel this and may naturally gravitate to us, knowing we are trustworthy.

Although the heroic context is intangible, it is not without substance. There are at least three primary bonding agents that together act as glue to keep our heroic context intact and give it strength; *Truth, compassion, and values*. Each element is needed to create the internal cohesion that brings meaning and purpose to our experiences. It is this cohesion that fortifies our courage and tenacity to remain steadfastly committed to our *Heroic Journey* when the going gets tough.

- **Bonding Agent 1 – *Truth*: Keep a firm grip on your personal *Truth*.** *"All truth passes through three stages. First, it is ridiculed. Second, it is violently opposed. Third, it is accepted as being self-evident."* **Arthur Schopenhauer**, German philosopher.

  The thread that runs throughout all three phases of personal transformation is a commitment to tell the *Truth* to ourselves and act on it, whatever that *Truth* may be. In the beginning it may be difficult to discern what we even mean by "*Truth*." In the heroic sense of the word, when we access *Truth*, we tap into and align with universal *Truth*s of human existence, whether they are fundamental laws of nature, historical constants in human experience, or the collective wisdom of humanity.

  While we can never know all the *Truth* there is to know, we can access its vast reservoir to retrieve our personal slice of *Truth*. Uncovering what stands between us and our *Truth* is much of the challenge of the first phase of our journey. Listening to our inner whisperings of *Truth* and practicing letting them grow strong enough to take center stage in our lives is the task of the second phase. Acting on our *Truth* from a place of wisdom in day-to-day reality is the task of the third phase, which completes the heroic quest of living by our personal *Truth.*

When we do not stand in our *Truth,* we may flounder and find it difficult to get a firm footing on our heroic path. Choices may be more difficult to make if we let other people's perspectives take precedence over our own or if we desperately want to avoid doing what we are called to do. We may try to justify (usually futilely) why we need to remain in a current situation that feels familiar or safe, but is hampering us from living on the growing edge of our *Heroic Journey.*

Forgiveness is a strong ally to *Truth.* Once we have forgiven ourselves and others, we tend to struggle less and align more easily with our personal *Truth.* As we forgive, the old stories we used to tell ourselves to justify living in a false or smaller reality naturally begin to fall away. We are then open to taking our place in a larger, more expansive and authentic story. We realize, sometimes only in hindsight, how each of our previous experiences contributed to building our story from the inside out.

- **Bonding Agent 2 – *Compassion*: Expand your heart-felt compassion for human frailties.** *"Compassion is the antitoxin of the soul: where there is compassion even the most poisonous impulses remain relatively harmless."* **Eric Hoffer**, American philosopher and social author of *The True Believer.*

  In *Chapter 3*, we discussed the importance of following the logic of the heart in our unfolding heroic story of self-forgiveness. As our heart softens internally and fills with self-forgiveness, it naturally spills out as empathy for others and compassion toward those who may still be experiencing pain and fear in their own lives. From this heart-centered perspective, we can relate to people differently. We may find it easier to be around those who used to irritate or drain us. We may find that people who routinely used to violate our personal space no longer do since we radiate better boundaries. Since we are more adept at self-listening, we may be able to hear the logic of other people's hearts, sometimes even when they are not able to hear it themselves.

Compassion does not set us apart from others, but rather allows us to experience a deeper connection to the humanity we all share in common. We know from going to the depths of our own being how challenging and scary that process can be. When coupled with personal wisdom, the very act of forgiveness can magically erase residual angst, persistent trauma, and longstanding anger we may have harbored toward ourselves or others. From personal experience we know that it is possible to come out the other side stronger and happier for having embarked on this most difficult, but valuable journey.

The positive power of our experience often makes us passionate about sharing our internal process. Just as others helped us on our journey, we may feel the urge to "pay it forward." One of the most rewarding and joyful experiences in life can be providing loving guidance and hope to others when they need it most.

From our place of compassion, though, we are not pushy. We are sensitive to the timeline of others' journeys. Sometimes they are not ready or do not want to hear our perspective. We only share guidance with those who are open to hearing what we have to say. Being available to others, whether or not they choose to accept our assistance, demonstrates how much we have matured as human beings and just how far we have come on our personal self-forgiveness journey.

- **Bonding Agent 3 – *Values*: Draw strength from your core values.** *"Authentic values are those by which a life can be lived, which can form a people that produces great deeds and thoughts."* **Allan Bloom**, American academic, philosopher, and political commentator.

  Many people, if asked, would say that it is important to live a principled life based on positive personal values. From a heroic perspective values are our internal reference point.

They are the strength that we draw upon in every facet of our lives.

There are overtly stated values and there are the values that we live by on a daily basis. "Walking our talk" is about living our core values. When we are clear about our core values and draw on them, walking our talk becomes second nature. Decision-making becomes easier and actions more purposeful and powerful. Items on our "to do" list are easier to prioritize by what is truly important and what is just extraneous busy work. We choose to do the "right thing" for the sake of doing it, not because we feel we have to or because it will get us external brownie points.

Having clear values is especially important in times of stress when we tend to default to what comes to us most naturally. When we live a principled life based on values, we tend to be less tempted to take the easy route in favor of the path we intuitively know will get us where we ultimately want to go, even if that path is more arduous.

Living by our values builds self-respect and draws to us people and situations that reflect external respect. Having a strong value system at the core of our being gives us a heightened sense of structural integrity. As a result we are less buffeted by the hurricane of chaos, constant changes, and external challenges. We are operating from the calm "I" at the center of ourselves.

Having a strong heroic context fundamentally changes our perception of reality and how we experience life. It is the fount from which meaning springs. It brings richness, purpose, and significance to all we do.

As storyteller and author Annette Simmons, says, "Once you choose your story, life makes more sense. Ridiculous things still happen. Random events and tragedy don't end. But they can be interpreted within the context of your story."[1] With a clear context for your self-forgiveness challenges, it becomes much easier to transform them into meaningful elements in your ever evolving heroic plot.

CHAPTER 28
WRITE YOUR PERSONAL HEROIC NARRATIVE

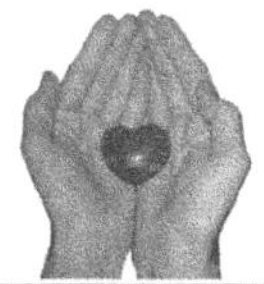

"Perhaps if we could really listen to what the myths are telling us we could hear what I heard myself saying not so long ago: 'Everybody has to be the hero of one story: his[her] own.' I said it lightly; or rather something said it in me, For we know more than we know, more than we understand. And if it is true, what an awesome undertaking!"

—P. L. Travers

British novelist remembered for her *Mary Poppins* children's novel series

Years ago I presented self-esteem workshops to Twelve Step Program groups in Seattle. I was struck by how generally there were two kinds of people who attended these meetings. One type committed to their growth and really delved internally to figure out how they could become more functional and happy people. They took personal responsibility for their beliefs and actions that had contributed to their stories of victimhood.

The other type seemed stuck in their old stories, repeating them week after week without seeing the patterns of misery they continued to recreate in their current relationships. It was also clear that this second group often had a very difficult time forgiving others and themselves. Retelling their stories became a way to re-justify each week why they or others deserved *not* to be forgiven.

I remember once hearing internationally acclaimed teacher and author Marianne Williamson say in a workshop, "May you become tired of your own story." That made a profound impact on me. I realized that as long as I was still attracted to my old story, I was destined to repeat it. Once I lost interest in the old story, it naturally evolved.

Writing your heroic narrative is about relinquishing the story that may have been scripted for you by others or that you unconsciously wrote when you had less awareness. It is about getting tired of being stuck in your unforgiving past and instead making a decision to rewrite your story from a transformational perspective. As counseling and human resources consultant, Michael H. Brown describes, "[Transformation] represents a complete change of consciousness from one level of operation to a higher more integrated level of operating."[1]

Retelling your past from a transformational perspective can help facilitate this process. In *Chapter 1*, we discussed how forgiveness helps us "re-member" the broken pieces of our lives into something whole. From a heroic perspective we take the painful incidents, fears we faced, anger we experienced, and the doubts we had and transform them into positive elements in our ongoing story of character development. We do this by finding the treasures under the pain, the value in facing our fears, the root of our anger and the wisdom we have accessed under our doubt. Each time we activate these hidden resources, we help reshape our story into a new context that is filled with hope, purpose and possibilities.

Based on my personal experience, I have developed a *seven step heroic narrative* process, to help you create your unique transformative story. Each step builds on the previous one and has associated tools or exercises to guide you through the story building process. (***Appendices G.1 – G.7*** contains those detailed exercises and tools.) When coupled with the heroic framework (winding inward, arriving at the center and winding back out again), you can develop a new script that more accurately reflects your authentic self and the qualities you are learning to embody for the remainder of your journey. As this new script becomes more fully ingrained in your psyche, it will be easier to recalibrate your thoughts and actions as you go. In the process you may find that the need to forgive yourself and others has naturally dropped away, since you are now living out a more fulfilling heroic story.

- **Step 1: Identify the heroic character traits you bring to your self-forgiveness journey**. We each have unique traits that help us activate our heroic character. There are other traits that we know we would benefit by strengthening to help us better weather our self-forgiveness challenges. The list of traits in **Table 28.1** contains some of the most common heroic character traits. It is by no means exhaustive and it may not contain the ones that specifically fit for you, but the list may evoke within you the heroic traits you want to consider strengthening.

- See ***Heroic Character Self-Evaluation Tool*** (***Appendix G.1a)*** to learn more detail about each of these traits and to test your heroic mettle on each of them.
- See ***Exercise 1: Heroic Character Trait Re-Examination (Appendix G.1b)*** to help you review your past in terms of how each experience helped you develop a particular heroic trait. By seeing your past, including the painful parts, as contributing to your heroic trait development, it helps you appreciate how the pain, difficult as it was, strengthened your heroic character and contributed to your personal story of heroism.

Heroic Character Traits	
Clear Sense of Self - Choices and actions are guided from within	**Leadership** - Demonstrate leadership capabilities regardless of title or position in an organization
Authenticity - Internal and external harmony	**Service-Oriented Perspective** - Willingness to serve extends beyond self interests
Heart-Felt Connection to Others - Open-hearted in contact with other human beings	**Awareness** - Internal observer plays an active role in life
Passionate Enthusiasm - Live life fully and boldly	**Commitment to Excellence** - Aspire to do one's best
Seeker of Purpose and Meaning - Find value in everyday experiences	**Resilience** - Ability to bounce back from adversity

Table 28.1. Common heroic traits. Can you think of others that fit for you, which are not on the list?

- **Step 2: Write a preliminary version of your heroic narrative**. Once you have completed *Exercise 1* referenced in Step 1 above, you are ready to begin filling in details of your heroic story of self-forgiveness. As we discussed in the *Part 1 Introduction*, in any good story, there is a beginning, middle and end. When you think of your life as a *Heroic Journey*, in addition to having all of the elements of any good story, your heroic story is about how your personal experiences are helping you develop wisdom and a more mature perspective of life. This is what places your story into a context of transformation. To help you with this process, see ***Exercise 2: Create Each Plot Element for Your Heroic Narrative (Appendix G.2)***.

- **Step 3: Integrate your inner whisperings into your heroic narrative**. In *Chapter 17* we discussed how shedding what no longer serves you helps clear the way to hear the inner whisperings that call to you from inside out. In ***Exercise 3: Create Your Inner Whisperings Journal (Appendix G.3)*** you will keep a journal that lists your inner whispering as they come to you. Seeing them written down gives them a more prominent role in your unfolding story. As Barry Neil Kaufman, author, teacher and co-founder of *The Option Institute* points out, "A loud voice cannot compete with a clear voice, even if it's a whisper."[2]

- **Step 4: Let your *Wise Narrator* tell your story.** You can quicken the role that your inner whisperings play in your life by allowing your internal *Wise One*, the aspect of you that does the inner whispering, to become the narrator of your life story. As the *Wise Narrator*, this part of you can bring to awareness why certain aspects of your life occurred the way they did and, in fact, how each incident brought you to transformational moments in your heroic development. See ***Exercise 4: Let Your Wise Narrator Retell Your Story (Appendix G.4)*** to help you with this process. As a member of your own audience listening to your *Wise Narrator*, you may feel more engaged in your story and eager to listen intently for what the next whispering will reveal to you. You may also find yourself waiting expectantly for new clues that will help you discover more about who you are and who you are capable of becoming.

- **Step 5: Anchor the new story in every fiber of your being.** As your new heroic story comes more clearly into focus with the assistance of your *Wise Narrator,* this step of the process helps root out everything that doesn't fit into your new story. The ***Anchor Your New Story Tool*** in ***Exercise 5 (Appendix G.5)*** is designed to help you bridge from the old story to the new. As you drop what no longer fits, you may feel a lightness that lifts your spirits and makes the rest of your journey more enjoyable, especially knowing what it took for you to get this far in your transformational story.

- **Step 6: Adapt your story as you go to reflect your expanding perception.** In *Part 1* we discussed that one of the great values of experiencing your life as a *Heroic Journey* is that it is not a static story, but it evolves with you as you change. One of the paradoxes of your journey is that while you are busy anchoring your new story in every fiber of your being, you will also be nudged to evolve your story as you expand your internal and external perceptions of reality. Learning to live with this dichotomy is a valuable step in your heroic maturity. It helps you evolve beyond *either/or thinking,* which narrows perception, and move into *both/and thinking,* which expands perception. There are often clues that help you know it is time for your story to evolve. ***Exercise 6: Take Action to Evolve Your Story (Appendix G.6)*** will help you recognize those clues and know what to do with the information once you receive it.

- **Step 7: Merge your personal story into the collective story.** As you progress through your transformation, you may find that your focus shifts from how you can change yourself to how you can use what you have learned to improve the lives of your family, the community, the world, or the global human condition. At the point you merge your personal *Heroic Journey* into the collective journey, you take a quantum leap forward in strengthening your story and deepening your connection to the world around you. The ***Expand Your Story Tool*** in ***Exercise 7 (Appendix G.7)*** is designed to assist you in bringing your expanded story into sharper focus.

Working through the steps involved in creating your heroic narrative may take time, but the pay off can be enormous. Prior to having a cohesive narrative, you may not have seen as well how all of your experiences or behaviors related. Once you have a clear story, though, you are able to step back from it and see what a powerful story you created, much of it without your conscious control. Once you are aware of what you created, it is much easier to live out your story in a more conscious way from this point forward.

I found this to be the case in writing this book. It was only after creating my own heroic narrative based on this process that my personal story of self-forgiveness, as it stands now, came more clearly into focus. (See the *Epilogue* for how I put my personal story together related to writing this book.)

As you discover how each of your experiences fit into your unique self-forgiveness story, don't be surprised if you make huge shifts in consciousness. Your self-love may blossom without any effort. Your heart may overflow with compassion for others, especially those who are living out their stories from a less conscious perspective. You also may find yourself excitedly anticipating the next chapter in your unfolding story.

CHAPTER 29
FULLY ENGAGE WITH LIFE

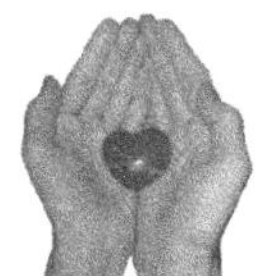

"I could not, at any age, be content to take my place by the fireside and simply look on. Life was meant to be lived. Curiosity must be kept alive. One must never, for whatever reason, turn his[/her] back on life."
—Eleanor Roosevelt
First Lady of the United States from 1933 to 1945

Reconstructing your story of self-forgiveness from inside out can unleash a power that makes you feel more fully engaged with life and excited about each new experience. Full engagement is about allowing your authentic self to take its rightful place in the world. It is about being more open-hearted and genuine in your interactions with the people around you. It is about seeing each new situation as an opportunity to let your wisdom take the lead. It also is about finding meaning and purpose in whatever you do.

Fully engaging with life, calls for activating your childlike curiosity, no matter what your age. It is approaching and living life with a playful attitude. It is actively looking for the magic in the mundane. And it is seeing life with the eyes of wonder and awe.

Mythologist Joseph Campbell once said, "People say that what we're all seeking is a meaning for life…I think what we are seeking is an experience of being alive, so our life experiences on the purely physical plane will have resonances within our own inner most being and reality, so that we actually feel the rapture of being alive."[1] The heroic path of self-forgiveness is a journey of continually opening to greater aliveness. It is at its core a profound love story. It is by fully loving ourselves, including the shadow aspects of ourselves, that we truly appreciate the magic and mystery that makes life worth living. It is my hope that you personally experience this sense of aliveness and that joyful moments will expand into a joyful way of being!

EPILOGUE
JOURNEY TO SELF-ATONEMENT

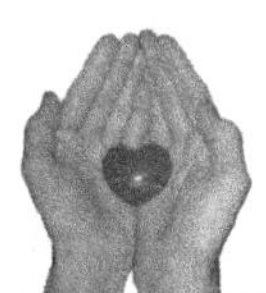

"Atonement is the making right, the reestablishing of balance, the restoration of sanity, alleviation of grief and the resumption of life."
—Douglas George-Kanentiio
American Indian journalist and Indian rights activist

When I began to write this book about self-forgiveness, other than a title and a cursory outline, I had only a faint inkling of how it would eventually evolve or how it would help me rewrite my own story from inside out. I did know from past personal growth work that to help structure my process of self-discovery, I was going to use the *Heroic Journey* process of winding inward, arriving at the center, and winding outward as a context to guide me on this quest. With this tool in hand, I ventured inside my "labyrinth of self-forgiveness challenges."

As I mentioned in the *Introduction*, my journey toward forgiving myself began with a realization that it has generally been easier for me to walk in the shoes of others than my own. While I have easily forgiven people for committing horrible acts of violence that severely affected me, my family, and friends, I have not always been able to feel this same level of compassion for myself and my own humanness, even for minor offenses. The discoveries I have made on my personal quest and those I share here have helped me step more fully into my own shoes. In the process I have developed a greater capacity for compassion of others.

Two questions became the focus of my contemplation as I began winding inward on this journey: 1) "*Why am I unwilling to feel the same level of compassion and forgiveness for myself that I have for attackers and murderers?*" and 2) *"If I forgive myself completely, how will it change my life?"* Close to the end of writing this book, I came across an anthology, *Beyond Forgiveness: Reflections on Atonement*[1] that helped me answer these questions more fully than I would have otherwise been able to do had I not read this book.

In the Preface of *Beyond Forgiveness*, editor and author Phil Cousineau points out that as important as forgiveness is to move on with our lives, there is another aspect that cannot be left out of this personal equation:

> [A]nother equally profound action is needed for real reconciliation, which Arun Gandhi, grandson of Mohandas Gandhi, calls the "other side of the coin." Turning over the coin of forgiveness, we discover *atonement*, the semi-hidden, much overlooked half of the reconciliation process.[2]…[A]tonement speaks to the secret part of us that needs to *prove* we are sorry for committing a terrible wrong, to show some proof that our words—*"I'm sorry"*—are not empty, but will be backed up by an *action* that stops the soul-rust threatening to corrode our lives.[3]

Edward Tick, one of the contributors to Phil Cousineau's anthology is a mythologist, psychotherapist, and co-director of *Soldier's Heart*, a veteran's healing program in New York. He uses "atonement therapy" to work with returning war veterans. He provides a clear definition of atonement, "The root of *atonement* is 'oneness,' 'becoming one with.' In essence, atonement entails not just awakening or exchanging feelings of empathy, friendship, or forgiveness but *performing acts of repair that bring what was separated, divided, or broken back into union*."[4]

Kate Dahlstedt, also a contributor in the *Beyond Forgiveness* anthology and co-director of *Soldier's Heart* points out:

> Restitution is another essential ingredient in the act of atonement. Making a sacrifice of some kind, a metaphoric gesture, seeks to repair, if only in miniature, that which has been lost. Restitution gives the individual the opportunity to create meaning from the original offense by offering to do something that he or she would not have done otherwise. It allows people to give when they have taken, to create when they have

> destroyed. Rebalancing the universal scales in this way is powerfully healing.[5]

I originally thought this book was simply about self-forgiveness. While this is a noble quest in itself, I was pleased to find that it has actually evolved into much more. I didn't realize until reading *Beyond Forgiveness* that I had intuitively created, through my personal self-discovery process, a book about *self-atonement* as well as self-forgiveness.

While self-forgiveness is woven throughout the book, the self-atonement side of the reconciliation coin is more specifically addressed in *Chapter 19: Discover the Gifts of Your Shadow* and integrated into the remainder of the book. Working with our shadow side helps bring the fractured parts of us back together into a sense of wholeness. Transforming our shadow selves into allies, who help us on the remaining part of our journey, gives the shadow selves an opportunity to make restitution to us for the internal trauma they caused us from their previous misguided perspective. By agreeing to step out of the shadow and become active forces in creating a positive future, these former shadow parts of us demonstrate that they are genuinely making amends. This transformational act repairs the deep pain inflicted on our psyche, rebalances our personal scale of justice, restores internal peace, and cleanses us of the heaviness from our past so we feel whole again.

In her work with veterans, Kate Dahlstedt has found that rituals, particularly when done ceremonially, help with this transformational atonement process. As she points out, "An essential ingredient of atonement and forgiveness ceremonies is *storytelling*...We can forgive and even have compassion and empathy for those who have hurt us. But we must first hear their story. We can then find the human and universal aspects that touch our own heartstrings."[6] Her co-director, Edward Tick also adds *public witnessing and healing ceremonies as important components of atonement.*[7]

As a context for change, the *Heroic Journey* helps us atone with ourselves through all three components. Throughout the book, we've discussed the transformational power of storytelling. We've cultivated our ability to witness our own thoughts and actions from a detached, but loving public witness perspective. We've also worked through a variety of exercises that can act as "mini healing ceremonies" along the way.

From a self-atonement perspective, though, there is no part of our journey where all three of atonement components, *storytelling*, *public witnessing* and *healing ceremonies*, coalesce more than when we do our shadow work. Our *Internal Dream Team* acts as our *internal community*, creating a ceremonial space to hold witness for each of the shadow's sub-personality transformational stories. (See *Chapter 19*, pages 139-144 for more details.)

During this witnessing process, a sub-personality is given the opportunity to openly and honestly share its story of self-forgiveness challenges in a safe, nurturing, and heart-centered environment. As our internal community members witness what is said, they listen intently for whether the sub-personality genuinely has remorse and sincerely seeks contrition for its thoughts and deeds that caused past damage to members of its inner community. Once the community members know that a real transformation has taken place, they acknowledge this and affirm the sub-personality for its efforts to repair the past metaphorical rip in the community fabric that was caused. Having their own personal contrition for past shortcomings, the community members accept the sub-personality's story as part of their shared legacy. They demonstrate their compassion by conferring the sub-personality with a new identity that is free of the past stain of shame or guilt.

The sub-personality's commitment to accept this change in role is formalized by signing a contract. (See *Chapter 19*, pp. 145-146 for an example.) With the contract signed, the public witnessing process is complete. The sub-personality is ushered forth into the world with a new identity that better serves itself and the community. In serving the community in a positive way, restitution is made and the sub-personality is reintegrated into the inner community again, but from a place of wholeness and liberation from the past.

Understanding the self-atonement process I intuitively created has given me a sense of completion about this book, which wouldn't have been possible before I integrated both sides of the reconciliation coin into my personal story. I am proud of the fact that I listened to my inner whisperings to go deeper, even while my *Internal Taskmaster* was telling me to move on and wrap up the book. By following my wisdom, I have been able to answer my two original questions with a greater clarity than I would have otherwise had.

The answer to my first question about why I was unwilling to feel the same level of compassion for myself as I do for others is that I wanted to hold "others" (particularly those I perceived as negative) away from me. By stepping into "their" shoes and leaving my own, I was able to maintain their "otherness" and disown the shadow parts of myself that "they" represent. Feeling compassion for "them" allowed me to adopt a superior stance that kept me from seeing them eye-to-eye, soul to soul. At some level I knew if I looked into their soul, I would have to face the parts of myself that they mirrored for me.

Working with my shadow selves has helped me face many of the parts of myself that used to repulse or terrify me. Although this work is never ending, I have been willing to look at many parts of myself that were attacking, mean spirited, angry, jealous, crazy, and had murderous intent toward my other shadow sub-personalities. By acknowledging that these parts of me existed, I took an important step toward working in concert with them rather than have them work covertly against me. This alliance has helped me better understand them, softened my self-judgment, and it has made the self-forgiveness process easier along the way. What has also been helpful is having a sense of curiosity about each shadow self's perspective, deeply listening to what it has to say, taking full responsibility for my reactions to it, and remaining open-hearted about how to forge a new path of cooperation in moving forward.

Having gone through the shadow process of self-atonement is making it easier for me to atone with others. When I feel more of a sense of personal wholeness, I feel less defensive. I can more easily access the part of myself that is genuinely remorseful for my actions. Having personally experienced the pain inflicted on me prior to my shadow's atonement, I feel more compassionate for the pain I may have caused others. I recognize that just as others have played valuable parts for me in my evolving story, I may be playing a valuable part for them in their own growth and development.

When my defenses are triggered by someone I feel needs to atone with me, rather than lash out in retaliation, I am committed to going within. While still holding others accountable for their actions, I ask myself if they are externally reflecting a shadow part of me that still needs to atone with my internal community. I also look for ways I can genuinely open my heart in compassion to the part of them that is struggling with atonement. I now know that their struggle is part of our shared legacy as human beings who are all "works in progress."

The answer to my second question about how my life would change if I forgave myself is that I now appreciate many more of the gifts that these shadow parts bring to my life. Knowing that these parts of me are blessings in disguise, I am more willing to explore their true identity under the façade of the shadow. The best part of all is that I have made peace with many of these parts of myself and transformed them into allies. In some cases they have become close friends and confidants, who I trust deeply and know will be by my side for the remainder of my life journey. Now that I know I can count on them to work with me instead of against me, I feel liberated from much of my past angst. My energy is now free to focus on using my talents and gifts to help shape a positive future for both my internal and external community.

As a result of this continuing inner work, I have less need to hold other people, with undeveloped shadow traits, at a distance. It is easier for me to stand open-hearted in my own shoes *and* simultaneously stand in theirs. I can do this because *I now know it is the same place, just seen from a different perspective*. We are all interconnected and we each act as reflections for one another.

When I came across the *Beyond Self-Forgiveness* anthology close to the end of writing this book, it was a great synchronicity and confirmation that I was on the right track with my internal process. The *Heroic Journey* self-forgiveness and self-atonement process was not something that I consciously created. It was an organic process that arose from my internal need to fundamentally change my relation to myself. Developing this process bypassed my intellect and reached deep into the core of my being to tap into my internal wisdom. It has been a wonderful surprise to me how the process has unfolded.

Many years ago when I lived in Seattle, I attended a *Heroic Journey* workshop led by mythologist Peter Wallis.[8] One of the exercises we did close to the end of the day was to create a drawing of our personal *Heroic Journey*. My drawing was very childlike, but powerful. I drew myself standing on the top of a structure that looked like the Great Wall of China. On one side of the wall was a beautiful grassy, peaceful meadow. On the other side of the wall were throngs of people in misery unaware of the other side. From my vantage point I could see the two sides and I knew that the wall was not insurmountable, but instead an artificial barrier we create within ourselves from a place of unawareness. When I saw the *Truth* of this I realized that one of my tasks in life was to help others in misery, who were ready to make a change, learn how to experience firsthand what was on the other side of the wall. But, I knew intuitively that to be a good guide for others, first I had to figure out how to get the parts of myself that were still stuck in misery over the wall.

Writing this book about self-forgiveness and self-atonement and doing my inner work along the way has helped me get many of the parts of myself over the invisible wall. This book is a gift I share with you on your personal journey of self-forgiveness and self-atonement. Hopefully, it will help you rise above your own wall and see there was actually nothing keeping you from experiencing the grassy peaceful meadow, except the artificial barriers you created within yourself. It is my heart-felt wish that knowing this from inside out will propel you in a meaningful and fulfilling direction that you cannot yet envision!

APPENDICES

APPENDIX A
SKILLS TO TAME UNRULY EMOTIONS

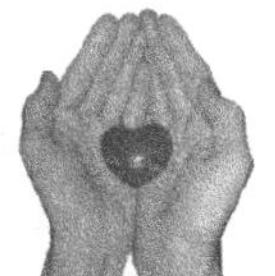

(This appendix is adapted with permission from Rev. Dr. Judith Larkin Reno's book, *Self-Interview.*[1])

Emotions are one of the best teachers on the planet. They can guide you to deeper self-knowledge and greater wisdom. They can teach you who you are and who you are not in the world. They can teach you healthy boundaries and entitlement. They can teach you how to effectively communicate, deal with confrontation, and develop conflict resolution skills.

But, just as your toes are not who you are, your emotions are not your identity. Attachment to emotions can cause problems. When you are attached to your emotions, you reduce your identity to an emotion. You also may confuse your worth as a human being with a particular emotion.

Do not let excessive and intense emotionality rob your life. Keep in mind that, although emotions are not your identity, you are responsible for resolving them. It does not work to repress or pretend you do not feel emotions. Nor does it work to collapse into excessive emotional indulgence as a lifestyle. Neither over-expression nor under-expression is healthy. Maturity comes with finding the middle road.

Think of emotions as the water element of your nature. Like the mighty tsunamis, emotions can be powerful. They can create stormy seas. They can be muddy, foggy, turbulent, stagnant, steamy, or crystal clear. Or, water can be so still that it perfectly reflects the world around it. As the myth of Narcissus tells us, water can act as a mirror.

Turbulent emotions can feel like a houseful of unruly children. It is your job to parent them in a healthy way. When there is a conflict among children, healthy parents listen to each child without judgment. They validate the emotions that arise. They identify the conflict between the children and then strive to resolve it. Here are some practical tips to help you tame unruly emotions:

1. **Identify and name emotions.** Throughout the day, name emotions the moment they arise. Repeatedly ask yourself, "What am I feeling now?" Be alert to imbalances of numbing or excessive emotionality. Simply naming an emotion can remove its disproportionate charge.
2. **Detach from your emotions.** Imagine you are filming the movie of your inner life. See your emotion, like an actor moving through the arena of your mind. Shift identification with your emotion from saying, for example, "I am sad," to instead asking, "What part of me is sad?"
3. **Track emotions back to their source.** Some emotions may be trying to flag your attention to deal with unresolved traumatic issues in your past. They may be calling you to go back in time to discover when they first entered your life. It may be helpful to ask yourself, "Where did I first learn this emotion? Does this negative emotion remind me of anyone? What event first created this negative emotion? What beliefs about life did I create as a result of this negative emotion?
4. **Stay present with negative emotions**. Sometimes emotions want to come to the surface, but we hold them back. Maybe we are afraid they will overwhelm us or bring with them unwanted consequences. If we repress emotions, though, they may become even more unruly. By letting out our emotions and being fully present with the associated feelings, the energy often dissipates quickly or sometimes completely disappears.
5. **Train your emotions.** The same way you train a dog to stay off the sofa, you can train negative emotions, so they do not overwhelm your life. By being consistent with your training, your emotions will learn that although they play a valuable part in your life, they do not rule the roost. Some of the specific training methods include:
    a. **Place a time limit on emoting.** Do not allow negative emotions to consume all of your time. For instance, tell yourself, "This anger is not allowed into my space until

3:00 p.m. At that time, I will spend 15 minutes thinking/writing about what is on my mind."

b. **Make a deal with your emotions.** Some negative emotions respond to bargaining or delay tactics. For instance, if you have a very strong emotion that triggers your desire to eat unhealthy junk food, tell yourself, "If I still want this snack on Sunday, I will have it. In the meantime, instead of acting on my emotional trigger, I am going to nurture myself by eating very healthy food." This statement acknowledges the emotion, which will often reduce its intensity in that moment. Also, by using this delay tactic, by the time Sunday comes, you may feel so good from eating healthy food that the desire for the unhealthy snack may no longer appeal to you or be totally forgotten.

c. **Stop negative emotions and refocus your attention.** Letting emotions consume your time can be habit forming. To break the habit, it may be helpful when negative, undermining emotions pop into your mind to say, "Stop!" Then do something else, like a project that takes your full attention. If you consistently do this each time the negativity comes to mind, eventually, it will likely get bored and go away. By not giving the negativity anywhere to anchor internally, you break the grip of the emotional spell so you can move on with your life.

6. **Release intense emotions.** Some intense emotions require release to clear them. Examples of release techniques include:
   a. **Anger.** To get anger out of your body, try hitting a pillow with your lower arm, screaming in the car (where no one else can hear you), or hitting a tennis racket on a mattress.
   b. **Sadness.** To dissipate sadness, rather than trying to hold it back, let yourself cry intensely. While you may be concerned that if you start crying you will never stop, actually giving yourself permission to cry fully and deeply often usually consumes less time and energy than trying to hold it in.
   c. **Pain.** To let go of a particularly painful past experience, you may want to write a letter about it and then burn it, bury it or throw it into a river to symbolically get rid of it.

d. **Fear.** To reduce abject fear, you may want to create a dance, poem, or picture that expresses your fearful feelings. The very act of expression gets your creative juices flowing, which can reduce the paralyzing and destructive effect of fear's hold over you.
e. **Any negative emotion.** To rid any negative emotion from your system you can use your breathing. On the exhale breath, forcefully expel the negative energy associated with the emotion. Pause several seconds and then on the in breath, purposefully and commandingly take in the positive. After even five minutes of practicing this type of deep breathing, you may find that the intense emotion has drastically dissipated and it is replaced with an indwelling sense of peace.

7. **Get support.** You do not have to release intense emotions completely on your own. Sometimes you may want to get the support of a skilled counselor or therapist, who can guide you in a way that helps you achieve a complete release of the emotions, so they do not remain stuck within you. Do not let negative emotions fester unresolved. They can multiply like an untreated infection.
8. **Find the part of you that is untouched by negative emotions.** Within each of us there is a calm center, or calm "I" that is unaffected by the emotional hurricane that may whirl around us. This is the source from which we draw solace, peace, refuge, and renewal. It is the place where we feel most "present" in the world. Before you are in times of stress, practice going there, so you can easily locate it when you need it most. Meditation and prayer can help take you there. By making this a daily practice, you will more naturally be able to stay present and calm, no matter what happens around you. (See *Exercise 3: Extract Yourself from the Whirlwind of Emotions* in *Chapter 22* on page 167 for more detail about how you can practice accessing your calm center.)

APPENDIX B
AFFIRMATION AND VISUALIZATION RESOURCES

Affirmation Resources

Definition of Affirmation

Affirmations constitute positive, controlled and directed self-talk, which gives focus and impact to one's plans for personal goals and fulfillment. —Lee Pulos

Books

Bloch, Douglas. *Words That Heal: Affirmations and Meditations for Daily Living.* New York: Bantam, 1990.

Evers, Anne Marie. *Affirmations-Your Passport to Happiness.* North Vancouver, B.C.: Affirmations-International Publishing, 1999.

Fishel, Ruth. *Change Almost Anything in 21 Days: Recharge Your Life with the Power of Over 500 Affirmations.* Deerfield Beach, FL: Health Communications, Inc., 2003.

Hay, Louise. *Heal Your Body A-Z: The Mental Causes for Physical Illness and the Way to Overcome Them.* Carlsbad, CA: Hay House, 1998.

Walters, J. Donald. *Affirmations for Self-Healing.* Nevada City, CA: Crystal Clarity Publishers, 2005.

Wilde, Stuart. *Affirmations.* Carson City, CA: Hay House, Inc., 1987.

Websites

- **Affirmations: The Power of Thought**
  http://www.philipshapiro.com/art-affirmations
  Affirmations and the subconscious mind, creating powerful and effective affirmations, and the technique for affirmations during periods of rest and meditation.

- **Positive Mindset Website**
  http://www.vitalaffirmations.com/affirmations
  What are affirmations, do affirmations work, how to create affirmations, sample affirmations.

- **Success Consciousness: Awakening the Wisdom and Power within You**
  http://www.successconsciousness.com/affirmations
  The power of affirmations, affirmations and self-talk, affirmations and how to affirm.

Visualization Resources

Definition of Visualization

To form a positive mental image to achieve a particular goal.

Books

Capacchione, Lucia. *Visioning: Ten Steps to Designing the Life of Your Dreams.* New York: Jeremy P. Tarcher/Putnam, 2000.

Gwain, Shakti. *The Creative Visualization Workbook.* Novato, CA: Nataraj Publishing, 1995.

Gwain, Shakti. *Creative Visualization: Use the Power of Your Imagination to Create What You Want in Your Life.* Novato, CA: Nataraj Publishing, 2002.

Just, Shari L. and Flynn, Carolyn. *The Complete Idiot's Guide to Creative Visualization.* New York: Penguin Group, 2005.

Phillips Osborne and Denning, Melita. *Practical Guide to Creative Visualization: Manifest Your Desires.* St. Louis, MN: Llewellyn Publications, 2001.

Webster, Richard. *Creative Visualization for Beginners: Achieve Your Goals and Make Your Dreams Come True.* Woodbury, MN: Llewellyn Publications, 2005.

Websites

- **Visualization Techniques Website**
  http://www.visualizationtechniques.net/
  What is visualization, benefits, goals, and visualization exercises.

- **Create Your Reality with Visualization Techniques**
  http://www.visualization-techniques.com/
  Achieving goals with mental visualization, list of visualization techniques, creative visualization facts and information.

- **Revolutionize Your Mind with Incredible Visualization Techniques**
  http://evisualizationtechniques.com/
  Creative visualization exercises, mental imagery, creative visualization videos.

APPENDIX C
RESOURCES FOR EFFECTIVE COMMUNICATION

General Communication Skills

McKay, Matthew, Martha Davis, and Patrick Fanning. *Messages: The Communication Skills Book.* Oakland, CA: New Harbinger, Publications, Inc., 2009.

Swets, Paul W. *The Art of Talking So That People Will Listen: Getting Through to Family, Friends and Business Associates.* New York: Fireside Books, 1983.

Negotiation and Conflict Resolution Skills

Bolton, Robert. *People Skills: How to Assert Yourself, Listen to Others, and Resolve Conflicts.* New York: Simon & Schuster, 1979.

Bramson, Robert M. *Coping with Difficult People.* New York: Dell Publishing, 1981.

Fisher, Roger and William Ury. *Getting to Yes: Negotiating Agreement Without Giving In.* New York: Penguin Group, 1991.

Patterson, Kerry, Joseph Grenny, Ron McMillan, and Al Switzler. *Crucial Conversations: Tools for Talking When Stakes Are High.* New York: McGraw Hill, 2002.

Patterson, Kerry, Joseph Grenny, Ron McMillan, and Al Switzler. *Crucial Confrontations: Tools for Resolving Broken Promises, Violated Expectations, and Bad Behavior.* New York: McGraw Hill, 2005.

Scott, Susan. *Fierce Conversations: Achieving Success at Work and in Life One Conversation at a Time.* New York: Berkley Publishing Group, 2002.

Stone, Douglas, Bruce Patton, and Sheila Heen. *Difficult Conversations: How to Discuss What Matters Most.* New York: Viking Press, 1999.

Weeks, Dudley. *The Eight Essential Steps to Conflict Resolution: Preserving Relationships at Work, at Home and in the Community.* New York: Jeremy P. Tarcher/Putnam, 1992.

Listening Skills

Brady, Mark. *The Wisdom of Listening.* Somerville, MA: Wisdom Publications, 2003.

Burley-Allen, Madelyn. *Listening: The Forgotten Skill: A Self-Teaching Guide.* New York: John Wiley & Sons, Inc., 1995.

Donoghue, Paul J. and Mary E. Siegel. *Are You Really Listening?: Keys to Successful Communication.* Notre Dame, IN: Sorin Books, 2005.

Goulston, Mark. *Just Listen: Discover the Secret to Getting Through to Absolutely Anyone.* New York: American Management Association, 2010.

Trust

Covey, Stephen. *The SPEED of Trust: The One Thing That Changes Everything.* New York: Simon & Schuster, 2006.

Morgan, Nick. *Trust Me: Four Steps to Authenticity.* San Francisco, CA: Jossey-Bass, 2009.

APPENDIX D
VOICE DIALOGUE RESOURCES

Definition of Voice Dialogue

A technique developed in the early 1970's by Drs. Hal and Sidra Stone, which identifies the different aspects of our personality or "sub-personalities." It gives voice to these sub-personalities, so we can better understand them and reintegrate them into our lives in more functional ways. This process also helps us access our untapped potential that lies hidden in the shadows.

Books

Dyak, Miriam. *The Voice Dialogue Facilitator's Handbook, Part I: A Step By Step Guide to Working with the Aware Ego.* Seattle, WA: L.I.F.E. Energy Press, 1999.

Stamboliev, Robert. *The Energetics of Voice Dialogue: An In-depth Exploration of the Energetic Aspects of Transformational Psychology.* Mendocino, CA: Liferhythm, 1992.

Stone, Hal and Sidra Stone. *Embracing Ourselves: The Voice Dialogue Manual.* Novato, CA: New World Library, 1989.

Stone, Hal and Sidra Stone. *Embracing Your Inner Critic: Turning Self-Criticism into a Creative Asset.* New York: HarperCollins, 1993.

Stone, Hal and Sidra Stone. *Partnering: A New Kind of Relationship.* Novato, CA: Nataraj Publishing, 2000.

Websites

- **Voice Dialogue** for Relationships, personal growth and transformation
  http://www.voicedialogue.com/index.html
  What is Voice Dialogue, articles, blogs, and more.

- **Voice Dialogue Institute**
  http://www.thevoicedialogueinstitute.org/index.html
  Including article, *Voice Dialogue* and *The Psychology of the Aware Ego*, by Miriam Dyak.

- **Voice Dialogue Connection**
  http://www.voicedialogueconnection.com
  Website by Judith Tamar Stone, daughter of Hal Stone and step-daughter of Sidra Stone, the developers of Voice Dialogue.

- **Transpersonal Dialogue International**
  http://www.TranspersonalDialogue.com
  The integration of Voice Dialogue and Transpersonal Dialogue, which supports the development of our full human potential.

APPENDIX E
AUTHENTICITY RESOURCES

Definition of Authenticity

To live life according to the needs of our inner being, rather than the demands of society or early conditioning.

Books

Anton, Corey. *Selfhood and Authenticity.* Albany, NY: State University of New York Press, 2001.

Cappannelli, George and Sedena. *Authenticity: Simple Strategies for Greater Meaning and Purpose at Work and at Home.* Cincinnati, OH: Emmis Books, 2004.

Guignon, Charles. *On Being Authentic: Thinking in Action.* New York: Routledge, *2004.*

Madden, Deirdre. *Authenticity.* Saint Paul, MN: Graywolf Press, 2005.

Robbins, Mike. *Be Yourself, Everyone Else is Already Taken: Transform Your Life with the Power of Authenticity.* San Francisco: Jossey-Bass, 2009.

Yifa. *Authenticity: Clearing the Junk: A Buddhist Perspective.* New York: Lantern Books, 2007.

Links to Articles

- **Journey into the Wilderness of Yourself**
  http://www.heroicjourney.com/pages/resources/articles/wildernessofself.htm
  by Marion Moss Hubbard.

- **Markers on the Path to Personal Authenticity**
  http://personal-authenticity-project.com/markers-path-personal-authenticity
  by Michael Nagel.

- **Who are You? Who is the Self that Would be Authentic?**
  http://personal-authenticity
  by Michael Nagel.

- **Some Psychological Skills which Enable Authentic Living**
  http://personal-authenticity
  by Michael Nagel.

- **The Power of Personal Authenticity**
  http://www.richardbrooke.com/blogs/blog_011509.asp
  by Richard B. Brooke.

- **Authenticity**
  http://www.authenticityconsulting.com/
  by Carter McNamara, MBA, PhD.

- **Sharing your Authentic Self**
  http://managementhelp.org/blogs/spirituality/2010/04/25/sharing-your-authentic
  by Linda Ferguson.

Websites

- **Heroic Journey Consulting**
  http://www.heroicjourney.com/pdfs/heroicevaluation.pdf
  Authenticity – One of the Ten Heroic Characteristics
  Take the Resilience Challenge - How evolved you are on each of the heroic parameters?

- **Personal Authenticity Project**
  http://personal-authenticity-project.com/
  Exploring the path, practice, and significance of personal authenticity.

- **Authenticity** as a Philosophy (Wikipedia)
  http://en.wikipedia.org/wiki/Authenticity
  The philosophy of the conscious self coming to terms with being in a material world.

APPENDIX F

BODY WISDOM RESOURCES

Definition of Body Wisdom

In addition to housing the physical components that allow us to exist, our body stores the memories of our thoughts, emotions and psyche. Body wisdom is listening to the overt and subtle signals about what is going on within us that our body naturally emits. Particular body parts more readily hold particular messages. Back problems may indicate feeling a lack of support. Chest tightness may be an effort to protect the heart. Leg problems may relate to difficulty with moving forward in life. As we become more adept at tuning into our body's signals and deciphering their meaning, our body can relax knowing we have received the communication. Listening to our body's wisdom can invigorate our body and make it come alive. It also can transform it into one of our strongest allies on our journey of self-discovery.

Books

Chopra, Deepak. *Perfect Health: The Complete Mind/Body Guide.* New York: Harmony Books, 1991.

David, Marc. *Nourishing Wisdom: A Mind-Body Approach to Nutrition and Well-Being.* New York: Random House, 1991.

Hartley, Linda. *Wisdom of the Body Moving: An Introduction to Body-Mind Centering.* Berkley, CA: North Atlantic Books, 1995.

Hay, Louise. *Heal Your Body A-Z: The Mental Causes for Physical Illness and the Way to Overcome Them.* Carlsbad, CA: Hay House, 1998.

Kabat-Zinn, Jon. *Full Catastrophe Living: Using the Wisdom of Your Body and Mind to Face Stress, Pain, and Illness.* New York: Bantam Dell, 2005.

Kamm, Laura Alden. *Intuitive Wellness: Using Your Body's Inner Wisdom to Heal.* New York: Atria Books, 2006.

Knaster, Mirka. *Discovering the Body's Wisdom.* New York: Bantum Books, 1996.

LaMothe, Kimerer. *What a Body Knows: Finding Wisdom in Desire.* Ropley, Hants, UK: O Books, 2009.

Levine, Peter. *Healing Trauma: A Pioneering Program for Restoring the Wisdom of Your Body.* Bolder, CO: Sounds True, Inc., 2005.

Lowen, Alexander. *Bioenergetics*, New York: Penguin/Arkana, 1994.

Northrup, Christiane. *The Wisdom of Menopause: Creating Physical and Emotional Health and Healing During the Change.* New York: Bantam Books, 2003.

Northrup, Christiane. *Women's Bodies, Women's Wisdom: Creating Physical and Emotional Health and Healing.* New York: Bantam Books, 2010.

Sarno, John. *The Mindbody Prescription: Healing the Body.* New York: Warner Books, Inc., 1998.

Scurlock-Durana, Suzanne. *Full Body Presence: Learning to Listen to Your Body's Wisdom.* Novata, CA: Nataraj Publishing, 2010.

Weiselfish-Giammatteo, Sharon. *Body*. Berkley, CA: North Atlantic Books, 2002.

Audiobooks

Dyer, Wayne and Christiane Northrup. *Inside-Out Wellness: The Wisdom of Mind/Body Healing*. (Audiobook, CD). Hay House, 2009.

Northrup, Christine. *Women's Bodies, Women's Wisdom 2-CD set* (Audiobook, CD). New York: Bantam Dell, 2006.

APPENDIX G.1a

HEROIC CHARACTER SELF-EVALUATION TOOL

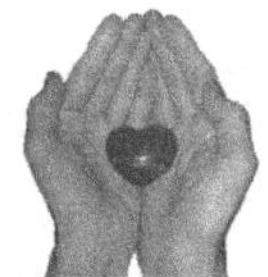

Test Your Heroic Mettle. See how evolved you are on each of these heroic parameters.

Description of Heroic Trait	Undeveloped → Fully Developed
1. **Clear Sense of Self** My choices and actions are guided from within.	Total Score from **1. a-d** ☐ divided by 4 = ☐
a. I am able to distinguish between society's values and beliefs and those reflective of my own nature and choosing.	1 2 3 4 5 6 7 8 9 10
b. I have a strong moral compass that directs my actions.	1 2 3 4 5 6 7 8 9 10
c. I love myself and appreciate who I am.	1 2 3 4 5 6 7 8 9 10
d. I radiate self-confidence.	1 2 3 4 5 6 7 8 9 10
2. **Authenticity** I have internal and external harmony.	Total Score from **2. a-d** ☐ divided by 4 = ☐
a. I am dedicated to discovering and living from my personal *Truth*.	1 2 3 4 5 6 7 8 9 10
b. I walk my talk.	1 2 3 4 5 6 7 8 9 10
c. I acknowledge and forgive myself for my shortcomings.	1 2 3 4 5 6 7 8 9 10
d. I am able to laugh at my "humanness."	1 2 3 4 5 6 7 8 9 10

Description of Heroic Trait	Undeveloped → Fully Developed
3. **Heart-Felt Connection to Others** I am open-hearted in my contact with other human beings.	Total Score from **3. a-d** ☐ divided by 4 = ☐
a. I listen deeply to what others have to say.	1 2 3 4 5 6 7 8 9 10
b. I have compassion for the challenges others face.	1 2 3 4 5 6 7 8 9 10
c. I appreciate the differences between people and value the richness and diversity those differences bring to life.	1 2 3 4 5 6 7 8 9 10
d. I actively seek collaboration and partnership opportunities.	1 2 3 4 5 6 7 8 9 10
4. **Passionate Enthusiasm** I live life boldly and fully.	Total Score from **4. a-d** ☐ divided by 4 = ☐
a. I have an optimistic attitude about life.	1 2 3 4 5 6 7 8 9 10
b. I am eager to discover and fulfill my life's mission.	1 2 3 4 5 6 7 8 9 10
c. I take personal responsibility for my thoughts and actions.	1 2 3 4 5 6 7 8 9 10
d. I accept challenges that push me to evolve beyond my perceived limitations.	1 2 3 4 5 6 7 8 9 10

Description of Heroic Trait	Undeveloped → Fully Developed
5. **Leadership** I demonstrate my leadership capabilities regardless of my title or position in an organization.	Total Score from **6. a-d** ☐ divided by 4 = ☐
a. I am a visionary, who can see practical bridges to the future.	1 2 3 4 5 6 7 8 9 10
b. I focus on finding creative solutions in the midst of difficulty.	1 2 3 4 5 6 7 8 9 10
c. I courageously take right action even when the personal consequences may be high.	1 2 3 4 5 6 7 8 9 10
6. **Seeker of Purpose and Meaning** I find value in everyday experiences.	Total Score from **5. a-d** ☐ divided by 4 = ☐
a. I see life in a context that brings me fulfillment, joy, and inner peace.	1 2 3 4 5 6 7 8 9 10
b. I have a healthy sense of my place in the world.	1 2 3 4 5 6 7 8 9 10
c. I am open to learning from both positive and negative experiences.	1 2 3 4 5 6 7 8 9 10
d. I am alert to synchronicities (meaningful coincidences) knowing that they provide me with important messages or answers.	1 2 3 4 5 6 7 8 9 10
e. I act as an example for others to follow even when no one is looking.	1 2 3 4 5 6 7 8 9 10

Description of Heroic Trait		Undeveloped → Fully Developed
7.	**Service-Oriented Perspective** My willingness to serve extends beyond my self-interests.	Total Score from **7. a-d** ☐ divided by 4 = ☐
a.	I feel a strong sense of responsibility for the good of all concerned.	1 2 3 4 5 6 7 8 9 10
b.	I am able to balance my needs with the wellbeing of others.	1 2 3 4 5 6 7 8 9 10
c.	I use my special talents as an outlet of self-expression and for the benefit of others.	1 2 3 4 5 6 7 8 9 10
d.	I am an effective agent of change in service to society and the planet.	1 2 3 4 5 6 7 8 9 10
8.	**Awareness** My internal observer plays an active role in my life.	Total Score from **8. a-d** ☐ divided by 4 = ☐
a.	I easily access both intuitive and logical ways of knowing.	1 2 3 4 5 6 7 8 9 10
b.	I am able to be both a player in my life and the director choosing how I play out the role.	1 2 3 4 5 6 7 8 9 10
c.	I am open to learning and evolving based on new input and experiences.	1 2 3 4 5 6 7 8 9 10
d.	I see the key factors in situations that can lead to transformational change.	1 2 3 4 5 6 7 8 9 10

Description of Heroic Trait	Undeveloped → Fully Developed
9. **Commitment to Excellence** I aspire to do my best.	Total Score from **9. a-d** ☐ divided by 4 = ☐
a. I am self-motivated to achieve my goals and dreams.	1 2 3 4 5 6 7 8 9 10
b. I have a clear understanding of the differences between "excellence" and "perfection."	1 2 3 4 5 6 7 8 9 10
c. I have a healthy balance in my life between "doing" and "being."	1 2 3 4 5 6 7 8 9 10
d. My success is based not only on external outcomes, but also on my ability to do the best I can on a moment by moment basis.	1 2 3 4 5 6 7 8 9 10
10. **Resilience** I am able to bounce back from adversity.	Total Score from **10. a-d** ☐ divided by 4 = ☐
a. I persevere despite difficulties.	1 2 3 4 5 6 7 8 9 10
b. I easily adapt to changing environments.	1 2 3 4 5 6 7 8 9 10
c. I am hopeful about the future.	1 2 3 4 5 6 7 8 9 10
d. I am able to see humor in the human drama.	1 2 3 4 5 6 7 8 9 10

Scoring:

1 - 4 Needs a lot of attention. Could be severely hampering you from effectively functioning in the world

5 - 7 Focus on further development can help you achieve your full potential

8 - 9 With some fine tuning, could help you become even more effective

10 A great strength that allows you to maximize your potential and fulfill your dreams

APPENDIX G.1b

EXERCISE 1: HEROIC CHARACTER TRAIT RE-EXAMINATION

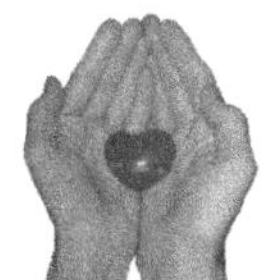

This exercise helps you review your past experiences in terms of how each one helped you develop a particular heroic character trait. The list of traits below is by no means exhaustive or the ones that specifically fit for you, but they may exemplify heroic traits you want to consider more fully embodying.

Heroic Character Traits	
Clear Sense of Self Choices and actions are guided from within	**Leadership** Demonstrate leadership capabilities regardless of title or position in an organization
Authenticity Internal and external harmony	**Service-Oriented Perspective** Willingness to serve extends beyond self interests
Heart-Felt Connection to Others Open-hearted in contact with other human beings	**Awareness** Internal observer plays an active role in life
Passionate Enthusiasm Live life fully and boldly	**Commitment to Excellence** Aspire to do one's best
Seeker of Purpose and Meaning Find value in everyday experiences	**Resilience** Ability to bounce back from adversity

Follow the steps below for this exercise:

- **Step 1:** As you read each trait above, see if you have any associated past experiences that flash into your mind. If so, without thinking too much about them, jot them down under the related trait below. If you thought of other traits, add them to this list and write down any past experiences that relate to them.
- **Step 2:** Now, go back and write down what these experiences taught you about the related character trait.

1. **Clear Sense of Self -** Choices and actions are guided from within
   a. Relevant experiences:
   Example: *When I was ten years old, two of my friends decided to shoplift at the corner drugstore. I wouldn't participate even though they called me "chicken."*

   b. What these experiences taught me:
   Example: *This was the first time I realized that I had a good sense of who I was and that I would adhere to my values no matter what the consequences. I was proud of myself for having a strong enough character not to bend to peer pressure.*

2. **Authenticity** - Internal and external harmony
   a. Relevant experiences:

   b. What these experiences taught me:

3. **Heart-Felt Connection to Others** - Open-hearted in contact with other human beings
   a. Relevant experiences:

b. What these experiences taught me:

____

____

____

4. **Passionate Enthusiasm** - Live life fully and boldly
   a. Relevant experiences:

____

____

____

   b. What these experiences taught me:

____

____

____

5. **Seeker of Purpose and Meaning** - Find value in everyday experiences
   a. Relevant experiences:

____

____

____

   b. What these experiences taught me:

____

____

____

6. **Leadership** - Demonstrate leadership capabilities regardless of title or position in an organization
   a. Relevant experiences:

____

____

____

b. What these experiences taught me:

____

____

____

7. **Service-oriented Perspective** - Willingness to serve extends beyond self interests
   a. Relevant experiences:

   ____

   ____

   ____

   b. What these experiences taught me:

   ____

   ____

   ____

8. **Awareness** - Internal observer plays an active role in life
   a. Relevant experiences:

   ____

   ____

   ____

   b. What these experiences taught me:

   ____

   ____

   ____

9. **Commitment to Excellence** - Aspire to do one's best
   a. Relevant experiences:

   ____

   ____

   ____

b. What these experiences taught me:

____

____

____

10. **Resilience** - Ability to bounce back from adversity

a. Relevant experiences:

____

____

____

b. What these experiences taught me:

____

____

____

11. **Other Trait** - ______________________________________

a. Relevant experiences:

____

____

____

b. What these experiences taught me:

____

____

____

12. **Other Trait** - ______________________________________

a. Relevant experiences:

____

____

____

b. What these experiences taught me:

____

____

____

APPENDIX G.2

EXERCISE 2: CREATE EACH PLOT ELEMENT FOR YOUR HEROIC NARRATIVE

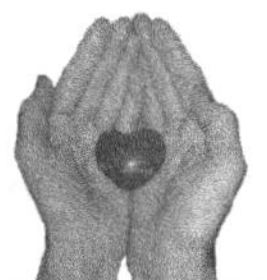

Once you have completed *Exercise 1:Heroic Character Trait Re-examination* (*Appendix G.1b*), you are ready to create the individual of your heroic narrative. Using the heroic story framework provided below, on a separate piece of paper, write your specific narrative details. Allow yourself time for this exercise and do not put undue pressure on yourself to finish it all at once. If you don't feel that you have progressed through a particular phase of your journey yet, fill in the details as best as you can for now. You can always come back to this or any of the other exercises at a future time when you have a different, and likely more evolved perspective about your self-forgiveness journey.

Note: Write your narrative elements in the past tense, as if it is an autobiography you are writing at the end of your life. By seeing your story as already having occurred, it helps you develop your observer skills and it acts as a visualization that facilitates your ability to see your heroic story as already fulfilled.

Hint About Creating Your Story:
Although the story elements are presented sequentially, your journey does not actually unfold in a logical linear fashion. As you come to awareness on one aspect of your life, it informs another aspect, which also may change in the process. Allow yourself to write your story elements in whatever order naturally emerges. As one part of your story becomes more crystallized you may want to go back and change something you previously wrote. Writing in this iterative way is an important technique in storytelling, which engages all levels of your being, including body, mind, emotions, and spirit. It allows you to weave together your story elements into a personalized and cohesive

whole. Some of the later exercises and tools referenced in *Chapter 28* will also help you evolve and crystallize your story.

Heroic Narrative Plot Elements

- **Plot Element 1: *My Introduction* - My "Heroic Call to Adventure."** This is the situation, either externally or internally, that drew you into your *Heroic Journey* of self-forgiveness. From a story perspective it is the challenge, conflict or problem you faced as the main character of your story that set you on your current path of introspection, learning, and growth.
  Example: *I was at my wits end. My life seemed to be falling apart. I had tried everything I could think of to pull the pieces back together with no success. It was when I thought about suicide and dismissed it as an option that my Heroic Journey of self-forgiveness truly began.*

- **Plot Element 2: *My Journey Inward* - What I had to shed that no longer served me.** What did you have to forgive yourself for believing, feeling or doing? You may want to review the chapters in *Part 2* to remind yourself about some of your major challenges. The very act of thinking deeply about this question and physically writing down your response can help you put additional distance between painful past experiences and who you are becoming. Reviewing the following questions and answering the ones that have the most relevance to you may help with this process:
  - What was my biggest regret in life? What helped me the most with my self-forgiveness process concerning this regret?
  - What were the most difficult emotional challenges I had to face related to self-forgiveness? What emotional strengths did I drawn upon to get through these challenges?
  - What bad habits of thought did I have to change to let go of guilt or shame about my past? How did I reframe those thoughts to release myself from the past?

- In what ways did I feel like a victim of circumstance? What helped me the most to stop feeling like a victim?
- What form did my personal criticism take? Was there someone else's voice that I had internalized, which I needed to release?
- Was there an area of my life where I unrealistically demanded perfectionism? What helped me to release my unrealistic demands?
- In what ways did I compare myself to others that didn't serve me? What insight helped me stop doing that?
- In what areas of life did I demonstrate self-righteousness? What did I do to take myself off my own pedestal?
- In what ways did I hold myself hostage to my past? What did I do to release myself from this self-imposed prison?
- What were some of my biggest challenges with my family? Were there any specific situations that especially triggered me? What did I do to clear my issues related to particular family members?
- Were there areas of my life that I used to worry about incessantly? Did I have anxiety about anything that caused negative physical side effects? What helped me break my worry habit?
- Are there ways I used to trap myself in a negative thinking cycle? What did I do to extract myself from my thought trap?
- Are there ways I used to punish my body, such as putting myself down for innate traits I couldn't change, being over/underweight, or being addicted to food/alcohol/illegal substances? What did I do to stop punishing myself?

- **Plot Element 3: *Arriving at the Center of Myself* – The process of claiming my inner wisdom.** Answer the following questions: (You may want to review the chapters and answers to exercises you worked through in *Part 3* to jog your memory.)
    - What shadow aspects of myself did I have to claim and forgive that I previously rejected or didn't even consciously recognize that I had?
    - What were the gifts under each of these shadow aspects of myself?
    - What core pain did I have to face? How did I come to terms with this pain?
    - How did my wisdom help me gain insight and transform these shadow aspects of myself?
    - What deeper insights concerning self-forgiveness did I learn from this phase of my journey?

- **Plot Element 4: *Winding Outward* – How I honed my authenticity.** Answer the following questions: (You may want to review the chapters and answers to exercises you worked through in *Part 4* to jog your memory.)
    - How was I challenged to become more authentic?
    - What incidents most tested my authenticity?
    - What people skills were most challenging for me to learn in this phase?
    - What helped me the most to live more fully in the present moment?
    - What aspects of life most challenged my patience? What helped me become a more patient person?
    - What special gifts have I given to the world? What were some of my biggest impediments to bringing those gifts into reality? Did I have to forgive any aspects of myself for holding myself back from sharing my gifts with others? If so, what steps did I take that helped propel me forward on my personal path?

- What were some of the consistent messages my body told me that were most challenging for me to hear? What helped me the most in listening to my body wisdom? Were there specific instances related to listening to my body that were epiphanies in self-understanding or self-forgiveness?
- How did I grow in wisdom as I aged? What did I learn in each decade of my life, particularly as it related to self-forgiveness? What words of wisdom do I have for the next generation?

- **Plot Element 5: *My Happy Ending* – What I learned and cherished the most about my amazing self-forgiveness journey.** This is the plot element where you synthesize what your experiences meant to you. You will write it as if you are at the end of your life, leading yourself through a retrospective overview of your self-forgiveness journey. You will show yourself what made your life so valuable and special. Below are some questions that may help you write this element:
  - What are three of the key situations in my past that helped me become more self-forgiving?
  - Who were the people who were most meaningful to me on my self-forgiveness journey? What made them so special? How did having them in my life at strategic times help me blossom and mature?
  - In what ways did I demonstrate my heroic maturity?
  - What brought me the most joy about my experiences in life?
  - What am I most proud of about myself and how my life evolved?

APPENDIX G.3

EXERCISE 3: CREATE YOUR INNER WHISPERINGS JOURNAL

For purposes of this exercise you will create a journal designed to record your inner whisperings that call to you from inside out as they occur. The very act of keeping a journal activates your conscious awareness to pay attention to what your inner whisperings have to say. The following steps may help you consciously affirm your inner whisperings and give them a stronger voice in your life.

- **Step 1: Let your inner artist take the lead on creating your journal.** Your *Inner Artist* is, by its very nature, much more in touch with the intuitive levels of creation. By giving this creative part of you the task of creating your *Inner Whisperings Journal*, you invite the communication between the inner aspects of yourself and your conscious awareness. Let your *Inner Artist* select your journal and decorate it. What colors and textures speak to you? Are there pictures that have a particular meaning or represent an archetypal symbol that is important to you? Let your journal evolve as you feel guided to add more embellishment over time.

- **Step 2: Invite your inner whisperings to come forth**. Once you have created your *Inner Whisperings Journal* there are some actions you can take to help invite your inner whisperings to reveal their wisdom to you. In addition to reviewing *Chapter 17* and doing the exercise, *Take Notes with a Grateful Heart* on page 123, here are some idea to help activate your receptivity:
  - See yourself as a reporter ready to take down what this very important subject of your story has to say.
  - Ask yourself, just before you go to sleep, "Is there something you want to share with me through my dreams?" When you first wake up, while you are still in that twilight state, be ready to write down any dreams you

remember. They may contain very important messages of wisdom that will make sense only to you.

- Ask yourself several times throughout the day as you think of it, "What do I need to know now to get to a deeper level of self-forgiveness?" Then let go of the thought and allow yourself to mull it over in your unconscious. Don't be surprised if your inner whisperings bubble to the surface when you least expect them. Having your *Inner Whisperings Journal* by your side allows you to be ready to record the messages whenever they come to light.

- **Step 3: Revise your heroic narrative based on the insight gained from your inner whisperings**. Each time your inner whisperings speak a deep *Truth* to you, look back at your heroic plot elements in *Exercise 2 (Appendix G.2)* and see if this revelation changes your story in any way. Adjusting your story to incorporate your new insight, helps you reclaim another strand of your past into the here and now and makes it less likely that your new insight will recede back into your unconscious.

APPENDIX G.4
EXERCISE 4: LET YOUR *WISE NARRATOR* RETELL YOUR STORY

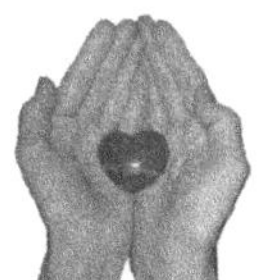

For purposes of this exercise, your internal *Wise One* becomes the narrator of your heroic story of self-forgiveness. By seeing your story through the eyes of your *Wise One*, you understand why the details of your story unfolded just as they did and how what you experienced helped you create a more meaningful and joyful life.

- **Step 1: Review your answers in the Voice Dialogue exercise, *Transform Your Shadow's Sub-Personalities into Trusted Allies*.** (See *Chapter 19*, pages 139-144.) This review, especially if you have had a little distance in time from when you first did the exercise, can help you see how each shadow aspect of your personality contributed to creating a greater sense of wholeness and an internal self-forgiving environment.

- **Step 2: Create transformative mini stories about your shadow sub-personalities.** From the information that you filled out in **Table 19.2** (page 141), create a one or two sentence story about each shadow sub-personality you worked with in that exercise. (Remember to write your stories in past tense.)
    - ***Example 1***: For the *Harsh Critic*: "I used to have a *Harsh Critic,* who relentlessly berated me when I made mistakes. But, I transformed this part of me into a *Coach,* who was able to discern when to push me and when to gently provide encouragement when I felt frustrated."
    - ***Example 2***: For the *Saboteur:* "My internal *Saboteur* used to undermine my ability to move forward. This part of me evolved into my *Advocate of Reason,* who slowed me down long enough to evaluate the situation and determine the best course of action."

- ***Example 3:*** For the *Whiny Child*: "My *Whiny Child* used to constantly demand my attention with nagging and complaining, which cut into my work time and made me really resent her. But, I realized in really listening to her that she was actually my *Playful Child*, who wanted the best for me and kept my workaholic from totally taking over my life.

- **Step 3: Create your larger *Internal Dream Team* story.** For this step in the exercise, you will take the perspective of your internal *Wise One,* who is the director of your life play. Integrate the individual stories of your sub-personalities from step 2 above into a more cohesive plot about how each of your *Internal Dream Team* members contributed to your heroic story of self-forgiveness. After you have completed your story, read it back to yourself several times. As you do, notice if your story feels richer and has a more vibrant texture than it did before you began this exercise. Hopefully this integration process will give you a greater appreciation for the wisdom you bring to your unfolding storyline. (Remember to also write this story in past tense.)
Example: As I owned my shadow sub-personalities, I came to appreciate my *Internal Dream Team* for how well it protected me and helped me succeed in life. My *Advocate of Reason* slowed me down and kept me from making rash decisions that might otherwise have sabotaged my ability to fulfill my goals. When I was hard on myself for taking too long in my decision-making, my *Coach* reminded me to be gentle with myself and encouraged me to take all the time I needed to make the best decision possible. My *Playful Child* reminded me not to take myself so seriously and enjoy the journey along the way. Understanding the value of each of the team members gave me immense gratitude for the role they played in helping me better understand my internal motivations,

refocusing my attention on what was important in life, and helping me forgive myself for all the punishment I inflicted on myself in the past due to my lack of awareness.

- **Step 4: Refine your *Internal Dream Team* story.** As more of your shadow sub-personalities come to light and are transformed, refine your self-forgiveness story in step 3 above to incorporate these new team members. Each time you bring sub-personalities out of the shadows and recognize their contribution, you develop a deeper level of self respect and allow them to become co-creators in your storyline of personal evolution.

- **Step 5: Incorporate your *Internal Dream Team* story into your heroic narrative.** Now that your *Wise Narrator* has helped you create your *Internal Dream Team* story, you are ready to fold it into your heroic narrative. Insert your story from step 3 above into *Plot Element 3*, in ***Exercise 2: Create Each Plot Element for Your Heroic Narrative (Appendix G.2***). Allow your *Wise Narrator* to fill in gaps that make your story more cohesive. Here are some questions that may help you see your heroic narrative from your *Wise Narrator* vantage point:
  - Does adding my *Internal Dream Team* story into *Plot Element 3* change my understanding of what I previously wrote for this element?
  - Does adding my *Internal Dream Team* story into *Plot Element* change my understanding of any of my other plot elements?
  - What is the most memorable insight I have learned about myself from this process?
    - Did this insight help me forgive any additional aspects of myself?
    - Did this insight help me discard any additional pieces of my story that no longer fit who I became?
  - Is there something that I appreciate more fully about myself from having completed this exercise?

APPENDIX G.5

EXERCISE 5: ANCHOR YOUR NEW STORY

This exercise is designed to anchor your new story more firmly within by bridge from your old story to the new. For purposes of the exercise, you will use **Table G.5** below as you work through each step.

- **Step 1:** In column 1, list all of the elements of your old story that still feel true, but do not contribute to a transformational storyline. It may help to go back to the chapters in *Part 2* to remind yourself what you still need to shed that does not serve you. You may want to review *Chapter 19* to see the shadow parts of yourself that have not yet been fully integrated. You may also want to review *Chapter 20* and check in with yourself about any core pain that still stings when you think about it.
- **Step 2**: Using the second column, let your *Wise Narrator* tell you, from the past tense, how you transformed these residual elements in ways that were more consistent with your new heroic storyline.
- **Step 3**: Using this completed exercise, update the plot elements in your heroic narrative (*Appendix G.2*) with how your *Wise Narrator* helped you transform the old story.

Residual Pieces of My Old Story	How My *Wise Narrator* Helped Me Transform This Old Story (Write in past tense)
Example: *I still have a lot of anxiety about what the future holds.*	***Example***: *When I started to feel anxious, my* Wise Narrator *reminded me that I was resourceful and I had the life experiences and internal wisdom necessary to deal with whatever came my direction.*
Example: *I still feel I "should" know more about love relationships than I actually do.*	***Example:*** *When I was hard on myself for not being more enlightened in my love relationship, my* Wise Narrator *reminded me that it was unrealistic for me to expect that I would know everything. It takes practice to do the dance of relationship without stepping on one another's toes.*

Table G.5. Examples of how your *Wise Narrator* can reframe your story.

APPENDIX G.6

EXERCISE 6: TAKE ACTION TO EVOLVE YOUR STORY

This exercise is designed to help you recognize when it is time to change your self-forgiveness story. It also gives you some simple action steps you can take to evolve your story to the next level. With practice, these steps will become a natural way of processing past experiences and integrating them into your continually evolving story.

- **Step 1**: Put a check mark in the box next to any statement below that you feel pertains to you right now. Statements you checked may be clues alerting you that it is time to evolve a particular aspect of your self-forgiveness story. Reading this list may help you realize there are other clues you didn't previously recognize, but are actually significant as well. Add those to your list.
  - ❑ I have a nagging feeling I need to go deeper to examine another aspect of myself that I have studiously avoided for years or built defenses to deny.
  - ❑ I have lost interest in material possessions and I feel I need to simplify my lifestyle.
  - ❑ I feel irritated about my job or living situation, but I don't know specifically why.
  - ❑ I feel a strong desire to explore a childhood dream or talent I never developed, but I haven't actually done it yet.
  - ❑ I feel bored with my life and know it is time to spice it up in some way.
  - ❑ I feel a magnetic pull beyond my conscious control toward a particular person, place, new interest, or path not yet explored. This strong pull I feel is:

    ____

    ____

- ❑ Other ______________________________
- ❑ Other ______________________________
- ❑ Other ______________________________

- **Step 2**: Put a star by the clue you checked that you most identify with at the moment.
- **Step 3**: For the clue you put a star by, write an action statement that reflects what you will do to help you evolve your story.
  - **Action Statement Example**: *I've always wanted to paint, but never pursued it because I felt I wasn't very creative. I forgive myself for suppressing my creative urge. I will sign up for a painting class this fall to explore this lifelong desire.*
  - **My Action Statement:**

    ____

    ____

    ____
- **Step 4**: Based on your action statement above, now write an addendum to your evolving story. (Write this statement in the past tense.)

  Story Addendum Example: *I used to tell myself I wasn't creative, but then I realized that I was a creative person, continually exploring new avenues that expressed my creativity.*

  My Story Addendum:

  ____

  ____
- **Step 5**: Using your statement from step 4 above, update the plot elements in your heroic narrative (*Appendix G.2*) to better reflect your evolving journey.

APPENDIX G.7
EXERCISE 7: EXPAND YOUR STORY

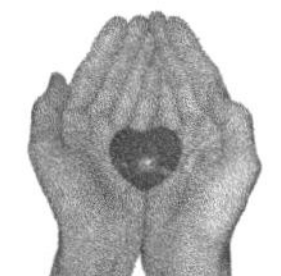

This exercise is designed to help you merge you personal story into the collective story of transformational change. You will examine how you used what you learned to contribute to society in positive ways. For purposes of this exercise, you will use the table below as you work through each step.

- **Step 1:** Look back over the previous exercises and pull out the top three nuggets that you learned about self-forgiveness from your amazing journey. Write each of them down in column 1.
- **Step 2:** Use column 2 to see how your previous experiences gave you the personal wisdom to pay your knowledge forward and help change the collective story. (Remember to write your responses in the past tense.)
- **Step 3**: Using this completed exercise, update plot element 5 in your heroic narrative (*Appendix G.2*). Review the other plot elements to see if this new addition changes in any way what you previously wrote.

Major Lessons from My Journey	How I Used What I Learned to Further the Collective Story
Example: *I learned that holding onto bitterness and harboring long term anger gave me a false sense of power. Once I forgave myself for the past, all that energy I was using to hang onto false power melted away. What I was left with was an internal peace that was the real core of my power.*	***Example***: *I used what I learned about personal peace to support community organizations that teach peace to children. Throughout the remainder of my life I was dedicated to helping children grow up knowing what took me so many years as an adult to understand.*

BACK MATTER

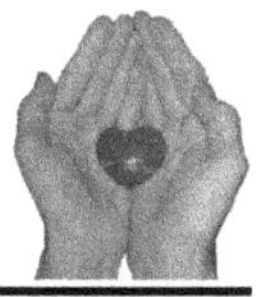

CHAPTER NOTES

Part 1: Create Your Heroic Story of Self-Forgiveness

1 Adapted from Annette Simmons, *The Story Factor: Secrets of Influence from the Art of Storytelling* (New York: Basic Books, 2001), p. 32.

2 Joseph Campbell, *The Hero with a Thousand Faces* (Princeton, N.J.: Princeton University Press, 1949).

3 Carol S. Pearson, *The Hero Within: Six Archetypes We Live By* (New York, Harper & Row, Publishers, Inc., 1986).

4 Carol S. Pearson, *Awakening the Heroes Within: Twelve Archetypes to Help Us Find Ourselves and Transform the World* (New York: Harper & Row, Publishers, Inc., 1991).

5 Carol S. Pearson, *The Hero Within: Six Archetypes We Live By* (New York: Harper & Row, Publishers, Inc., 1986), p. 152.

6 In both her books, *The Hero Within* and *Awakening the Heroes Within*, Carol S. Pearson acknowledges that there is a popular confusion in our society that equates "Hero" with "Warrior," in which the hero is seen as a combative figure. She presents a different perspective of the hero's journey that encompasses other archetypal plots (of which the *warrior* is only one). This perspective of the hero helps us identify with the more positive aspects of the archetype and further develop our heroic character. "Heroes fight for a principle, a cause, a way of life, or a future vision." Carol S. Pearson and Margaret Mark, *The Hero and the Outlaw* (New York: McGraw Hill, 2001), p. 106.

7 Adapted from Annette Simmons, *The Story Factor: Secrets of Influence from the Art of Storytelling* (New York: Basic Books, 2001), p. 51.

Chapter 1: To Forgive or Not to Forgive… That is the Question

1 Donald Kraybill, Steven Nolt, and David L. Weaver-Zercher, *Amish Grace: How Forgiveness Transcended Tragedy* (San Francisco, CA: Josey Bass, 2007).

2 Ibid, p. 182.

3 Mohandas Gandhi quote, *The Quotations Page*, accessed January 29, 2011, http://tinyurl.com/6hh7ttw.

4 Emmett E. "Bud" Welch in an interview with Sandy McPherson Carrubbam, "Oklahoma City Bombing: Two Fathers and Forgiveness," *AmericanCatholic.org*, accessed January 25, 2011, http://tinyurl.com/3fv84vd.

5 Ibid.

6 Malachy McCourt as quoted by Alex Witchel, "At Lunch with: Malachy McCourt—How a Rogue Turns Himself Into a Saint; The Blarney Fails to Hide an Emotional Directness," *The New York Times*, published July 29, 1998, accessed January 25, 2011, http://tinyurl.com/6b8a9vu.

7 Donald Kraybill, Steven Nolt, and David L. Weaver-Zercher, *Amish Grace: How Forgiveness Transcended Tragedy* (San Francisco, CA: Josey Bass, 2007), p. 126.

8 Rebecca Stoia-Caraballo, Mark S. Rye, Wei Pan, Keri J. Brown Kirschman, Catherine Lutz-Zois and Amy M. Lyons, "Negative Affect and Anger Rumination as Mediators Between Forgiveness and Sleep Quality," *Journal of Behavioral Medicine* 31: 6 (December 2008): 478-488.

9 J. W.Carson, F. J. Keefe, V. Goli, A. M. Fras, T. R. Lynch, S. R. Thorp, and J. L. Buechler, "Forgiveness and Chronic Low Back Pain: A Preliminary Study Examining the Relationship of Forgiveness to Pain, Anger, and Psychological Distress," *Journal of Pain* 6 (2005): pp. 84–91.

10 Martina A. Waltman, Douglas C. Russell, Catherine T. Coyle, Robert D. Enright, Anthony C. Holter, and Christopher M. Swoboda, "The Effects of a Forgiveness Intervention on Patients with Coronary Artery Disease," *Psychology & Health* 24:1 (January 2009): 11 – 27.

11 Sandi Dolbee, "The Healing Power of Forgiveness: Science Measures Physical as Well as Mental Benefits," *San Diego Union Tribune*, August 16, 2008, accessed January 24, 2011, http://tinyurl.com/6czfqyr. Writer Sandi Dolbee was one of ten participants in a 2008 Templeton-Cambridge Journalism Fellowships in Science and Religion. Her project was on the science of forgiveness, particularly how the ancient religious virtue is being popularized by studies showing that it has mental and physical health benefits. From the research on her project, she found hundreds of studies that linked forgiveness to improved physical and emotional well-being.

12 Loren L.Toussaint, David R. Williams, Marc A. Musick, and Susan A. Everson-Ross, *Mental Health, Religion & Culture* 11:5 (July 2008): 485.

13 Mike Celizic, "She Sent Him to Jail for Rape; Now They're Friends," *Today.com*, March 10, 2009, accessed March 2, 2011, http://tinyurl.com/3zvpqgz.

14 Ben Loeterman, "What Jennifer Saw: Cotton's Wrongful Conviction," *PBS Frontline Show # 1508*, Feb. 25, 1997.

15 Scot [sic] Abrahamson and Will Robinson, *"A Decade Behind Bars for a Rape he Didn't Commit," Center on Wrongful Convictions, Northwestern Law*, accessed on July 16, 2011, http://tinyurl.com/3qj84ol.

16 CBS News Online, 60 Minute Story, *Eyewitness Testimony*, March 8, 2009, accessed on YouTube.com Part 1 http://tinyurl.com/4y9kmgy and Part 2 http://tinyurl.com/3fz86g7.

Chapter 2: Follow Your Heroic Path of Transformation

1 Marion Moss Hubbard, *The Workplace Labyrinth: A Heroic Journey to the Center of Yourself*, an unpublished dissertation submitted in partial fulfillment of the requirements for the degree of Doctor of Philosophy in Transpersonal Psychology and Consciousness Studies, International University of Professional Studies (Maui, HI, 2001).

2 Marion Moss Hubbard, *Work as a Heroic Journey: Use the Workplace to Evolve Your Character and Consciousness* (San Diego, CA: Orion Publishing Company, 2005).

3 Hermann Kern, *Through the Labyrinth: Design and Meanings Over 5,000 Years* (New York: Prestel, 2000), p. 298.

4 Based on *Jeff Saward,* "The Centre of the Labyrinth," *Labyrinthos*, accessed on May 28, 2011, http://www.labyrinthos.net/centre.html.

5 Ibid.

6 It is no surprise that the Greek and Minoan versions of the labyrinth myth are so drastically different. Traditionally when dominator cultures take over another civilization, what they often do is destroy what the vanquished culture cherishes. Often symbols are declared to have the opposite meaning of what was previously culturally understood. "This demonization of earlier deities and religious symbols is a well-documented and recurrent mythical motif in recorded history." Riane Eisler, *Sacred Pleasures: Sex, Myth, and the Politics of the Body* (San Francisco: HarperSanFrancisco, 1995), p. 131.

7 Riane Eisler, *Sacred Pleasures: Sex, Myth, and the Politics of the Body* (San Francisco: HarperSanFrancisco, 1995), p. 130.

8 Ibid, pp. 131-132.

9 Marion Moss Hubbard, *Work as a Heroic Journey: Use the Workplace to Evolve Your Character and Consciousness* (San Diego, CA: Orion Publishing Company, 2005), pp. 16-24.

10 Ibid, p. 4.

11 Melissa West, *Exploring the Labyrinth: A Guide for Healing and Spiritual Growth* (New York: Broadway Books, 2000), p. 42.

12 Ibid, p. 156-158.

13 Ibid, p. 165.

Chapter 3: Let the Logic of Your Heart Guide You on Your Journey

1 Annette Simmons, *The Story Factor: Secrets of Influence from the Art of Storytelling* (New York: Basic Books, 2001), p. 56.

2 This rational perception of reality has greatly influenced the many areas of science, such as the interdisciplinary field of *cognitive science*. The term cognitive science was coined by theoretical chemist H. Christopher Longuet-Higgins in 1973 and it explores how the mind processes information. Scientific disciplines associated with cognitive sciences include cognitive linguistics, computational neuroscience, cognitive psychology, artificial intelligence, and the cognitive studies of memory and perception.

3 Physicist, philosopher and author Danah Zohar points out the limitation of the materialistic perception of reality. "For something to exist, the materialist says, it must be substantial, the substantial is the physical, and the physical is made out of matter, which in turn is made out of atoms. Thus we, the "selves" we perceive ourselves to be, are really just so many atoms briefly drawn together. We are our bodies, and our minds are a mere reflection of various atoms or neural processes." Danah Zohar, *Quantum Self: Human Nature and Consciousness Defined by the New Physics* (New York: William Morrow and Company, 1990), p. 95.

4 Kabir Helminski "The Heart: Threshold Between Two Worlds," in *Inner Knowing: Consciousness, Creativity, Insight and Intuition,* ed. Helen Palmer (New York: Jeremy P. Tarcher/Putnam, 1998), p. 245.

5 Ibid, p. 247.

6 Frances Vaughan, as quoted in Marilyn Mandala Schlitz, Cassandra Vieten, and Tina Amorok, *Living Deeply: The Art and Science of Transformation in Everyday Life* (Oakland, CA: New Harbinger Publications, Inc., 2007), p. 20.

7 Marilyn Mandala Schlitz, Cassandra Vieten, and Tina Amorok, *Living Deeply: The Art and Science of Transformation in Everyday Life* (Oakland, CA: New Harbinger Publications, Inc., 2007), p. 21.

8 Rollin McCraty, William A. Tiller, and Mike Atkinson, "Head-Heart Entrainment: A Preliminary Survey," *Proceedings of the Brain-Mind Applied Neurophysiology EEG Neurofeedback Meeting*. Key West, Florida, 1996, accessed on the *Institute of Heart Math* website, May 31, 2011, http://tinyurl.com/5s888oo.

9 Rollin McCraty and Mike Atkinson, "Cardiac Coherence Increases Heart-Brain Synchronization: Influence of Afferent Cardiovascular Input on Cognitive Performance and Alpha Activity," *Proceedings of the Annual Meeting of the Pavlovian Society*. Tarrytown, NY, 1999. Accessed on the *Institute of Heart Math* website, May 31, 2011, http://tinyurl.com/5s888oo.

Part 2:The Journey Inward: Shed What No Longer Serves You

1 Jill Purce, *Mystic Spiral: Journey of the Soul* (Great Britain: Thames & Hudson, 1974), p. 15.

2 Anne Wilson Schaef, *Beyond Therapy, Beyond Science* (New York: HarperCollins Publishers, 1992), p. 154.

Chapter 4: Do Your Emotional Housecleaning

1 Anonymous, "A Twelve-Step Approach to Atonement," in *Beyond Forgiveness: Reflections on Atonement,* ed. Phil Cousineau (San Francisco: Jossey-Bass, 2011), p. 97.

2 A pseudonym has been used to protect the identity of the storyteller.

3 Marion Moss Hubbard, *Removing Your Mask: No More Hiding from Your Truth* (Orion Publishing Company: Seattle WA, 1992). *http://www.heroicjourney.com/pages/products.htm*.

Chapter 5: Look for Clues of What to Forgive

1 O. Patterson, *Slavery and Social Death: A Comparative Study* (Cambridge, MA: Harvard University Press, 1982).

2 A pseudonym has been used to protect the identity of the storyteller.

Chapter 6: Stop Bad Habits of Thought

1 Psychotherapist and author Ted Kuntz, as interviewed by Trudy Peskett, in "Daily Acts of Kindness Combat Stress," *Health Action Network Society,* January 24, 2008, accessed January 21, 2011, http://tinyurl.com/3ozumx8.

2 Oakley Ray, "How the Mind Hurts and Heals the Body," *American Psychologist* (January 2004): p. 32.

3 B. Justice, "Critical Life Events and the Onset of Illness," *Comprehensive Therapy 20* (1994): pp. 232–238.

4 M. Watson, J. S. Haviland, S. Greer, J. Davidson, and J. M. Bliss, "Influence of Psychological Response on Survival in Breast Cancer: A Population-based Cohort Study," *Lancet* 354:9187 (1999): 1331–1336. The study followed women with early stage breast cancer for five years and reported that their fighting spirit "was not associated with improved survival," 1335. But, "patients who had a high score on the helpless measure at baseline were more likely to have relapsed or died during the five years." 1335.

5 D. P. Phillips, T. E. Ruth, and L. M. Wagner, "Psychology and Survival," *Lancet* 342:8880 (1993): 1142–1145. Chinese-Americans, but not Whites, die significantly earlier than normal (1.3 to 4.9 yr) if they have a combination of disease and birth year, which Chinese astrology and medicine consider ill-fated. The more strongly a group is attached to Chinese traditions, the more years of life are lost. The results hold for nearly all major causes of death studied. 1142.

6 Becca R. Levy, Martin D. Slade, Suzanne R. Kunkel, and Stanislav V. Kasl, "Longevity Increased by Positive Self-Perceptions of Aging," *Journal of Personality and Social Psychology* 83:2 (2002): 261–270. The study found that the median survival of those in the more positive self-perceptions of aging group was 7.6 years longer than the median survival of those in the more negative aging self-stereotype group.

7 Staff writer, "Positive and Negative Stress," *StressFocus.com* website, accessed on January, 16, 2012, http://tinyurl.com/7f7drxf.

8 Muhammad Ali quote, Brainyquotes.com, accessed January 29, 2011, http://tinyurl.com/5s69l4x.

9 Phil Shapiro, "Affirmations: The Power of Thought," *Dr. Phil Shapiro, M.D.* website, accessed February 11, 2011, http://www.philipshapiro.com/art-affirmations.

10 Wayne Dyer, *You'll See It When You Believe It* (New York: HarperCollins, 1989).

11 Louise Hay, *Heal Your Body A-Z: The Mental Causes for Physical Illness and the Way to Overcome Them* (Carlsbad, CA: Hay House, 1998).

12 Shakti Gwain, *Creative Visualization: Use the Power of Your Imagination to Create What You Want in Your Life* (Novato, CA: Nataraj Publishing, 2002), p. 12.

Chapter 7: Rid Yourself of the Victim Mentality

1 Marion Moss Hubbard, *Removing Your Mask: No More Hiding from Your Truth* (Seattle, WA: Orion Publishing Company, 1992).

2 For more information about Eva Mozes Kor and her life's work see C.A.N.D.L.E.S Holocaust Museum and Education Center, http://www.candlesholocaustmuseum.org/.

3 *The Forgiveness Project* website, accessed June 18, 2011, http://theforgivenessproject.com/stories.

Chapter 8: Find the Corrective Value in Criticism

1 Carol Dweck, *Mindset: The New Psychology of Success* (New York: Random House, 2006).

2 Thomas Edison, *The Quotations Page*, accessed January 29, 2011 http://tinyurl.com/6deovmr.

3 A pseudonym has been used to protect the identity of the storyteller.

Chapter 9: Release Perfectionism

No note.

Chapter 10: Stop Comparing Yourself to Others

1 Jane Shure, "Comparing Ourselves to Others," *Huffington Post Living*, February 27, 2008, accessed July 17, 2011, http://tinyurl.com/65lwrdy.

2 The Clifton *StrengthsFinder* is the culmination of more than 50 years of Dr. Donald O. Clifton's lifelong work: leading millions of people around the world to discover their strengths. In 2002, Dr. Clifton was honored by an American Psychological Association Presidential Commendation as the Father of Strengths-Based Psychology. *Strengths* website, accessed July 23, 2011, http://tinyurl.com/d5wm39.

3 Marcus Buckingham and Donald O. Clifton, *Now Discover Your Strengths* (New York: Free Press, 2001).

4 A pseudonym has been used to protect the identity of the storyteller.

Chapter 11: Ditch Self-Righteousness

1 Story by Marion Moss Hubbard, Heroic Journey Consulting, www.heroicjourney.com.

Chapter 12: Quit Holding Yourself Hostage to Your Past

[1] Pseudonyms have been used to protect the identity of the storyteller and her ex-husband.

Chapter 13: Clear the Past with Family Members

[1] A pseudonym has been used to protect the identity of the storyteller.

[2] A pseudonym has been used to protect the identity of the storyteller.

Chapter 14: Break Your Addiction to Worry

[1] Staff writer, "Symptoms of Anxiety," *Healthy Place: America's Mental Health Channel*, October 2, 2008, accessed January 28, 2011, http://tinyurl.com/5utqhyt.

[2] *Psychology Today* staff writer, "Anxiety Attack Symptoms: When Worry Takes Control," *WebMD* website, accessed on January 28, 2011, http://tinyurl.com/5wpz6lu.

[3] Dennis Gersten, CFS Radio Program, February 1, 1998, *Imagerynet* website, accessed June 26, 2011, http://tinyurl.com/3bcs7tf.

[4] Margaret Paul, "Addiction to Worry," *Heart 'n Souls* website, accessed June 26, 2011, http://tinyurl.com/3evuedw.

Chapter 15: Extract Yourself from Thought Traps

[1] A pseudonyms have been used to protect the identity of the storyteller and her brother.

Chapter 16: Stop Berating Your Body

[1] Mirka Knaster, *Discovering the Body's Wisdom* (New York: Bantum Books, 1996), p. 42.

[2] Cher, Quoteland.com, accessed May 1, 2011, http://tinyurl.com/6l5kb82 .

[3] Judith Larkin Reno, *Elephants in Your Tent: Spiritual Support as a Mystic Survives Cancer* (Philadelphia, PA: Xlibris Corp., 2005).

[4] For more about Cameron Clapp's life see http://www.cameronclapp.com/ and Google videos at http://tinyurl.com/3be7x9e .

[5] John Kreiser, "A Real Bionic Man," *CBS News.com*, February 11, 2009, accessed September 2, 2011, http://tinyurl.com/3kbhfgy.

[6] Sherry Metzger, "Unquenchable Spirit: The Cameron Clapp Story," *oandp.com* website, February 2006, accessed on September 2, 2011, http://tinyurl.com/3qfej33.

[7] Ibid.

[8] For more information about Dr. Randy Pausch see the *Carnegie Mellon University* website at http://tinyurl.com/59plgu.

[9] Sheryl-Lee Kerr, "Famous Last Words," *Sunday Times*, April 27, 2008, p. 22, accessed on September 3, 2011, http://tinyurl.com/4x694hb.

[10] Randy Pausch, "The Last Lecture: Really Achieving Your Childhood Dreams," *Carnegie Melon University* as seen on *YouTube*, accessed on April 6, 2011, http://tinyurl.com/2z3wsx.

[11] "Randy Pausch: An Incredible Outlook," *Caring4Cancer Magazine*, Spring 2008, accessed September 2, 2011, http://tinyurl.com/3o5wks3.

[12] Sheryl-Lee Kerr, "Famous Last Words," *Sunday Times*, April 27, 2008, p. 22, accessed on September 3, 2011, http://tinyurl.com/4x694hb.

[13] Ram Dass, *Still Here: Embracing Aging, Changing, and Dying* (New York: Riverhead Books, 2000), p. 199.

[14] For more about Lee Atwater, see John Brady, "I'm Still Lee Atwater" *Washington Post*, Sunday, December 1, 1996, accessed May 1, 2011, http://tinyurl.com/592wg.

[15] Tom Turnipseed, "What Lee Atwater Learned; And the Lesson for His Protégés," *Washington Post*, Apr 16, 1991, p. A19.

[16] Lee Atwater and T. Brewster, "Lee Atwater's Last Campaign?" *Life Magazine*, February 1991, p. 67.

[17] Beth Hedva, *Betrayal, Trust, and Forgiveness: A Guide to Emotional Healing and Self-Renewal* (Berkley, CA: Ten Speed Press, 2001), p. 123.

[18] A pseudonym has been used to protect the identity of the storyteller.

Part 3: Arrive at the Center of Yourself: Claim Your Inner Wisdom

1 Michael S. Schneider, *A Beginner's Guide to Constructing the Universe: The Mathematical Archetypes of Nature, Art, and Science* (New York: HarperCollins Publishers, 1994), p. 9.
2 Ibid.
3 Shakti Gawain, *The Path of Transformation: How Healing Ourselves Can Change the World* (Mill Valley, CA: Nataraj Publishing, 1993), pp. 121-122.
4 James Hollis, *Why Good People Do Bad Things: Understanding Our Darker Side* (New York: Gotham Books, 2007), p. 218.
5 Ibid, p. 219.

Chapter 17: Listen to Your Inner Whisperings

1 John Demartini, "Listening to Your Guiding Whispers: The Secret Wisdom of the Inner Voice," *About.com Holistic Healing* website, accessed September 9, 2011, http://tinyurl.com/cqv9jy.
2 Adapted from John Demartini, "Listening to Your Guiding Whispers: The Secret Wisdom of the Inner Voice," *About.com Holistic Healing* website, accessed September 9, 2011, http://tinyurl.com/cqv9jy.
3 Catherine Pratt, "Your Inner Voice—4 Reasons to Listen to It Instead of Limiting Beliefs," *Life with Confidence* website, accessed September 16, 2011, http://tinyurl.com/3n42gvc.

Chapter 18: Own Your Shadow

1 Joseph Campbell, *Pathways to Bliss: Mythology and Personal Transformation* (Novato CA: New World Library, 2004), p. 73.
2 Individuation is the process of becoming a separate and unique, but whole human being.
3 James Hollis, *Why Good People Do Bad Things: Understanding Our Darker Side* (New York: Gotham Books, 2007), p. 185.
4 Debbie Ford, *The Shadow Effect: Illuminating the Hidden Power of Your True Self* (Carlsbad, CA: Debbie Ford Films and Hay House, Inc., 2009), DVD.
5 Ibid.

[6] Sam Keen, *Faces of the Enemy: Reflections of the Hostile Imagination* (New York: Harper & Row, Publishers, Inc., 1986), p. 11.

[7] Rodney Smith, "Abuse, Guilt, Self-Abuse, and Forgiveness," *InnerSelf.com,* accessed on January 28, 2011, http://www.innerself.com/Essays/abuse.

[8] Story by Marion Moss Hubbard, Heroic Journey Consulting, www.heroicjourney.com.

Chapter 19: Discover the Gifts of Your Shadow

[1] Adapted from Colin Tipping, *Radical Forgiveness: Making Room for the Miracle* (Marietta, GA: Global 13 Publications, Inc., 2002), p. 280.

[2] In addition to Voice Dialogue, other disciplines have arisen from Psychosynthesis that incorporate sub-personalities into their work including, Gestalt therapy developed by Fritz Perls, Laura Perls and Paul Goodman; Alchemical Hypnotherapy developed by David Quigley; Inner Child Work developed by John Bradshaw; Internal Family Systems therapy developed by Richard C. Schwartz; and others.

[3] Hal and Sidra Stone, "Me Me Me! Sub-Personality Tug of War," published originally in *Yen Magazine* and republished in *What is Voice Dialogue*, accessed on December 17, 2010, http://tinyurl.com/3mquglj.

Chapter 20: Get to the Root of Your Core Pain

[1] Elizabeth Hamilton, *Untrain Your Parrot: And Other No-Nonsense Instructions on the Path of Zen* (Boston, MA: Shambhala Publications, Inc., 2007), p. 154.

[2] Debbie Ford, *The Shadow Effect: Illuminating the Hidden Power of Your True Self* (Carlsbad, CA: Debbie Ford Films and Hay House, Inc., 2009), DVD.

[3] Excerpt used with permission from Elaine Rozelle's forthcoming book, *Journey to the Naked Soul: Seven Evolutions to the Center of Yourself* to be published by Orion Publishing Company. See more detail at http://www.heroicjourney.com/pages/products.htm.

Chapter 21: Love Yourself - Shadow, Pain, and All

1 Story by Marion Moss Hubbard, Heroic Journey Consulting, www.heroicjourney.com.

Part 4: Wind Outward: Hone Your Authenticity

1 Lauren Artress, *Walking a Sacred Path: Rediscovering the Labyrinth as a Spiritual Tool* (New York: Riverhead Books, 1995), p. 67.

2 Marilyn Mandala Schlitz, Cassandra Vieten, and Tina Amorok, *Living Deeply: The Art and Science of Transformation in Everyday Life* (Oakland, CA.: New Harbinger Publications, Inc., 2007), p. 157.

3 Lance Secretan, *Spirit@Work Cards: Bringing Spirit and Values* (Caledon, Ontario, Canada: Secretan Center, 2002), p 2.

4 Marion Moss Hubbard, *Messengers of Wisdom: Ten Ways the People You Work with Can Help Evolve Your Heroic Character* (San Diego, CA: Orion Publishing Company, 2006).

5 Brian Tracy, *Quoteland.com*, accessed February 21, 2011, http://tinyurl.com/3jr7rg6.

Chapter 22: Learn to Live in the Present Moment

1 A pseudonym has been used to protect the identity of the storyteller.

Chapter 23: Strengthen Your Patience

1 Ralph Blum, *The Book of Runes: A Handbook for the Use an Ancient Oracle: The Viking Runes with Stones: 10th Anniversary Edition* (New York: St. Martin's Press, 1993), p. 117.

2 A pseudonym has been used to protect the identity of the storyteller.

Chapter 24: Give Your Authentic Gifts to the World

1 Joseph Campbell as quoted in Diane Osbon, *Reflections on the Art of Living: A Joseph Campbell Companion* (New York: HarperCollins, 1991), p. 18.

2 James Hollis, *Why Good People Do Bad Things: Understanding Our Darker Side* (New York: Gotham Books, 2007), p. 190.

3 Ibid, p. 194.
4 Ibid, p. 193.
5 Edward Estlin Cummings, *Quoteland.com*, accessed October 15, 2011, http://tinyurl.com/3wzmkxo.
6 Steve Jobs, Commencement address delivered at Stanford on June 12, 2005, see transcript at http://www.heroicjourney.com/pdfs/stevejobs.pdf.
7 Ibid.
8 Ibid.
9 Marion Moss Hubbard, *Work as a Heroic Journey: Use the Workplace to Evolve Your Character and Consciousness* (San Diego, CA: Orion Publishing Company, 2005), pp. 25-53.

Chapter 25: Align with Your Body's Wisdom

1 For more information about Bioenergetics Analysis see Alexander Lowen, *Bioenergetics* (New York: Penguin/Arkana, 1994).
2 For more information about how our bodies prevent us from feeling emotions and how we can energetically shift that dynamic, see Tarra Judson Stariell's article, "Bioenergetics, Body Language Translated," *Southern California Institute for Bioenergetics Analysis* website, accessed July 28, 2011, http://tinyurl.com/3b24rca.
3 Louise Hay, *You Can Heal Your Life* (Carlsbad, CA: Hay House, 1984).
4 Louise Hay, *Heal Your Body A-Z: The Mental Causes for Physical Illness and the Way to Overcome Them* (Carlsbad, CA: Hay House, 1998), p. 3.
5 Ibid, p. 97.
6 Ibid, p. 63.
7 Ibid, p. 97.
8 Ibid, p. 75.
9 Ibid, p. 75.
10 Pseudonyms have been used to protect the identities of the storyteller and interviewer.

Chapter 26: Embrace Aging as Life's Ultimate Lesson

1 Dr. Leonard W. Poon, Ph.D. as quoted in Lynn Peters Adler, *Centenarians: The Bonus Years* (Santa Fe, NM: Health Press, 1995), p. 272.

2 Adapted from Lynn Peters Adler, *Centenarians: The Bonus Years* (Santa Fe, NM: Health Press, 1995), p. 308-310.

3 Joseph Campbell, *The Power of Myth* (New York: Doubleday, 1988).

4 Joseph Campbell, *The Power of Myth* (New York: Doubleday, 1988), pp. 70-71.

5 Ram Dass, *Still Here: Embracing Aging, Changing, and Dying* (New York: Riverhead Books, 2000).

6 Ibid, p. 7.

7 Theodore Roszak, *America the Wise: The Longevity Revolution and the True Wealth of Nations* (New York: Houghton Mifflin Company, 1998), p. 1.

8 Ram Dass, *Still Here: Embracing Aging, Changing, and Dying* (New York: Riverhead Books, 2000), p. 18.

9 For more information about "sage-ing" see Zalman Schachter-Shalomi and Ronald S. Miller, *From Age-ing to Sage-ing: A Profound New Vision of Growing Older* (New York: Warner Books, Inc., 1995) and Shirley MacLaine, *Sage-ing While Age-ing* (New York: Atria Books, 2007).

Part 5: Reconstruct Your Story from Inside Out

1 Shelley Carson, "From Tragedy to Art: Meaning-Making, Personal Narrative, and Life's Adversities: Using Expressive Narrative Writing to Transform Pain into Art," *Psychology Today* blog, published June 18, 2010, accessed on February 26, 2011, http://tinyurl.com/3p7t6ap. As quoted in Dr. Carson's blog, James Pennebaker at the University of Texas in Austin and his colleagues have "discovered that writing about an emotional life event during short sessions of 20 minutes each on just four consecutive days can reduce the number of sick days people report, improve immune functioning, and decrease dysphoria and anxiety." K. A. Baikie, and K.Wilhelm, "Emotional and Physical

Health Benefits of Expressive Writing. *Advances in Psychiatric Treatment,* 11 (2005): *338-346.*

2 Ibid.

3 Robert Karen, *The Forgiving Self: The Road from Resentment to Connection* (New York: Anchor Books, 2003), p. 6.

Chapter 27: Build a Strong Heroic Context

1 Annette Simmons, *The Story Factor: Secrets of Influence from the Art of Storytelling* (New York: Basic Books, 2001), p. 221.

Chapter 28: Write Your Personal Heroic Narrative

1 Michael S Brown, *A Psychosynthesis Approach to Organizational Transformation*, accessed February 26, 2011, http://tinyurl.com/3sfbodb.

2 Barry Neil Kaufman quote, *Quotationspage.com*, accessed February 26, 2011, http://www.quotationspage.com/quotes/Barry_Neil_Kaufman/.

Chapter 29: Fully Engage with Life

1 Joseph Campbell, *The Power of Myth* (New York: HarperCollins Publishers, 1988), p. 1.

Epilogue: Journey To Self-Atonement

1 Phil Cousineau, ed. *Beyond Forgiveness: Reflections on Atonement,* (San Francisco: Jossey-Bass, 2011).

2 Phil Cousineau, "The Next Step in Forgiveness and Healing," *Beyond Forgiveness: Reflections on Atonement,* (San Francisco: Jossey-Bass, 2011), p. xxiv.

3 Ibid, p. xxxiv.

4 Edward Tick, "Healing the Wounds of War: Atonement Practices for Veterans," *Beyond Forgiveness: Reflections on Atonement,* (San Francisco: Jossey-Bass, 2011), p. 116.

5 Kate Dahlstedt, "Burying the Stone: Rituals and Ceremonies of Atonement," *Beyond Forgiveness: Reflections on Atonement,* (San Francisco: Jossey-Bass, 2011), p. 65.

6 Ibid.

[7] Edward Tick, "Healing the Wounds of War: Atonement Practices for Veterans," *Beyond Forgiveness: Reflections on Atonement,* (San Francisco: Jossey-Bass, 2011), p. 121

[8] Peter Wallis' workshops combine mythology with concrete activities such a movement, artistic expression, active games, guided imagery, and dramatic skits, to help people develop a different frame of reference for experiencing their lives.

Appendix A: Skills for Taming Unruly Emotions

[1] Adapted with permission from Rev. Dr. Judith Larkin Reno, *Self Interview* (Gateway University, Vista, CA, 2010), pp. 61-65. Contact for Dr. Reno: jreno@roadrunner.com, 760-727-6600, www.GatewayUniversity.org.

BIBLIOGRAPHY

Abrahamson, Scot [sic] and Will Robinson. "A Decade Behind Bars for a Rape He Didn't Commit." *Center on Wrongful Convictions, Northwestern Law*. Accessed on July 16, 2011. http://tinyurl.com/3qj84ol.

Adler, Lynn Peters. *Centenarians: The Bonus Years.* Santa Fe, NM: Health Press, 1995.

Anonymous. "A Twelve-Step Approach to Atonement." In *Beyond Forgiveness: Reflections on Atonement,* edited by Phil Cousineau, 91-100. San Francisco: Jossey-Bass, 2011.

Artress, Lauren. *Walking the Sacred Path: Rediscovering the Labyrinth as a Spiritual Tool.* New York: Riverhead Books, 1995.

Atwater, Lee and T. Brewster. "Lee Atwater's Last Campaign?" *Life Magazine*. February 1991.

Baikie, K. A. and K.Wilhelm. "Emotional and Physical Health Benefits of Expressive Writing." *Advances in Psychiatric Treatment, 11 (2005):* 338-346.

Benson, Sally. *Stories of the Gods and Heroes*. New York: Dial Press, 1940.

Blum, Ralph. *The Book of Runes: A Handbook for the Use an Ancient Oracle: The Viking Runes with Stones: 10th Anniversary Edition.* New York: St. Martin's Press, 1993.

Brady, John. "I'm Still Lee Atwater." *Washington Post*. Sunday, December 1, 1996. Accessed May 1, 2011. http://tinyurl.com/592wg.

Brown, Michael S. *A Psychosynthesis Approach to Organizational Transformation*. Accessed February 26, 2011. http://tinyurl.com/3sfbodb.

Buckingham, Marcus and Donald O. Clifton. *Now Discover Your Strengths*. New York: Free Press, 2001.

CBS News Online 60 Minute Story. *Eyewitness Testimony*, March 8, 2009. Accessed on YouTube.com. Part 1 http://tinyurl.com/4y9kmgy and Part 2 http://tinyurl.com/3fz86g7.

Campbell, Joseph. *The Hero with a Thousand Faces*. Princeton, N.J.: Princeton University Press, 1949.

________________. *Pathways to Bliss: Mythology and Personal Transformation*. Novato CA: New World Library, 2004.

________________. *The Power of Myth*. New York: Doubleday, 1988.

________________. As quoted in Diane Osbon. *Reflections on the Art of Living: A Joseph Campbell Companion*. New York: HarperCollins, 1991.

Carrubbam, Sandy McPherson. "Oklahoma City Bombing: Two Fathers and Forgiveness," *AmericanCatholic.org*. Accessed January 25, 2011. http://tinyurl.com/3fv84vd.

Carson, J. W., F. J. Keefe, V. Goli, A. M. Fras, T. R. Lynch, S. R. Thorp, and J. L. Buechler. "Forgiveness and Chronic Low Back Pain: A Preliminary Study Examining the Relationship of Forgiveness to Pain, Anger, and Psychological Distress." *Journal of Pain* 6 (2005): 84–91.

Carson, Shelley. "From Tragedy to Art: Meaning-Making, Personal Narrative, and Life's Adversities: Using Expressive Narrative Writing to Transform Pain into Art." *Psychology Today* (blog). Accessed on February 26, 2011. http://tinyurl.com/3p7t6ap.

Casarjian, Robin. *Forgiveness: A Bold Choice for a Peaceful Heart.* New York: Bantam Books, 1992.

Celizic, Mike. "She Sent Him to Jail for Rape; Now They're Friends." *Today.com*. March 10, 2009. Accessed March 2, 2011. http://tinyurl.com/3zvpqgz.

Clifton, Donald. *StrengthsFinder*. *Strengths* website. Accessed July 23, 2011. http://tinyurl.com/d5wm39.

Cousineau, Phil. ed. *Beyond Forgiveness: Reflections on Atonement.* San Francisco: Jossey-Bass, 2011.

Dahlstedt, Kate. "Burying the Stone: Rituals and Ceremonies of Atonement." In *Beyond Forgiveness: Reflections on Atonement,* edited by Phil Cousineau, 61-72. San Francisco: Jossey-Bass, 2011.

Dass, Ram. *Be Here Now.* San Cristobal, NM: Lama Foundation, 1971.

________________. *Still Here: Embracing Aging, Changing, and Dying.* New York: Riverhead Books, 2000.

________________. "Dealing with Suffering and Seeing it as Grace." *Ram Dass* website. Accessed April 16, 2011. http://tinyurl.com/64allhq.

Demartini, John. "Listening to Your Guiding Whispers: The Secret Wisdom of the Inner Voice." *About.com Holistic Healing* website. Accessed September 9, 2011. http://tinyurl.com/cqv9jy.

Dweck, Carol. *Mindset: The New Psychology of Success.* New York: Random House, 2006.

Dyer, Wayne. *You'll See It When You Believe It.* New York: HarperCollins, 1989.

Eisler, Riane. *Sacred Pleasures: Sex, Myth, and the Politics of the Body*. San Francisco: HarperSanFrancisco, 1995.

Ford, Debbie. *The Shadow Effect: Illuminating the Hidden Power of Your True Self.* Carlsbad, CA: Debbie Ford Films and Hay House, Inc., 2009, DVD.

Gawain, Shakti. *Creative Visualization: Use the Power of Your Imagination to Create What You Want in Your Life.* Novato, CA: Nataraj Publishing, 2002.

________________. *The Path of Transformation: How Healing Ourselves Can Change the World.* Mill Valley, CA: Nataraj Publishing, 1993.

Gersten, Dennis. CFS Radio Program, February 1, 1998. *Imagerynet* website. Accessed June 26, 2011. http://tinyurl.com/3bcs7tf.

Hamilton, Elizabeth. *Untrain Your Parrot: And Other No-Nonsense Instructions on the Path of Zen*. Boston, MA: Shambhala Publications, Inc., 2007.

Hay, Louise. *Heal Your Body A-Z: The Mental Causes for Physical Illness and the Way to Overcome Them.* Carlsbad, CA: Hay House, 1998.

________________. *You Can Heal Your Life.* Carlsbad, CA: Hay House, 1984.

HealthPlace.com staff writer. "Symptoms of Anxiety." *Healthy Place: America's Mental Health Channel.* October 2, 2008. http://tinyurl.com/5utqhyt.

Hedva, Beth. *Betrayal, Trust, and Forgiveness: A Guide to Emotional Healing and Self-Renewal.* Berkley, CA: Ten Speed Press, 2001.

Helminski, Kabir. "The Heart: Threshold Between Two Worlds." In *Inner Knowing: Consciousness, Creativity, Insight and Intuition,* edited by Helen Palmer. New York: Jeremy P. Tarcher/Putnam, 1998.

Hollis, James. *Why Good People Do Bad Things: Understanding Our Darker Side.* New York: Gotham Books, 2007.

Hubbard, Marion Moss. *Messengers of Wisdom: Ten Ways the People You Work with Can Help Evolve Your Heroic Character.* San Diego, CA: Orion Publishing Company, 2006.

________________. *Work as a Heroic Journey: Use the Workplace to Evolve Your Character and Consciousness.* San Diego, CA: Orion Publishing Company, 2005.

________________. *The Workplace Labyrinth: A Heroic Journey to the Center of Yourself.* Unpublished dissertation submitted in partial fulfillment of the requirements for the degree of Doctor of Philosophy in Transpersonal Psychology and Consciousness Studies. International University of Professional Studies. Maui, HI, 2001.

________________. *Removing Your Mask: No More Hiding from Your Truth.* Seattle WA: Orion Publishing Company, 1992.

Justice, B. "Critical Life Events and the Onset of Illness." *Comprehensive Therapy 20* (1994): 232–238.

Karen, Robert. *The Forgiving Self: The Road from Resentment to Connection.* New York: Anchor Books, 2003.

Keen, Sam. *Faces of the Enemy: Reflections of the Hostile Imagination*. New York: Harper & Row, Publishers, Inc., 1986.

Kern, Hermann. *Through the Labyrinth: Design and Meanings Over 5,000 Years*. New York: Prestel, 2000.

Kerr, Sheryl-Lee. "Famous Last Words," *Sunday Times*, April 27, 2008, pp. 22-24, accessed on September 3, 2011, http://tinyurl.com/4x694hb.

Knaster, Mirka. *Discovering the Body's Wisdom.* New York: Bantum Books, 1996.

Kraybill, Donald, Steven Nolt, and David L. Weaver-Zercher. *Amish Grace: How Forgiveness Transcended Tragedy.* San Francisco: Josey Bass, 2007.

Kreiser, John. "A Real Bionic Man." *CBS News.com*. February 11, 2009. Accessed September 2, 2011. http://tinyurl.com/3kbhfgy.

Kor, Eva Mozes. *The Forgiveness Project* website. Accessed June 18, 2011. http://theforgivenessproject.com/stories/eva-kor-poland/.

Kor, Eva Mozes. "Interwined Live." *C.A.N.D.L.E.S. (*Children of Auschwitz Nazi Deadly Lab Experiments Survivors) *Museum* website. Accessed June 25, 2011. http://tinyurl.com/6xs6tqa.

Kuntz,Ted as interviewed by Trudy Peskett. "Daily Acts of Kindness Combat Stress." *Health Action Network Society.* January 24, 2008. Accessed January 21, 2011.http://tinyurl.com/3ozumx8.

Levy, Becca R., Martin D. Slade, Suzanne R. Kunkel, and Stanislav V. Kasl. "Longevity Increased by Positive Self-Perceptions of Aging." *Journal of Personality and Social Psychology* 83:2 (2002): 261–270.

Loeterman, Ben. "What Jennifer Saw: Cotton's Wrongful Conviction." PBS Frontline Show # 1508. Feb. 25, 1997.

Lowen, Alexander. *Bioenergetics*. New York: Penguin/Arkana, 1994.

MacLaine, Shirley. *Sage-ing While Age-ing.* New York: Atria Books, 2007.

McCourt Malachy as quoted by Alex Witchel. "At Lunch with: Malachy McCourt—How a Rogue Turns Himself Into a Saint; The Blarney Fails to Hide an Emotional Directness." *The New York Times*, published July 29, 1998. Accessed January 25, 2011. http://tinyurl.com/6b8a9vu.

McCraty, Rollin, William A. Tiller, and Mike Atkinson. "Head-Heart Entrainment: A Preliminary Survey." *Proceedings of the Brain-Mind Applied Neurophysiology EEG Neurofeedback Meeting*. Key West, Florida, 1996. Accessed on the *Institute of Heart Math* website. May 31, 2011. http://tinyurl.com/5s888oo.

McCraty, Rollin, and Mike Atkinson. "Cardiac Coherence Increases Heart-Brain Synchronization: Influence of Afferent Cardiovascular Input on Cognitive Performance and Alpha Activity." *Proceedings of the Annual Meeting of the Pavlovian Society*. Tarrytown, NY, 1999. Accessed on the *Institute of Heart Math* website. May 31, 2011. http://tinyurl.com/5s888oo.

Metzger, Sherry. "Unquenchable Spirit: The Cameron Clapp Story." *oandp.com* website. February 2006. Accessed on September 2, 2011. http://tinyurl.com/3qfej33.

Osbon, Diane. *Reflections on the Art of Living: A Joseph Campbell Companion.* New York: HarperCollins, 1991.

Palmer, Helen. *Inner Knowing: Consciousness, Creativity, Insight and Intuition*. New York: Jeremy P. Tarcher/Putnam, 1998.

Patterson, O. *Slavery and Social Death: A Comparative Study.* Cambridge, MA: Harvard University Press, 1982.

Paul, Margaret. "Addiction to Worry." *Heart 'n Souls* website. Accessed June 26, 2011. http://tinyurl.com/3evuedw.

Pausch, Randy. "The Last Lecture: Really Achieving Your Childhood Dreams." *Carnegie Melon University* as seen on *YouTube*. Accessed on April 6, 2011, http://tinyurl.com/2z3wsx.

"Randy Pausch: An Incredible Outlook," *Caring4Cancer Magazine*, Spring 2008, accessed September 2, 2011, http://tinyurl.com/3o5wks3.

Pearson, Carol S. *Awakening the Heroes Within: Twelve Archetypes to Help Us Find Ourselves and Transform the World.* New York, Harper & Row, Publishers, Inc., 1991.

________________. *The Hero Within: Six Archetypes We Live By.* New York, Harper & Row, Publishers, Inc., 1986.

Pearson, Carol S. and Margaret Mark. *The Hero and the Outlaw*. New York: McGraw Hill, 2001.

Phillips, D. P., T. E. Ruth, and L. M. Wagner. "Psychology and Survival." *Lancet* 342:8880 (1993): 1142–1145.

Poon, Leonard as quoted in Lynn Peters Adler. *Centenarians: The Bonus Years.* Santa Fe, NM: Health Press, 1995.

"Positive and Negative Stress." *StressFocus.com* website. Accessed on January, 16, 2012. http://tinyurl.com/7f7drxf.

Pratt, Catherine. "Your Inner Voice—4 Reasons to Listen to It Instead of Limiting Beliefs." *Life with Confidence* website. Accessed September 16, 2011. http://tinyurl.com/3n42gvc.

Psychology Today staff writer. "Anxiety Attack Symptoms: When Worry Takes Control." *WebMD* website. Accessed on January 28, 2011. http://tinyurl.com/5wpz6lu.

Purce, Jill. *Mystic Spiral: Journey of the Soul.* Great Britain: Thames & Hudson, 1974.

Ray, Oakley. "How the Mind Hurts and Heals the Body." *American Psychologist* (January 2004): 32.

Reno, Judith Larkin. *Elephants in Your Tent: Spiritual Support as a Mystic Survives Cancer.* Philadelphia, PA: Xlibris Corporation, 2005.

________________. *Self Interview.* Vista, CA: Gateway University, 2010.

Rozelle, Elaine. Forthcoming book, *Journey to the Naked Soul: Seven Evolutions to the Center of Yourself.* San Diego, CA: Orion Publishing Company.

Roszak, Theodore. *America the Wise: The Longevity Revolution and the True Wealth of Nations.* New York: Houghton Mifflin Company, 1998.

Saward, Jeff. "The Centre of the Labyrinth." *Labyrinthos*. Accessed on May 28, 2011. http://www.labyrinthos.net/centre.html.

Schachter-Shalomi, Zalman and Ronald S. Miller. *From Age-ing to Sage-ing: A Profound New Vision of Growing Older*. New York: Warner Books, Inc., 1995.

Schaef, Anne Wilson. *Beyond Therapy, Beyond Science*. New York: HarperCollins Publishers, 1992.

Schlitz, Marilyn Mandala, Cassandra Vieten, and Tina Amorok. *Living Deeply: The Art and Science of Transformation in Everyday Life*. Oakland, CA.: New Harbinger Publications, Inc., 2007.

Schneider, Michael S. *A Beginner's Guide to Constructing the Universe: The Mathematical Archetypes of Nature, Art, and Science*. New York: HarperCollins Publishers, 1994.

Secretan, Lance. *Spirit@Work Cards: Bringing Spirit and Values*. Caledon, Ontario, Canada: Secretan Center, 2002.

Shure, Jane. "Comparing Ourselves to Others." *Huffington Post Living*. February 27, 2008. Accessed July 17, 2011. http://tinyurl.com/65lwrdy.

Shapiro, Phil. "Affirmations: The Power of Thought." *Dr. Phil Shapiro, M.D.* website. http://www.philipshapiro.com/art-affirmations.html.

Simmons, Annette. *The Story Factor: Secrets of Influence from the Art of Storytelling*. New York: Basic Books, 2001.

Smith, Rodney. "Abuse, Guilt, Self-Abuse, and Forgiveness." *InnerSelf.com*. Accessed on January 28, 2011. http://www.innerself.com/Essays/abuse_guilt.htm.

Stariell, Tarra Judson. "Bioenergetics, Body Language Translated," *Southern California Institute for Bioenergetics Analysis* website. Accessed July 28, 2011. http://tinyurl.com/3b24rca.

Stoia-Caraballo, Rebecca, Mark S. Rye, Wei Pan, Keri J. Brown Kirschman, Catherine Lutz-Zois and Amy M. Lyons. "Negative Affect and Anger Rumination as Mediators Between Forgiveness and Sleep Quality." *Journal of Behavioral Medicine* 31: 6 (December 2008): 478-488.

Stone, Hal and Sidra Stone. "Me Me Me! Sub-Personality Tug of War." *What is Voice Dialogue*. Accessed on December 17, 2010, http://tinyurl.com/3mquglj.

"Symptoms of Anxiety." *Healthy Place: America's Mental Health Channel*, October 2, 2008. Accessed January 28, 2011, http://tinyurl.com/5utqhyt.

Tick, Edward. "Healing the Wounds of War: Atonement Practices for Veterans." In *Beyond Forgiveness: Reflections on Atonement,* edited by Phil Cousineau, 115-134. San Francisco: Jossey-Bass, 2011.

Tipping, Colin. *Radical Forgiveness: Making Room for the Miracle.* Marietta, GA: Global 13 Publications, Inc, 2002.

Toussaint, Loren L., David R. Williams, Marc A. Musick, and Susan A. Everson-Rose. *Mental Health, Religion & Culture* 11:5 (July 2008): 485.

Turnipseed, Tom. "What Lee Atwater Learned and the Lesson for His Protégés." *Washington Post*. Apr 16, 1991, p. A19.

Vaughan, Frances, as quoted in Marilyn Mandala Schlitz, Cassandra Vieten, and Tina Amorok. *Living Deeply: The Art and Science of Transformation in Everyday Life.* Oakland, CA: New Harbinger Publications, Inc., 2007.

Waltman, Martina A., Douglas C. Russell, Catherine T. Coyle, Robert D. Enright, Anthony C. Holter, and Christopher M. Swoboda. "The Effects of a Forgiveness Intervention on Patients with Coronary Artery Disease." *Psychology & Health* 24:1 (January 2009): 11 – 27.

Watson, M., J. S. Haviland, S. Greer, J. Davidson, and J. M. Bliss. "Influence of Psychological Response on Survival in Breast Cancer: A Population-based Cohort Study." *Lancet* 354:9187 (1999): 1331–1336.

West, Melissa. *Exploring the Labyrinth: A Guide for Healing and Spiritual Growth.* New York: Broadway Books, 2000.

Zohar, Danah. *Quantum Self: Human Nature and Consciousness Defined by the New Physics.* New York: William Morrow and Company, 1990.

CREDITS

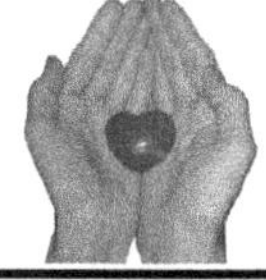

Cover	Author composite design using: • *Spiral Staircase* @ 2011 Photos.com, a division of Getty Images, Permission granted under licensing agreement; • *Hands and Heart* photo by Richard A. Hubbard © 2011; • *Book 15* @ Photo-Objects 25,000 Premium Image Collection, Copyright 1997-1999, Hemera Technologies, Inc., Permission granted under licensing agreement; • Labyrinth graphic designed by author © 2011; • Orion Publishing logo design by author © 1997; and • Heroic Journey logo design by author © 2001.	
Chapter Headers:	*Hands and Heart* photo by Richard A. Hubbard © 2011	
Introduction:	Adventure photo –Author photo © 2011	xxiii
Part 1:	*Movie Reel* © 2011 Photos.com, a division of Getty Images., Permission granted under licensing agreement	1
Chapter 2:	Labyrinth graphics - Figures 2.1 designed by author © 2011	14

I wish to thank all of the people who agreed to share their personal self-forgiveness stories. In instances where the storytellers' identities have not previously been published, I have used pseudonyms to protect them and others mentioned in their stories. While I cannot authenticate the veracity of each of the personal stories that I have included, I hope that you, as a reader, will be able to relate to the *subjective experience* of the storytellers.

INDEX

A

B

C

D

E

G

H

I

L

M

O

P

Q

R

S

T

U

V

W

Z

Other Books by Dr. Marion Moss Hubbard

Removing Your Mask:
No More Hiding from Your Truth

Work as a Heroic Journey:
Use the Workplace to Evolve Your Character and Consciousness

Workplace Heroism Series Booklet
Messengers of Wisdom:
Ten Ways the People You Work with
Can Evolve Your Heroic Character

Available through
Heroic Journey Consulting
www.heroicjourney.com

Praise for *Removing Your Mask*

"This book may replace years of therapy! Marion Moss [Hubbard] gives us the inspiration to uncover the happiness that is just waiting to embrace us."
DJZ, Edmonds, WA

"Your book has been a tremendous help. I have read my share of self-help books. But your book had almost a singular effect upon me....You gave the best, the clearest description yet, I've ever seen in print or ever heard of!...There are so many meaningful passages that I expect this book to be one of my 'all time favorites' for some time to come!"
TG, Conwall, NY

"This is a 'must read' if you are interested in living your truth while connecting from your heart."
Velma Peace, Bellevue, WA Bookstore Reviewer

"I have read books and articles on being real and authentic, but this book made it the clearest for me to see my own mask—my own false self—and the destruction of living an inauthentic life."
RL, Richmond, Indiana

"This book is a great book. It gives a lot of insight to those who don't understand and witness to those who do."
SF, Wilsonville, OR

"I really value and appreciate the book! I value its simplicity and clarity. I found it [confrontational], *supportive and empowering!!"*
RY, Koloa, HI

Praise for *Work as a Heroic Journey*

"[This book] is inspiring and enlightening! Dr. Moss Hubbard crystallizes those issues that we are vaguely aware of which filter and block our ability to cope with the work environment. Her lessons are practical and her suggestions are thought provoking. Great for a workgroup to review and study together."

Linda Giannelli Pratt

Chief, Office of Environmental Protection and Sustainability (OEPS)
City of San Diego Environmental Services Department

"Marion Moss Hubbard has created a valuable framework in which change, confusion, frustration and success can all be viewed as a cycle of growth within an organization. A very helpful tool for both individuals and organizations!"

Peter Wallis

Group Facilitator/Consultant, Kirkland, WA

"Take this book on your next vacation or retreat, read it and mark the parts that speak to you. You'll return home refreshed, with a new sense of purpose. And if you have a major life decision to make, don't do anything until you have read this book. It is first aid for the soul."

Clyde Farrell

Attorney, Austin, Texas

"Drawing from mythology as well as her personal experience as a trainer, consultant, supervisor, and employee, Dr. Hubbard guides the reader through the ten stages of the heroic workplace journey. This book is concise and readable and contains questions and exercises that help bring the message alive for readers."

Holly Bell, Ph.D., LCSW

Research Scientist, School of Social Work,
University of Texas, Austin, Texas

ABOUT THE AUTHOR

Photo by Richard A. Hubbard

Dr. Marion Moss Hubbard has a Ph.D. in Transpersonal Psychology. She specializes in helping individuals and organizations move through change with greater clarity, ease, and long lasting positive results. She has over 30 years of experience in coaching, mentoring, communication, leadership development and organizational change work.

In her coaching practice, *Heroic Journey Consulting*, Marion works with individuals to strengthen their resilience, more fully develop their awareness, and find greater meaning and depth to their personal and professional lives. She shares her own path of self-forgiveness and personal development to help her clients deprogram old belief patterns, clear past traumas, and release energy blocks that keep them from fulfilling their goals and dreams.

Marion is an inspirational keynote speaker and has facilitated hundreds of training classes and workshops on personal, professional, and leadership development topics. She is author of two books including *Work as a Heroic Journey: Use the Workplace to Evolve Your Character and Consciousness* and *Removing Your Mask: No More Hiding from Your Truth.* She also has written the first booklet in her *Workplace Heroism Series – Messengers of Wisdom: Ten Ways the People You Work with Can Evolve Your Heroic Character.*

Marion lives in San Diego, California with her husband, Richard, and enjoys exploring both her internal and external world. She can be contacted through her website at www.heroicjourney.com.

www.ingramcontent.com/pod-product-compliance
Lightning Source LLC
Chambersburg PA
CBHW060238100426
42742CB00011B/1568

* 9 7 8 0 9 6 3 1 3 4 1 9 6 *